MONTESQUIEU'S COMPARATIVE POLITICS AND THE SPIRIT OF AMERICAN CONSTITUTIONALISM

MONTESQUIEU'S
COMPARATIVE POLITICS
AND THE
SPIRIT OF AMERICAN
CONSTITUTIONALISM

ANNE M. COHLER

UNIVERSITY PRESS OF KANSAS

© 1988 by the University Press of Kansas

Published by the University Press of Kansas (Lawrence, Kansas 66045), which was organized by the Kansas Board of Regents and is operated and funded by Emporia State University, Fort Hays State University, Kansas State University, Pittsburg State University, the University of Kansas, and Wichita State University

Library of Congress Cataloging-in-Publication Data

Cohler, Anne M.
    Montesquieu's comparative politics and the spirit of American constitutionalism / Anne M. Cohler.
        p.   cm.
    Bibliography: p.
    Includes index.
    ISBN 0-7006-0376-X (alk. paper)
    1. Montesquieu, Charles de Secondat, baron de, 1689–1755. De l'esprit des lois. 2. United States—Constitutional history.
I. Title.
JC179.M753C64   1988
321.8'0973—dc19   88-17647
                                                              CIP

Printed in the United States of America
10 9 8 7 6 5 4 3 2 1

The paper used in this publication meets the minimum requirements of the American National Standard for Permanence of Paper for Printed Library Materials Z39.48-1984.

To Jonathan and James

CONTENTS

ACKNOWLEDGMENTS

Before beginning this book, I had often thought of writing on Montesquieu but had not begun. When I first took a course in modern political philosophy, I considered Montesquieu but wrote on Burke. When I took a graduate course in the Enlightenment, I finally turned to Hume, and when I contemplated a dissertation, Rousseau seemed more plausible. My reluctance to tackle Montesquieu was well founded. In addition, this book came to be inextricably entangled with my work on a new translation of *The Spirit of the Laws,* which gave me both a new view of the text and some new colleagues as well. For years, Basia C. Miller and I argued interminably over the meaning of sentences and together discovered much about the way the book was written. Keith Baker, François Furet, and their students provided me with a thorough grounding in the history of the eighteenth century. Their knowledge of Montesquieu and of Tocqueville has always been worth thinking about and taking into account. Although the argument in this book is grounded in an analysis of the book itself, not of its historical circumstances, I hope to have followed a chain of thought that is not implausible for those circumstances. The staff and the students of the Basic Program of Liberal Education for Adults of the University of Chicago have provided a more than gracious community in which to think out some of these problems. More recently, Leonard R. Sorenson, John Cook, Joseph Alulis, and the readers at the University Press of Kansas have all been willing to read carefully and offer useful thoughts about what I could do to make myself clearer.

A fellowship for independent study and research from the National Endowment for the Humanities in 1985/86 gave me the time and the incentive to finish this book. A piece called "Moderate and Free Government: The Division of Powers," published in *E Pluribus Unum: Constitutional Principles and the*

Institutions of Government, vol. 2 of *Constitutionalism in America,*
edited by Sarah Baumgartner Thurow (Lanham, Md.: University
Press of America, 1988), shares a common ancestry with chapter
7 of this work, and I am grateful to the publisher for permission to
print parts of that work.

Anne M. Cohler
Chicago, Illinois
November 1987

1

INTRODUCTION

Although Montesquieu's *The Spirit of the Laws* is acknowledged to have had a direct influence on the shape of the United States Constitution and although Montesquieu is often mentioned along with Hobbes, Locke, and Rousseau as having been influential in shaping liberalism, he has not been studied as carefully as have other early liberals and other sources of the Constitution. There are any number of possible explanations for this relative neglect. The book appears to be altogether without organization. It has only traces of traditional thinking about natural law or of the analysis of the movement from a state of nature to a civil and political society built upon that nature, which Hobbes, Locke, and Rousseau have made so familiar. One is never sure of the relative weight of Montesquieu's support for the nobility, of his advocacy of legal process and equality, of his admiration for ancient republicanism. His description of the balance of power in English government was an inspiration for the U.S. Constitution, but that English government does not seem to fit into Montesquieu's scheme of three forms of government. It seems to be an addition that was not worked back into the thought of the beginning of the book. Efforts to see Montesquieu as a precursor of sociology and economics tend to falter on his use of political categories in both social and economic analyses. In this book, I am going to step back and take another look, recalling Montesquieu's own description of his project and trying to follow his lead. The men who designed and defended the U.S. Constitution in *The Federalist* and Alexis de Tocqueville serve here as examples of those who did likewise, and their understanding serves as a kind of defense and support of my analysis of Montesquieu.

Montesquieu's early works offer some clues to the project; in his Preface to *The Spirit of the Laws,* Montesquieu offers us some reflections on the book that follows. Let us look at these two briefly. Montesquieu wrote in the 1748 Preface that it had taken him twenty years to produce this book. Twenty-seven years earlier he had published his first, and other, major work, *The Persian Letters*. It might be plausible to look to this work, not for his principles, but for the considerations that led him to look somewhere in particular for his principles. The premise of *The Persian Letters* is the illumination that comes from the clash of two points of view, the Persian and the French.[1] Two Persians come to France and observe; they write letters to each other and to other persons about their discoveries, while one, Usbek, writes letters home to try to keep his harem under control. From one point of view the book offers the French a view of themselves from the outside, as specimens. But Usbek may well also be a model for how not to travel, how not to look at another country. His is a moralizing, universalizing point of view. He never comes to be able to do what the French who read the book are to do—namely, to see himself from another point of view, as the French would see him. In the end, when he finally realizes that his wives have not been waiting for his return for ten years but instead have been amusing themselves and proceeding with their own purposes— that is, their own men—he responds by ordering their punishment.

The autonomous life of the harem interferes with the carrying out of Usbek's order. The old eunuch, who has been in charge of the harem, dies; his replacement is suspiciously scrupulous about not opening Usbek's correspondence with his predecessor. Finally, a younger, ambitious eunuch suggests that the replacement is not doing the job and that he himself could do it properly. Negotiating all this through the mail takes about two years. Having obtained permission, the young eunuch sets about disciplining the harem. First the wives write and complain about his barbarous injustice, but before Usbek answers, two final letters from the eunuch arrive—the first reports finding the virtuous Roxana with a young man, and the second promises to punish, to exterminate crime, to spill blood. The final letter is from Roxana, who writes while dying of a poison that she has taken: "How could you have imagined me credulous enough to believe that I existed only to adore your caprices, that in permitting yourself everything, you had the right to thwart my every desire? No: I have lived in slavery, but I have always been free. I reformed your laws by those of nature, and my spirit has always held to its independence" (letter 161).[2]

Montesquieu places the series of letters between Usbek and his harem at the end of the book, isolating them from the letters between Usbek and his friends in Europe. But upon reinserting them in that series, it becomes clear that this letter of Roxana's was received before the last two letters of Usbek's to other persons, in which he complains that men of knowledge and wisdom are despised in society and in which he blames the ministers of a government for the moral disintegration of the society: "What crime can be greater than that committed by a minister, when he corrupts the morals of an entire nation, degrades the souls of the most upright, tarnishes the splendor of rank, obscures virtue itself, and confounds those of the highest birth with the most despised?" (letter 146). Is Usbek's conclusion that he is a man of such wisdom that society can never really understand and sympathize with him and that the eunuchs, as his ministers, are to be blamed for the moral dissolution of his harem? In Usbek we have a man who, like Tocqueville's French intellectuals, arrogantly sets himself, his rational general principles, and his sentimental virtue apart from any responsibility for the results of putting his principles into effect in a society of real—that is, eccentric, willful, opinionated, and spirited—people.[3]

The universality that is, in effect, the generalization of one's own life and prejudices is unsatisfactory, even dangerous. In a little work written in 1724, shortly after *The Persian Letters,* Montesquieu has the Roman dictator Sulla say: "I believed that taking liberty from a city where I was a citizen was the worst crime. I punished that crime, and I was not concerned whether my genius would be good or bad for the republic. Nevertheless the government of our fathers was reestablished; . . . and Rome has never been so tranquil."[4] Here it becomes clear that Sulla's imposition of his version of liberty hastened the end of liberty in Rome.

These brief sketches suggest Montesquieu's concern with making a distinction between the external rules and the particular internal processes of a government. Upholding or enforcing standards may not be the same as seeing to it that those standards govern the actions of the people who are ruled. *The Persian Letters* has often been included among the works of the writers the French call the *moralistes*—Pascal, La Rochefoucauld, and La Bruyère. In these works the distinction between the appearance of virtue—of life lived according to rules—and its internal reality is dissected with great rigor. People are altogether capable of fooling themselves about the import of their actions while they suppose themselves to be acting on some good, important, clever, or even intelligent principle. People who fool themselves in such a way become incapable of seeing what is really happening, and thus of acting well.

Montesquieu himself moves to take the variety of political life more seriously, to construct a comparative government that is something other than a hierarchical series in which each government is measured against a single universal standard. This order must somehow be a reflection of the internal structure of governing, of the principles of action of those in political life. In book 1 Montesquieu says that he is following the order of the spirit of the laws, rather than of the laws—that is, an internal, not an external, principle. We are invited to inquire into the effects of governing strictly with respect to an external principle and, as we do in chapter 3, into the meaning of the spirit and even of its variety. That variety can produce forms of government that vary profoundly—tiny, consistent republics; vast, silent despotisms; complicated, turbulent monarchies.

In *The Federalist* and in the works of Tocqueville, as we shall see, something of this tradition of concern with the internal is maintained. The Federalists, as well as the members of the Constitutional Convention, were concerned primarily with trying to envision the ways the new government would work. They did not rely upon proposing a principle upon which the members of the government were to act, not even the principle of election. They created situations and jobs that were to shape the activity and the principles of action of the representatives. In this context they were interested in the internal processes of government and in the character of those who were to govern. Tocqueville turned his attention away from the governors to the governed, remarking upon the latter's character. From his point of view the election of all the officers of the government, however the election is done, makes possible the rule of an oppressive principle, democratic rule. Tocqueville interests himself in the particular ways this democracy shapes character and the democratic ways its harmful effects can be meliorated. Those means embody democracy as self-government, rather than democracy as rule. That is, they center upon the internal activity of democracy.

In his Preface and in the Foreword to the second edition of *The Spirit of the Laws*, Montesquieu offers some reflections on universals and particulars in the study of political life. His principles permitted him, he says, to make some sense of the diversity of laws and mores, to see that men are not led by their fancies alone. But Montesquieu's principles are the principles of governments, not principles of organization, as he explains in book 3. With those principles it is possible to establish clearly the spirit of antiquity and to avoid making false distinctions or seeing similarities where none exist. These principles order the facts and may well make a pattern, a design, themselves, as we shall propose in the conclusion to chapter 4.

Montesquieu says he hopes to offer his readers, as inhabitants of a particular country, true, not prejudiced, understandings of their duties. But to be unprejudiced is not to be universal; rather, it is to understand oneself and the basis of one's own government. What interests Montesquieu, as he points out in the Foreword, is the quality, the modification of the soul, or the virtue that makes a particular government work. Montesquieu does not ask us to abandon that virtue but to see it as singular and to look for the adjustments proper to it. Enlightenment here is neither abandonment nor universalization of the principle of a government. Then, perhaps, the *traits saillants*—"sallies" or "protuberances"—of the works that Montesquieu disapproves of in the Preface may be the result of their universalizing the point of view of a particular government, so that their work is out of shape, giving undue attention to some topics. Montesquieu's own work is, rather, inclusive—so inclusive that it seems to be shapeless. Perhaps *The Spirit of the Laws* presents us with the world organized so that relations are clearer than in our experience but not so clear that they are falsified by a linear organization along one principle.

Thomas Pangle, in his *Montesquieu's Philosophy of Liberalism: A Commentary on The Spirit of the Laws,* proceeds as if Montesquieu had organized his book along such a line of thought.[5] Pangle treats the description of kinds of law in book 1 as if it were the equivalent of Hobbes's or Locke's descriptions of the state of nature and the laws that derive from it. The conclusion that Pangle draws is that Montesquieu's version of natural law and right is a variation on those of Locke and Hobbes. Pangle thinks that although Montesquieu centers his theory on the importance of security, one cannot cut through the variety and particularity of history and experience to simple principles. However, Pangle proceeds to treat the discussion of governments in books 2 through 8 as a critical preliminary to the discussion of English constitutionalism in book 11. He sees the remainder of the book as a discussion of the variety of circumstances that must be taken into account in pursuing an English government. Moderation, or prudence, is required in order to adapt to those circumstances and to protect the security of individuals, the essence of the purpose of the English government as Montesquieu describes it. In order to give this linear structure to *The Spirit of the Laws,* Pangle must treat the discussion of forms of government as a critical interlude. In his view, ancient republics are mentioned to clarify the conflict between their internal organization and their foreign relations; the discussion of monarchies, which illuminates the false honor of the nobility, is ancillary to this analysis of the republics. This approach reconstructs the book so that it can be seen as a variation on Locke's *Second Treatise.*

It seems to me that Montesquieu's book is simply not written this way and that the form itself indicates a fundamental distaste for that way of thinking about political life. Instead, Montesquieu offers a comparative politics in which a variety of goods and the governments that embody them must be carefully considered.[6] Here I proceed quite differently. I begin by taking a look at the shape of the book as a whole, read from beginning to end, linearly. When one looks at it in this fashion, one can come up only with suggestions and questions for further inquiry. Montesquieu raises the question of spirit and law. He presents us with three governments whose structures are distinct. He introduces a government and its conditions of existence in external relations and taxations, where the aim is a universal principle, political freedom for its individual citizens. He offers an analysis of natural circumstances, of climate and terrain, which suggests that the more the government of a country must respond to natural necessity, the closer it is to despotism. Then he presents a history of commerce, a political economy, an analysis of religion as it relates to the kinds of political life already described, and some histories and versions of the relations of laws and the problem of legislation, which can only serve as remarks upon the discussions earlier in the book of the kinds of governments and the conditions of the existence of each. His is not an argument for, or an exposition of, a thesis. Rather, it proceeds by accretion, by introducing new considerations to the old ones, thus increasing the complexity and deepening the considerations.[7] In order to properly analyze the book, we must proceed in somewhat the same way. First, we must find some terms, some notions, that will permit us to go through the book following Montesquieu's underlying structure.

To begin with, one must take seriously Montesquieu's suggestion in book 1 that there is a difference between the order of the laws and that of the spirit, and that he intends to follow that of the spirit. When one takes the topics raised in book 1—the justice of intelligent beings, the natural law, and the variety of positive law—one finds that Montesquieu regularly, in many more places than I have mentioned, undermines and transforms those notions. He proposes a kind of typology of the spirit. That typology also makes sense of the forms of governments that he proposes in books 2 through 8. This becomes clear as one proceeds through an analysis of the forms of government in terms of their moderation, again taking the considerations throughout the book. That is, in order to get some understanding of the internal structure of *The Spirit of the Laws,* one must take topics that are raised in the beginning and consider their treatment throughout the book.

Only then can we turn to the English government and to the circumstances that would or would not serve as its support or as the support of similar governments. That government, then, is not the solution to the political problem but is an example of a modern government whose response to its circumstances and possibilities can teach much about those same circumstances and possibilities. By looking at the book in this way, we can get a clear view of the understandings that the Federalists and Tocqueville carried away with them from their reading of Montesquieu's book. They took away from him just those things he would have wanted. They took, not prescriptions or rules, but an assessment of their situation, of the possible solutions, and of ways of judging those solutions.

Let us turn, finally, to a brief suggestion about the substance of Montesquieu's thought as it emerges in this book. Montesquieu begins his book with a distinction between the law—divine, natural, and positive—and the spirit of the law. Commonly, the word *spirit (esprit)* referred to the spirit of God, or more ordinarily, it meant "mind" or "wit." This notion of mind is not passive; it is active, as its extension toward wit indicates. The curiosity here is, not the distinction between law and spirit, but the notion of the spirit of the laws. The problem, as I pursue it, is of the relation between the three kinds of law and the spirit in its political form. When we follow Montesquieu's analysis of the effect of rule in accord with divine and natural law as he presents them, we find that he criticizes each as being destructive of spirited political action and life. Understanding Montesquieu's notion of spirit presents the possibility that his liberalism may not be based on an assessment that politics is properly simply a protection of life, liberty, and property, but rather that it is to encourage human action of some kind.

Although recently Montesquieu has been identified as a liberal in the Lockean tradition and as a stern critic of the monarchy, traditionally Montesquieu was seen as an aristocratic liberal or a liberal monarchist—as someone whose acceptance of Lockean liberalism was, at best, tempered by something else. Jefferson, for example, regarded him with considerable suspicion as well as admiration.[8] It has even been suggested, along this line, that Montesquieu's was really a defense of the Fronde, of the French nobility's claim against monarchical rule. In general, as we shall see, I stand closer to the traditional view. But it seems to me that Montesquieu had unsentimental, precise reasons for his distrust of liberal natural right—and for his acceptance of something that often appears to be quite similar.

Spirit as a principle of action toward some end is naturally particular and limited. The passions are, by contrast, general.

Thus, there are the spirited small republics, in which the passions are constrained to serve the political life, and the large limitless despotisms, in which the passions are constrained only by fear. But when one returns to the problem raised by the Christian notion of spirit, the situation changes. Christianity presumes the possibility of the divine spirit in everyone. The universality of the spirit mimics the natural universality of the passions. Politics came to be based on the presumption of some underlying human similarity, not of profound differences. New forms of government emerged as a consequence of this change in opinion. The first such government was the monarchy. Its origin lay in the acceptance of the variety of barbarian and Roman laws, and its ranks and orders, built on inheritance, encourage the honor and vanity that implies similarity rather than fundamental difference. These notions underlie, it seems to me, the discussions of law and spirit and of moderation and the forms of government in Montesquieu. In chapters 3 and 4, I present the material from Montesquieu that makes this assessment plausible and that gives it further depth and content.

The question has become one of how to embody the particularity of the political spirit so that politics is not inevitably despotic. Monarchies are one solution to this problem, but their inherited hierarchy is undermined by the notion of natural and spiritual equality. This is Tocqueville's point of departure, as we shall notice in chapter 8. Montesquieu introduces another possiblity into his description of English government. That government presents the possibility of the modern moderate government with which we are concerned in chapter 5. There we will encounter problems with which we are much more familiar—representation, separated and balanced powers, and limited or constitutional government. This government seems to sit on top of the society. The representation is given form through the institutions, through the balanced and separated powers. Its actions back upon that society are limited to punishing visible actions and general policies. The latter are the topics of chapter 6, where we look at the ways such a government can act back upon the society it represents—at the way it must understand and treat the economy, the religion, and the historical experience of its society.

It is illuminating to see the formation of the United States

Constitution in the context suggested by this analysis. The limits on the government are, then, not a product of a principled notion of limited government, as in Locke. Rather, they are a consequence of the understanding of the limits within which a moderate government must act in order not to become despotic. Free government becomes a characteristic of that moderate government; it is a way of acting, a spirit. The balance of powers both preserves the distance required for moderate government and shapes the activity, and finally even the character, of the representatives. This is not to say that this is a whole account of the Founding; rather, it casts another light upon the thought behind the shape of the Constitution. Political action never has quite the consistency of political thought.

In chapter 8, we shall turn to Tocqueville and return to the problem of spirit and character. Tocqueville takes a look at the democratic man as he can be envisioned from the American experience. He fears the new despotism that was only suggested in Montesquieu. He dissects the character of the new democrat, which makes such a new despotism possible—the passions and the limited, crippled spirit that result from an acquiescence in the new principle of democratic rule.

In sum, it seems to me that a careful look at Montesquieu's *Spirit of the Laws* gives us another way to look at our common political experience. Montesquieu's concern with spirit and character, rather than law and principle, gave the Federalists and give us a way of considering politics that encourages thought about circumstance without losing sight of ends—that is, what was once called prudence.

2

NARRATIVE

The Spirit of the Laws is divided into thirty-one books, all but one of
which are divided into a number of small chapters. The books are
separated into six parts (1–8, 9–13, 14–18, 20–23, 24–26, and
27–31). An "Invocation to the Muses" was placed at the
beginning of book 20, about halfway through. These guides do not
appear in all the editions, largely because the man who was
Montesquieu's representative to the printer mistakenly left out
the parts in the first edition and objected to the "Invocation to the
Muses" as being inappropriate in such a work.[1] Here, however,
we shall make whatever use we can of as many guides as there are
throughout this work. We shall use these chapters, books, and
parts to find our way about the work, referring to books and then
chapters in parentheses.

Part 1 is made up of books 1 through 8, but book 1, "On Laws
in General," stands apart and appears to be an introduction to the
work as a whole. There Montesquieu says we are subject to divine
laws as intelligent beings, to natural laws as natural beings, and to
political and civil laws as subjects of some particular government;
but he assures us that it is the ensemble, the spirit of these laws,
with which he is concerned and that he will follow the order of its
relations. In its outline, the sketch of the orders of the laws implies
a traditional version of the various kinds of law and their
relations. But upon examination, it is extremely difficult to make
ordered sense of these brief remarks. Montesquieu may be
suggesting here that if we are seen as intelligent beings, as
Descartes's angels, we are minds without bodies whose justice is
an exact reciprocity (1.1).[2] Even when we are taken as natural
beings, as we are by Hobbes and Locke, our success in acquiring
knowledge results, according to Montesquieu, in a motive for
uniting in society beyond fear, hunger, or sexuality—the desire to
live in society (1.2). When we begin with particular law and

custom, as lawyers do, it is difficult to find any grounds for unity
other than our wanting to live together—that is, our wills; but the
things that are ruled by the civil, political, or international law
may well vary with some other circumstance or consideration
(1.3). Later, the reader will learn that religious law, whose aim is
the best, is a despotic guide to political life, whose realm is the
good (24.7), that nature's force is despotic (bks. 15–17), and that
property and even the potentiality for citizenship could become
universal, not the consequence of some particular political law
(bks. 9–10, 27–28). The political realm seems to escape from
these legal categories. Montesquieu finally offers spirit as an
encompassing category for political life.

In books 2–8, Montesquieu proposes a typology of three
governments: republics, monarchies, and despotisms. Each government has a nature, or source of sovereign power, and a
principle, or motive for its people's doing the things that maintain
the government. The typology is a consequence of a classification
of the nature or source of rule, in respect to the number of rulers
and in respect to whether that rule is according to the law. Thus, a
single ruler who rules according to the law is a monarch, and one
who rules according to his will is a despot. If there are few or
many rulers, the government is a republic.[3] One is led to wonder
about the status of rule under law in republics. Are there two
kinds of republics? To establish their rule, republics require laws
establishing suffrage; monarchies require intermediate, subordinate, and dependent powers which provide channels through
which power flows. Despotisms require a despot, who in turn
requires a vizier to rule for him.

Each government has a principle, a motive for the actions of the
people that maintain the government: political virtue, honor, or
fear. The citizenry is devoted to the country in a democratic
republic. That devotion is political virtue. In an aristocracy, the
aristocrats moderate their ambition for the sake of the republic. In
a monarchy, one's honor is identified with one's place within the
structure of the monarchy. That honor moves men to great actions,
as they try to act in accordance with the way men who have such a
place are supposed to act. Such actions both support the government and defend the honor of the person. The despot and all his
subjects act out of fear for their lives. In each case the relation

between the people and the government is altogether different—
shaped by the character of the citizens, by the structure of the
government, or directly by fear of the ruler.

Montesquieu ends book 3, on the principles of the three
governments, with a distinction between despotisms and moderate governments, between a government in which "men's portion,
like beasts', is instinct, obedience, and chastisement" (3.10), and
those in which "tempering, modification, accommodation, terms,
alternatives, negotiations, remonstrances" can be proposed
(3.10). Religion provides the only limit to the actions of a despotic
prince. If he is assumed not to be a man, natural right does not
apply, but the laws of religion do (3.10). Moderation appeared
first as the principle of aristocracies (3.4); but here it characterizes
governments that are not despotic (3.10); and later it appears as
the category within which are the governments free by their nature
(11.4). We shall put these notions together with the forms of
government in chapter 4.

These three governments are further described in book 4, on
education; in book 5, on the legislator's laws which support each
principle; in book 6, on the forms of justice; in book 7, on luxury;
and in book 8, on corruption. These books answer the questions:
How is the principle taught? Which laws allocating property,
particularly through inheritance, lead to the society that supports
each principle? How are the violators of the laws tried and
punished? Is luxury, or the excess required for leisure, necessary in
any of these governments? How are the three governments
corrupted? This discussion covers the ground customary in a
treatise on government. Why, then, we wonder, does Montesquieu
think this is such an incomplete account of political life that he has
scarcely written a fifth of his book? To answer this question one
needs to ask whether his treatment of these topics offers suggestions as to what has not been considered, as to other approaches to the same questions that ought to be pursued.

Let us return to book 4, on education. When monarchies are
compared to despotisms, they are said to elevate rather than
debase the heart (4.3). In monarchies the inconsistency between
the teachings of families, teachers, and society is ascribed to
religion. "This comes partly from the opposition there is for us
between the ties of religion and those of the world, a thing

unknown among the ancients" (4.4). Our religion—that is, Christianity—is not satisfied with the elevation of the heart of monarchies; it asks something else. Republican governments require the full strength of education (4.5). Fear is aroused by threats and punishments; honor is aroused by the divisions inherent in the monarchy; but virtue is a renunciation of oneself—a love of the laws in place of self-love (4.5). Political virtue must be taught, and Montesquieu reminds the reader about Plato, about music and gymnastics, about works on political life that turn on education. Here, however, education is that of the passions, a kind of habituation to constraint.

When Montesquieu, in book 5, turns to the laws that support republics and monarchies, he turns to laws that define families and establish the relations among those families. In republics, the laws must control the distribution of property so that each family has an equal share. The shares must also be small enough to ensure frugality (5.6). Then the attention and ambition of the citizens will turn to the good of their country. Monarchies, too, are supported by an inheritance law, but in their case the inheritance law ensures the preservation of the wealth and the prerogatives of great families (5.9). In both cases, commerce is disturbed. In monarchies "the laws must favor all the commerce that the constitution of this government can allow, so that the subjects can, without being ruined, satisfy the ever-recurring needs of the prince and his court" (5.9). Republics, when carried to their logical extension, have no commerce (4.6); nevertheless, there also seems to be an affinity between democracy and commerce (5.6). There are no laws in despotisms that support anyone or anything. "They cut down the tree to gather the fruit" (5.13). Despotic government is "uniform throughout; as only passions are needed to establish it, everyone is good enough for that" (5.14).

Although inheritance laws seem to determine the number and the relative wealth and importance of families, the question remains of the source and durability of that order (bks. 27 and 28) and of whether and the extent to which human government is thought to properly concern itself with the structure of families (bk. 26). In turn, the possibilities for commerce are shaped by inheritance laws, by the goods that can be traded and the men who can trade, and by increases or decreases in the number of each (bks. 20–22). In certain circumstances the prince himself can be the product of an inheritance law (18.31).

In book 6, the principles of each government are related to the simplicity of civil and criminal laws (6.1–3), the forms of judgments (6.4–8), and the establishment of penalties (6.9–21). In the first and second section, complexity is defended, and severe penalties are said to be typical of despotisms and markedly less effective than was often thought. Republics, like despotisms, have simple laws; but like monarchies, republics do not have severe penalties. Monarchies differ from republics and despotisms in the complexity of their laws and in the deliberation required in their judgments; they are like republics and unlike despotisms in the severity of their penalties. When actions are not altogether forced by necessity and when there is some space free for action, penalties are less severe. But what about penalties for crimes that appear to be so terrible that harsh punishment seems to be forced by necessity? Then the political freedom of the citizen is the question, as in book 12.

Luxury, the topic of book 7, is whatever one has beyond the necessary; this is not to say that a surplus is used "luxuriously" but that a surplus of a certain proportion beyond the necessary is required to support an order. If goods are doubled and the sequence begins with the necessary amount, luxury progresses in a sequence of 0, 1, 3, 7, 15, 31, 63, 127. In a monarchy, luxury increases from the laborer to the artisan, to the merchant, to the nobles, to the magistrates, to the great lords, to the principal tax collectors, to the princes. In Plato's republic the sequence of luxury was arithmetic, 1, 2, 3, 4, matching the division of its census. Luxury in a monarchy, unlike luxury in the republic, does not follow the constitutional order. The use of luxury is controlled by sumptuary laws. Such laws are not necessary in well-constituted democracies, are required in aristocracies, and are pernicious in monarchies. Luxury raises the issue of the condition of women, because goods beyond the necessary that are not expended in political activities are available for private, or women's, use. Incontinence in women Montesquieu connects with luxury, with liberty for the impulses of the heart, and with the weakness of the spirit (7.14). Two other possibilities for the use of luxury are not mentioned here. First, although the clergy is included as an intermediate order in monarchies, it is not included in the order of luxury. We are left to wonder about the goods that are made available to the church (25.5–6, 30.21, 31.9–10). Second, surplus goods, or luxury, can be used up in commercial activity when they are invested in further commerce, or they can be used by a warlike nobility (5.6, 20.22). Montesquieu ends book 7 with an observation that the weakness of women precludes their rule in households, but not in government (7.17).

Book 8, "On Corruption of the Principles of the Three Governments," can be divided into two sections, one on the corruption of the principles themselves (8.1–14) and one on the size appropriate for each government (8.15–20). The principle of a democracy is corrupted when it becomes either too egalitarian and despotic (8.3) or inegalitarian and aristocratic or monarchic. Aristocracies are corrupted when the nobles' rule becomes arbitrary; the extreme example is a hereditary aristocracy. Aristocracies hold more to the laws when they dread something, external power for example (8.5). Despotisms cannot decline. They are held together by external circumstances, or by religion's enforced order. In respect to size, republics are small; monarchies are of a middle size; and despotisms are large. Then, the conquests of a republic or of a monarchy threaten their principles.

Quite different patterns of governing are exhibited in republics, monarchies, and despotisms. In republics, government is the possession of the citizens, whose training and circumstances produce their devotion to the country. In monarchies, aspects of government are distributed to the heads of various families. In despotisms, there is only the power of the ruler, leaving everyone else equally subject to that power. Republics are singular, peculiar; despotisms are all alike, universal; monarchies are somehow in between. The question arises of the relation of these patterns of rule to the pattern suggested for justice in book 1, chapter 1—a question we shall examine in the next chapter.

In part 2, Montesquieu takes up the important issues in regard to liberty: whether the regime is of sufficient size that it can defend itself while remaining free, or moderate (bks. 9, 10); whether the constitution establishes political liberty and the security of the persons of the citizenry through the defense of the privacy of their thoughts (bks. 11, 12); and whether it sets taxes and some means of collecting those taxes in a way that does not violate the security of property (bk. 13). Here is the agenda of the Federal Convention of 1787, which proposed the Constitution of the United States, and its problem—namely, devising a new form of government that would be both by the many and free. In part 2, liberty is a concern of all governments and is the end of one. Part 1 identifies distinctive, peculiar kinds of government; part 2 identifies a government whose distinction is its peculiar devotion to a universal principle. This change in the content of civil, political, and international law reminds one of the emptiness of those categories in book 1, chapter 3, and raises the question of what can be behind this change or revolution.

Solitary small republics are indefensible against other kinds of governments. They must federate to survive. Rome did so and conquered the world; then Rome was conquered by federations of barbarian tribes. In addition, small countries may properly conquer in their own defense, to protect their liberty; but conquering for defense gives them no grounds for plundering the conquered. The aim is accomplished when the enemy is defeated. Either a confederation or respect for the civil laws and way of life of a conquered people implies the acknowledgment of similarities among the citizens of these distinctive governments, and thus the acknowledgment of a common humanity in a new international law (10.3). Then, it seems, the provisions for the defense of a republic for the sake of its liberty put in question its singularity.

Political liberty also implies certain constitutional arrangements and respect for the safety of each individual citizen. Political liberty is not in the nature of small republics, aristocratic or democratic, but rather is found in moderate governments (11.4). In governments that are moderate by their nature, liberty exists within laws. These laws establish boundaries and a space within those boundaries that is freed from compulsion. Free people are able to do what is within those boundaries; but they are neither constrained to do what is outside of them nor not to do what is within them (11.3). Free constitutions balance powers to this end (11.4). The English constitution is the constitution that has political liberty as its purpose. England is somehow both monarchical and republican (5.19). It appears that these moderate governments may be a kind of government of which the monar-

chies of part 1 and the English government are both examples.
Montesquieu's examination of the English government (11.6)
brings to the fore executive, legislative, and judicial powers that
seem closely related to those in the Constitution of the United
States. These powers are separated by their different sources and
are balanced through shared functions. A monarchy like that of
the English was unknown to Aristotle and the ancients (11.9–11).
The remainder of book 11 takes up the Roman balanced
government (11.12–20), in which the senate and the people
divide up the various powers. The constitution does not balance
the offices; instead, the offices express the balance between the
orders of the citizenry upon which the singularity of a small
republic was based. Montesquieu remarks that the ancients called
such governments *police,* "polities" (11.11). Nevertheless,
throughout the rest of the book he uses this word in the ordinary
sense of the everyday administrative arrangements for security
and safety that guard civility.

Part 2 ends with a consideration of the means of securing that
safety for one's person and possessions in the criminal law (bk.
12) and in taxation (bk. 13). In both cases, Montesquieu turns his
attention to the substance of the question, not to the form. The
question is how certain crimes are to be defined and what is to be
taxed and how much, not legal procedure and not who can
properly levy taxes. If we are to be able to act freely within the
space given to us by the law, the government must not inquire into
our thoughts, even when it suspects us of heresy or high treason. It
must not take so many of our goods or take them in such a way
that we cease to act, become lazy.

Once citizens are left with a space free of constraint and the
power to act within it, what will they do? What then drives them
and shapes them? What is the source of their spirit? These
questions imply the need for a wider search, and Montesquieu
begins such a search in part 3, in books about climate (14–17),
terrain (18), and finally about the various spirits (19). Part 3 ends
with a reconsideration of the English and an explanation of the
extent and way in which their character is shaped by their
constitution (19.27).

In his consideration of climate and terrain in part 3, Montesquieu presents the reader with two external, physical, things that

affect people and shape their souls, the one directly and the other indirectly. In examining these books, we can get a closer look at Montesquieu's view of the structure of the soul and the things that can shape it—at those things that make people alike and those that make people different. In this sense they are a kind of reconsideration of the questions about human nature raised in book 1, chapter 2. "If," he says, "it is true that the character of the spirit and the passions of the heart differ extremely in the various climates, laws should be relative both to the differences in these passions and to the differences in these characters" (14.1). In hot climates, people are extremely sensitive and subject to their passions, particularly to sexual passion; they are all equally subject to their passions and to their passions alone. In cold climates, people's sensations are more crude; people are more inclined to action and thus to pursuing their own ends. People then vary from those who are extremely sensitive and inactive to those who are very active and insensitive. Terrain limits the possibilities for action; this makes possible distinctions among the spirited as they pursue a particular way of life.

In books 15, 16, and 17, Montesquieu presents us with people who are subject to the despotic force of hot climates, to the circumstances of civil, domestic, and political slavery. Slavery, or despotic rule, is required when people are so subject to their passions that they will not work, when they are so involved in sexual passion that raising children is too much trouble, and when they are so fearful and cowardly that they do not protect themselves. In each case, only externally applied force can get people to do the things required for their preservation. Civil slavery that is founded on a natural reason occurs when, in a despotism, men put themselves under the protection of a lord or when "men come to perform an arduous duty only from fear of chastisement" (15.7). But such slavery goes against nature insofar as men are born equal. In Europe, civil slavery is not required by climate, and it was abolished by Christianity. Experience has demonstrated the workability of these arrangements (15.8). The remainder of book 15 is concerned with removing some of the abuses and dangers of slavery in the places where it exists and, finally, with prudent ways of freeing slaves. Distaste for slavery did not make an abolitionist of Montesquieu.

Turning from civil to domestic slavery, Montesquieu says that in hot climates, women have none of their natural modesty. Natural modesty is the shame intelligent beings feel for their imperfections; in this instance the imperfection is the conflict between their constant sexuality and the time-consuming care required for the preservation and education of children. This natural law is peculiarly applicable to women. "When the physical power of certain climates violates the natural law of the two sexes and that of intelligent beings, it is for the legislator to make civil laws which forcefully oppose the nature of the climate and reestablish the primitive laws" (16.12). The complexities, even the conflicts, in nature require legislation, choice. The grounds for that choice are the question. Montesquieu offers some suggestions in the succeeding books, and he invites the reader to reconsider the forms of government. I take up this problem in the consideration of forms of government and moderation in chapter 4.

Where do the despots come from in the climate of natural slavery? From elsewhere, unless they are eunuchs, from other climates where spirit and self-control are possible and encouraged. In places where there is no temperate zone, the strong and the weak meet directly, which leads to a succession of conquests, weakenings of the strong, and new conquests in turn. In a temperate zone, neighbors are more alike and can defend themselves from each other; and this encourages the liberty of those countries. According to Montesquieu, there is no temperate zone in Asia, and the terrain is one of broad expanses without major geographical divisions; in Europe there is a large temperate zone, and the terrain is divided by seas, major rivers, and snow-capped mountains. In both Asia and Europe the terrain adds to, rather than subtracts from, the effects of the climate.

Terrain—in the sense of both the quality of the land and its configuration—is a natural circumstance which channels the activities of people as they try to find food and shelter. Book 18 is divided into two sections: the first considers peoples who cultivate the land (18.1–8), and the second, those who do not and who depend on animals for their livelihood (18.9–31). In the first instance, only inhabitants of mountains and islands can defend themselves and remain free. In the second, savages, who hunt wild animals, are distinguished from barbarians, who herd domestic animals. The first were the source of ancient republics and the second, of the modern monarchy. Montesquieu considers two barbarian peoples, the Tartars (18.19–21) and the Franks (18.22–31). Each of these peoples leads a distinctive, peculiar, singular way of life. Book 18 adds spirited, small, poor, free peoples to the passive, large, rich, despotic peoples of books 15 through 17. Here we see a suggestion of the ground for the distinction between republics and despotisms.

Book 19 is titled "On Laws in Their Relation with the Principles Forming the General Spirit, the Mores, and the Manners of a Nation." Some principles form the spirit, mores, and manners of a nation. Laws are related to these principles. The question arises whether there are principles so different from each other that laws relate to the principles in distinctive ways. The peoples discussed in the preceding books of part 3 form particular ways of life as a result of their natural circumstances. Other than conquest, there is no change and no source of change. But in book 19 Montesquieu introduces a people with a sociable humor who appear to be in a constant state of flux in which the people constantly watch each other's activities while copying, honoring, scorning, and changing each other. These people—surely the French—are compared to the Spanish, the Chinese, and finally the English. The comparison between the French and the Spanish suggests that reform of the French toward greater seriousness and constancy could lead to their becoming lazy like the Spanish. The comparison between the French and the Chinese differentiates China, where public life is conducted in terms of familial distinctions (19.19), from those countries in which Christianity confounds these distinctions, unifying rather than separating people (19.18). With this conjunction, Montesquieu is suggesting, as we shall show, that Christianity forms the modern spirit, limiting political possibilities to those that take its unifying spirit into account.

English government, as we saw at 11.6, depended upon representative institutions which were balanced so that passions countered passions. The forms into which Englishmen step and through which they are shaped are determined by a division of political power, rather than by an establishment along divisions analogous to the natural ones. Such an organization is the opposite of China's. The English organization assumes the political irrelevance of the natural familial divisions within a people, upon which China was based. Rather, it proposes distinctions among rulers based upon the logic of ruling. In so doing, it assumes that there are no essential relations between ruling and a part of the population defined by nature. Montesquieu's descriptions of the effects of the balance of power in England are based on the possibility that a citizen might change allegiances from the executive to the legislative and back again as he seeks to influence the government. This is possible only if the population beneath the division of power contains no permanent divisions that can be related to political activity. Here we are in the arena of *Federalist* number 10. The population must be divided among a number of overlapping interests: those of geography, kinds of work, varied forms of wealth, and religions, no one of which is taken too seriously. If there are to be no permanent or ultimately important divisions among the people, economic life must be managed in a new way, and religion must be separated from direct involvement in political life. Montesquieu takes up these questions next in parts 4 and 5. Montesquieu marked the beginning of these sections of the second half of his book with his "Invocation to the Muses," in effect asking our patience for this most unpoetic consideration of the grounds of political life.

Like the French, the English have no fixed place, but unlike the French, one cannot tell from their appearance the place they claim. A leader of fashion, like a patrician or a mandarin and unlike a member of Parliament, can easily be picked out of a crowd. Of the English character, Montesquieu wrote, "But these men who are so proud, living mostly alone with themselves, would often find themselves among unfamiliar people; they would be timid and one would see in them, most of the time, a strange mixture of bashfulness and pride" (19.27). The question remains of the conditions under which a society can exist wherein men have no fixed place and have a character like that of the English.

The four books (20–23) of part 4 take up the questions that fit under the old title of political economy: the laws in relation with the nature and distinctions of commerce, the revolutions of commerce, the use of money, and the number of inhabitants. Montesquieu's discussion of commerce begins by presuming the relations of equality and inequality, described in books 5 and 7, that result from the political structure. Equality at its most extreme leads to a society without commerce, as Plato realized. As commerce spreads, so do relations among peoples, softening and corrupting the mores of singular peoples. Commerce is an activity that takes place between peoples; its shape is determined by the constitutions of those peoples (bk. 20), by changes in the broader patterns of the exchange of money (bk. 22), and by changes in the distribution of population (bk. 23).

In states that are governed by one person alone, commerce is founded primarily on luxury, on the wants and needs of those who have wealth and power. In states that have popular governments, commerce is founded on the needs and wants of the many. In the first case, a few goods of great value and considerable profit for each item are traded; in the second, many goods of lesser value and profit per unit are traded. But the traders and their trade are problematic for monarchies, despotisms, and ancient republics. For the traders to have any considerable wealth and power, trade must become a public affair and traders public men, but there is little or no place for either in these governments. Although economic commerce is ascribed to Tyre, Carthage, Marseilles, Florence, Venice, and Holland (20.4), these small republics could perhaps be seen, in this context, as trading companies in which the citizenry gathers the profits. This trading, like the agricultural labor of the helots, provides for the leisure of the citizenry. Here the growth of trade is hampered by the small size of the countries, as it is in monarchies and despotisms, because they have no place in public affairs (20.4). England is singled out as the country in which political interest gives way to the interest of its commerce, as the country that knows best how to take advantage of religion, commerce, and liberty simultaneously (20.7). In taking up the revolutions in commerce in book 21, Montesquieu shows the movement of commerce from that of Tyre to that of England.

In book 21, commerce is viewed as inevitable, and certain physical conditions such as climate and terrain are viewed as fixed. These latter provide the limits of commerce. Revolutions in commerce are the result, then, of the changes in the peoples of the world and of the consequent changes in their relation with one another. "Commerce, sometimes destroyed by conquerors, sometimes hampered by monarchs, wanders across the earth, flies from where it is oppressed, and remains where it is left to breathe" (21.5). In ancient times, each step to broaden international trade using sea power came to grief. Sea trade is identified with economic commerce, with commerce among the people and between the peoples for everyday goods, because the costs of sea transportation are so much less than those of overland transportation. Sea trade leads to an expansion of trade. Commerce, from the point of view of book 20, is natural in the sense of being inevitable, but its shape is a result of political actions and decisions.

Exploration during ancient times was primarily by land. The seas were discovered from the land, as lands are now discovered by sea (21.9). "The Romans cared only for land troops, whose spirit made them stand ever firm, fight in one place, and die there. They did not esteem the practice of seafaring people, who offer themselves for combat, withdraw, return, always evading the danger, employing stratagems, and rarely force" (21.13). The barbarian invasions destroyed the existent commerce in luxury, but because of the personal laws of the barbarians, those same invasions helped to create a situation that supported the revival of commerce in a new form. The Roman political constitution took no interest in commerce. The Roman right of nations was repugnant to commerce, as strangers had no property rights, either in things or in their own persons (21.14). The barbarians, by contrast, left the conquered peoples their former laws and their right to property and protection (21.18). This latter practice is taken up at some length in book 28.

The way for commerce was barred, temporarily, by the Christian theologians who condemned lending at interest (21.20). Not until letters of exchange were invented by Jews to save their goods from rapacious princes did commerce begin to develop (21.20). The invention of the compass and the discovery of America and much of Asia and Africa led to the expansion of commerce over the world. This new commerce is much less vulnerable to direct political control than was the commerce of the ancients. It is worldwide and outside of any particular political order, and it is not the mission of some small peoples, as it had been. This new commerce is the topic of book 22, "On Laws in Their Relation to the Use of Money."

With money as a topic, Montesquieu comes to the part of his discussion of economic things that is most like modern economics. In commerce, many commodities are traded. The kind of commodities and the extent of their trade are a result of the circumstances described in books 20 and 21; but once commodities are in commerce, they are all traded through the sign that represents them—money (22.2). That sign can be real, attached to a certain weight and grade of a metal; or it can be an idea, detached by debasement of the coinage from such certainty. Montesquieu preferred real monies (22.3). Money is rented for a price—interest—and is exchanged between countries. The price of goods, including that of money, is dependent upon the total quantity of goods marketed and upon the metals available for use as money. These variables are balanced out in the exchange (22.10). If it were not for the prevalence of international trade, particularly of an international trade that relies upon banks and letters of exchange rather than on precious metals, governmental action to control the relation between goods and money would be both possible and largely successful. Thus, although the Romans at the time of the Punic Wars could act directly to change the value of money in specie, they could not do so later, and modern governments have virtually no possibility of taking such direct action in regard to the value of money. Montesquieu concludes book 22 with a long description of Roman efforts to control usury in an economy whose prosperity depended upon wars. Those wars first required borrowing, and then the debts were repaid with the tribute from successful wars. He ends by remarking: "laws which are extremely good give birth to extreme evil. I shall continue to repeat: moderation governs men, not excesses" (22.22).

Population, like the value of money, has escaped from direct political constraint. Here Montesquieu is the sociologist, as he was the economist in the preceding chapter. In some circumstances population increases; in others it decreases. For the population to increase, families require fathers and some continuity; marriages must be prudently made; the government must not be harsh, although destitution in the midst of plenty leads the destitute to have many children; the land must be cultivated rather than left as pasture; the land must be equally divided, or the arts must be practiced, if land is unequally divided; countries must be small, as they were in Greece or as they were, in effect, under the Carolingians. The Romans made laws to encourage fertile marriages, but their circumstances gradually made it less likely that the population would increase, and the laws were changed yet further.

In books 22 and 23, in regard both to money or trade and population, the particular or individual tendencies and some universal, apparently natural ones encounter each other directly. There is no barrier between them, no space, no shape established by a government that gives a particular form to individual or family life. Montesquieu brings this to our attention through his discussion of the effect that Christianity has on population. Christianity promotes celibacy as the best way of life for everyone and denies that "the multiplication of mankind could be a result of our cares" (23.21). The spirit of distance from public affairs had already been introduced by the philosophic sects. Christianity was what prohibited usury in a universal way, making commerce possible only through the Jews, who developed a technique for commerce that took advantage of their statelessness. The shape that Christianity tried to give to private life had the effect, not of establishing that shape, but of leaving individuals to face universal, natural pressures.

Religion is the topic of part 5: the nature, principle, and place of its rule. In book 24 Montesquieu presents himself in opposition to Pierre Bayle. Impure religions are better than none, according to Montesquieu; there may be no religion pure enough for Bayle. That some obey both religions and governments is important, even if some disobey (24.2). In book 23 Montesquieu objects to Christianity because of its insistence on pushing everyone to a perfection that is appropriate only for a few. Here he says that Christianity is appropriate for moderate governments because of its gentleness (24.3). In addition, he distinguishes between laws that act as precepts and those that act as counsels, between command and inspiration, between the spirit in laws and the heart in religion (24.7). Political laws are a command, an order that speaks to the spirit, whereas religion speaks through counsels, inspirations, to the heart. The first can be general; the second should not be. Montesquieu's example is celibacy, which leads to an increasing number of rules when it is promulgated as a law for a certain order of people. Religion can support, run counter to, or replace aspects of political life, particularly those under the civil law, by proposing contemplation, penances of certain kinds, festivals, and other rules of conduct.

Religions build a way of life around their principle. The everyday activities their members pursue appear as an external police for the society at large. The sentiments or feelings of religion attach us to sensible things or to spiritual ones. The latter are stronger if they also contain the intellectual idea of a choice that the Divinity makes in their favor. Montesquieu's examples are Judaism and Mohammedanism (25.2). Religions have temples, ministers, wealth, monasteries, sacrifices, a pontificate. Tolerance, change in religion, persecution of other religions, or the relation between religions arise as topics in the context of their external police, not only with the state, but with each other. Here Montesquieu puts a dramatic condemnation of the Spanish Inquisition (25.13). In each case, Montesquieu explains that in their external relations, religious institutions must respect the limits set by political life.

In book 26 the varying orders of laws are related to the things over which the laws can have jurisdiction, particularly to rule over the structure of families (26.1). The bulk of this book is concerned with the proper place of laws whose claims are universal: namely, divine, natural, civil, and international law. Political laws—those laws that define the governments of a particular people—are defended against the civil law. The domain and order of succession of a royal family in a monarchy (26.16) and ostracism in a republic (26.17) are said to be matters for the rules of political, rather than civil, right. Montesquieu concludes with instances in which particular circumstances are of primary importance: the regulations of the police, which require prompt attention to everyday affairs (26.24), and cases such as a boat at sea, whose rules ought not be extended any further than the situation itself (26.25). This careful positioning of divine, natural, civil, and international laws is typical of modern, moderate governments. Perhaps a source of moderation is to be found in the very process of people's being subject to universal laws while being protected from the direct application of any one of them by their very number and variety of ends: God and the preservation of life, property, and societies.

In parts 3, 4, and 5, Montesquieu explores the conditions— natural, economic, and religious—that underlie the governments whose structure he explored in parts 1 and 2. He seems to suggest that the relation between governments and those underlying conditions has changed. Some governments—namely, republics— used to try to shape those conditions, and they had some success without becoming simply despotic. They had some kind of moderation, even if it depended on the character of the citizens. Ancient republics and despotisms have assumed that the natural divisions among the people, however understood, have a relation to political distinctions. Those divisions no longer seem to be commensurate with political life, with distinctive ways of life, but rather to be a response to the working out of universal natural laws. Moderate government—monarchies and what we now call democratic republics—need to get some distance from this universality, to give a space for particular political life and ends. These are the topics of my chapters 4, 5, and 6.

The remaining question is how political law has been and can be shaped for moderate governments. In book 26, Montesquieu said that royalty and ostracisms—that is, excluding citizens from citizenship—were to be guided by political principles. In part 6 (bks. 27–31) the origins of political law for a monarchy are taken up at length. In parts 1 and 2, monarchical institutions were treated as a given. To discuss the source of the political law that defines monarchies is to question the rule of the king. For Montesquieu the shape of the French monarchy is a result of circumstances and decisions that can be understood strictly within human and political terms.

Books 27 and 28 are peculiar in form; book 27 is one long chapter, and book 28 has 45 chapters, far more than any other. Book 27 traces how in Rome the civil law escaped from political law, and thus from political purpose; book 28 traces the slow development in France of a way of judging disputes that could be called political. Book 29 describes how law should be written when it establishes a way of judging, or a way of legislating—that is, when it acts indirectly. Books 30 and 31 take the reader from the origin of the French monarchy through some of its revolutions. The history of the variations of the institutions that form the monarchy—the nobility, the clergy, a separate judicial order—are the subject of these final books.

In book 27 Montesquieu analyzes how in Rome the control of inheritances by political laws was dissolved. Under Romulus, he says, the land was divided among the families, and inheritance laws designed to keep one plot for each family were established. The Romans believed in the absolute power of fathers over their children. This power seemed to extend logically to the share of the father's goods that each child inherited. These principles were in conflict, and the second principle pushed constantly toward individual testaments and toward accumulating the wealth or increasing the poverty of certain families. The citizenry was decimated by wars, and families that had children became markedly less prevalent. The restoration of the citizenry was encouraged by giving women with children the right to inherit. Then, the wealth of all nations inundated Rome. Finally, under Justinian, Roman law tried to follow natural equality, with no reference to the regime's interest in any kind of family or relation among families.

Book 28 describes the growth of French civil law, which was embedded in a way of judging rather than in a code of administered penalties. The conquerors of the Roman Empire did not impose their civil law on the conquered peoples. They thought of law as something attached to individuals, as something personal (28.2). The civil law of the barbarians was based on settlements that established satisfaction for wrongs done. Certain sums, called *freda,* were paid to the lord for his enforcement of the settlement; this constituted the justices of the lords, which was both a service and a payment. Quarreling families would have pursued their vendettas endlessly unless the lord could provide the justice for which he was paid—a settlement and an enforcement of that settlement. The codes that established settlements gradually ceased to be used. Because there were no canons of evidence, it was not clear how to tell the guilty from the innocent. Ordeals, of which combat was the chief example, were a way to leave the judgment to God. They also had the curious merit of solving the problem of appropriate penalties. There was no possibility for an appeal of the judgment.

According to Montesquieu, the reign of Saint Louis, about two hundred years after the first Capetian king of France, began the turnaround toward a new civil law. Saint Louis set a general restriction on judicial combat in his domain, and he restricted it in his baronies in the case of a challenge for false judgment (28.29). Appeals of both the judgment itself and of the proceedings became possible. This led to a whole sequence of changes, which set up something like judicial process as we now know it. These changes, however, established, not a code, but a way of proceeding. They led to a distaste for the old way of doing things. "Sometimes many centuries must pass to prepare for changes; events ripen, and then there are revolutions" (28.39). The parlement, which was the judge of last resort and which considered questions between the holders of great offices in relation to the political order, was obliged to become a sitting body. The continuing establishment of the king's jurisdiction is the subject of the end of book 28. Written law required a study of which the nobles and illiterate peoples were not capable (28.43). The king needed officers to record and enforce the new rules for the kingdom.

Two questions are taken up in the remainder of the book. First, in book 29, How are laws to be written, composed, that will serve as did those of Saint Louis to settle disputes? The question is not, as in book 5, which laws ought the legislator give in order to promote the principles of the government, but how should laws be written so that they will both settle disputes and do so in the direction preferred by the legislator. According to Montesquieu, laws often seem similar but are not or seem different but are similar in their aims, effect, motive, spirit. They must be compared in the context of other laws, their purpose, and their circumstances. Only then will it be clear that a given law is truly the same in two countries or times. Laws must be composed so as not to encourage more disputes (29.16). They must not rule either through opinions on particular cases (29.17) or with excessive uniformity (29.18). And finally, one must beware of the passions of the legislator, even of the greatest legislators, the political philosophers (29.19). This formal discussion of the laws is most appropriate for laws that establish relations rather than those that direct actions—for the laws that are typical of moderate governments and of their constitutions.

Second, the question for books 30 and 31 is, What changes in the structure of the government itself paralleled those in the civil law that led to the development of a civil law based on a way of judging rather than on a body of rules to be administered? The question of the political structure becomes the question of the source of the nobility and of the king. To begin with, the political law of the Frankish monarchy did not establish inherited fiefs, but it did distinguish nobles from other Franks. These nobles followed the kings to war, but they had to be asked to join (30.3). The kings constantly acquired goods in these wars and gave them to the nobles (30.4). These goods—benefices, honors, and fiefs—were regulated by the political, not by the civil, laws and were revocable (30.16). Then, although the nobility was as old as the monarchy, the nobility was not attached to particular rewards and duties; the distribution of particular goods was at the discretion of the king. At the beginning of the reign of the Merovingians, there were free cities and a large number of freemen, but by the beginning of the reign of the Capetians, the number of servitudes was prodigious. Only lords and serfs remained. Montesquieu ascribes this chiefly to the constant warfare in which booty and prisoners were constantly being taken and distributed (30.11).

Roman taxation by a central government had disappeared. The king's revenues came from his own domains (30.13). The words that had been used to describe that taxation were now used to describe altogether different practices (30.14). There were no taxes; instead, free men owed services. Military and civil jurisdiction was in the same person—the count, the bishops, or the vassals of the king. Fiscal rights were small, and judicial rights were shared with notables, so that the regime was not in fact despotic (30.18). The justice of the lords was the result of the original settlement; it was not a corruption of the government (30.20). When the church was given a fisc or fief in order to support itself, the church's fief was held in the same way as other fiefs. But there was a problem when it became the bishop's duty to lead his followers to war alongside the vassals and counts. Over the course of the entire period of rule of the Merovingians and the

Carolingians, fiefs and underfiefs came to be inherited, and freeholds were converted into fiefs.

Montesquieu describes the efforts by kings and queens to halt this transformation, all of which were ultimately unsuccessful. When they tried to reassert the revocability of fiefs, they were resisted. Some regularity was essential, even in this nation. As fiefs were settled, the question of where the king could get fiefs to give his followers became acute. The attention of the kings turned to the wealth of the clergy. Because the church can inherit from everyone and is a permanent body, its goods increase continuously, making it a constant source of goods that kings can take and give to the nobles.

In the French constitution of that time, all power resided in the king, the nobility, and the clergy. Good kings balanced the other two powers and joined interests with one or both (31.21). Charles Martel despoiled the clergy and formed fiefs a second time. He "put an end to an abuse which, unlike ordinary evils, was the easier to cure for being so extreme" (31.9). Pepin protected the clergy and established tithes (31.12). Charlemagne kept the power of the nobility within limits and curtailed the oppression of the clergy and of freemen (31.18). His successor, Louis the Pious, antagonized both: the clergy by enacting excessively strict regulations for their behavior, and the nobility by elevating commoners (31.21). The kings and the clergy continued to weaken each other (31.23). The Battle of Fontenay in 842 irreparably damaged the monarchy (31.25). Afterwards the nobility could choose whether a new fief was to be under the king or under a lord; they were obliged only to follow the king to a defensive war (31.27). Each effort to reassert the political control of the king over fiefs actually furthered the great transformation to inherited fiefs and underfiefs. There was no longer any way of stopping the disintegration. Finally, the crown was given to Hugh Capet, who held the largest fief. Political government ended, and feudal government began when the crown was given to the most powerful vassal and was inherited as the fief had been (31.32). Women inherited crowns in kingdoms established later, as in Normandy, because the feudal order eventually permitted women to inherit fiefs (31.33). Fiefs became the concern of civil, rather than of political, laws (31.34).

In sum, between book 28 and books 30 and 31, Montesquieu

has collected two political laws for the French monarchy: the first established a way of judging disputes; the second regulated the inheritance of the crown according to the practice of the Salic Franks before they conquered Gaul. Out of this bare material Montesquieu fashioned, in books 2–8, an understanding of a new kind of government based on intermediate institutions—a monarch and nobility, a judicial order, and a clergy—which could be compared to the ancient republics. That government, neither singular nor universal, has had many variations. This construction may well be what had made Montesquieu say in his Preface that, with Correggio, he too was a painter. Let us, then, return to the beginning of the book, examining it this time in respect to the way the topics of the beginning are treated throughout. The question now will be, not the order of appearance, but the internal structure of the book.

3

SPIRIT

Montesquieu begins *The Spirit of the Laws,* as we have already noticed, with what appears to be a discussion of the different kinds of laws—divine, natural, and human; but he concludes the first book by saying: "I shall examine all these relations; together they form what is called THE SPIRIT OF THE LAWS . . . as this spirit consists in the various relations that laws may have with various things, I have had to follow the natural order of laws less than that of these relations and of these things" (1.3). He contrasts the "natural order of the laws" to the order of "these relations and these things," or that of the spirit. The law and the spirit seem to operate in different ways, if not in different realms.[1]

Montesquieu's distinction between law and spirit would be immediately recognizable if the question were whether the law is obeyed in the spirit of God—that is, if one law and one spirit were contrasted. In this question we would immediately recognize Saint Paul and Martin Luther. In 2 Corinthians, Paul wrote: "Now if the dispensation of death, carved in letters on stone came with such splendor that the Israelites could not look at Moses' face because of its brightness, fading as this was, will not the dispensation of the Spirit be attended with greater splendor."[2] And in Romans he says, "But now we are discharged from the law, dead to that which held us captive, so that we serve not under the old written code but in the new life of the Spirit."[3] For Luther the important thing was faith, not works: ". . . so the person of a man must needs first be good or wicked before he does a good or wicked work, and his works do not make him good or wicked, but he himself makes his works either good or wicked."[4] These quotations serve only to remind us of the insistence and bluntness with which these two denigrated obedience to the law as a principle of action and insisted upon the importance of the intent, the spirit, or the faith in which acts were done. But they both turned around and insisted

34

upon obedience to the written law, to the authorities. The one thing required of this world is the peace that provides room for the spiritual life, and the rules of any society that provides that peace must be accepted and defended.

If Montesquieu's book relied on law rather than spirit as the organizing principle, the discussion of laws would provide what would be, in effect, an outline of the rest of the book; but it does not. In this chapter, I shall first present an examination of the criticism of each law suggested in book 1 and then follow the implications of that criticism throughout the whole book, as Montesquieu fills the despotism and emptiness of the legal categories with the spirit, with human activity directed toward a common, if limited, end. To summarize, the divine justice based upon precise reciprocity, equality, punishment, and universality turns, in practice, into endless punishment. Justice needs limits to be a human good. In practice, divine justice runs perilously close to the politics based upon the equality and the universality of the passions that is enforced by fear of punishment. But the citizens must have some weakness for each other; they must share a partiality, a spirit. Without the direction and action of natural spirits, only despotic force, or slavery, can enforce the activities required for survival. Those spirits have a natural basis in the ways of life that result from trying to make a living in a variety of terrains and climates. The relation between that partiality and the universality of the divine, even of the spirit of God, or of the natural, can vary. The variations imply different contents for and relations between political, civil, and international right, and therefore, republics, monarchies, or despotisms. The latter group is the topic of books 2–8, and of my fourth chapter.

DIVINE LAW

Chapter 1 of book 1, "Of Laws in Their Relation with Various Beings," is primarily concerned with the place of divine law and the justice it expresses. Divine law is not that law, or dispensation, given to people as a consequence of the intervention of God in human affairs. Rather, Montesquieu seems to begin with Descartes's list of the various beings that have laws of their own: the

divinity, the material world, angels, beasts, and men.[5] But
Montesquieu changes Descartes's angels into particular intelligent
beings.[6] Montesquieu says that the material world would not exist
or continue to exist without some regularity, some rule. That rule
and the intelligent beings that perceive it could not be created by a
blind fate. There must be, then, a primitive reason, or, perhaps by
implication, God. Here Montesquieu takes Descartes's argument
that the limited human spirit—which doubts, understands, af-
firms, denies, wills, rejects, perceives, and imagines—is inconceivable without a complete spirit upon which it depends; then he
allies it with the traditional argument for the existence of God
from the design of the world.

There are, according to Montesquieu, relations of equity prior
to any positive law for particular intelligences that regulate
relations between such intelligences and between the particular
intelligences and the divinity. If such intelligences fail to achieve
an equitable relation between themselves and with the divinity, or
primitive reason, it is because of their limited nature and because
it is in the nature of such beings to act by themselves. Each
example Montesquieu gives of this equity involves a principle of
strict reciprocity. Particular intelligent beings acknowledge their
debts to the laws and to their superiors and are themselves held
subject to the harm they have done to another being. This equity is
based on reciprocity—an eye for an eye; and if goods cannot be
repaid, one must remain dependent upon the god, the society, or
the man that provided the good. This justice assumes the equality
of the particular intelligences; no accommodation is made for the
strengths or weaknesses of the parties. It also depends exclusively
on punishment for enforcement; no sense of common good or
common activity promotes it, but simply the punishment of
individuals for wrongs done. Finally, this justice is universal; it
applies to all such intelligences in every situation. To understand
Montesquieu's assessment of this justice, we need to examine the
suggestions that he makes throughout the book about the justice
based upon exact reciprocity, equality, punishment, and universality. Here that justice is seen in action, in the political life of
passionate and spirited people. We shall examine its similarity to
the justice practiced in republics and in despotisms and then take

up the question of punishment. In practice, unconstrained by some limited, common way of life, this justice is despotic.

According to Montesquieu, republican law and justice follow the pattern for justice established in book 1. In republics, the citizens are treated equally by the law and are made literally equal through a distribution of lands and through inheritance laws that establish frugality as well as liberty; or the citizens are made to appear equal by a kind of commerce that does not encourage expenditure or by habits modeled on the frugality of a senate (5.5–7). This equality is expressed in political life as the equal devotion of the citizens to their country. "In a democracy, love of equality limits ambition to the single desire, the single happiness, of rendering greater services to one's homeland than other citizens. Men cannot render it equal services, but they should equally render it services. At birth one contracts an immense debt to it that can never be repaid" (5.3). Republics, then, are based on the obligation to repay an infinite debt to the society that sustains the equal citizens. However, the obligation is to be repaid, not out of fear of punishment, but out of love of country. Therefore, punishments are moderate and rare (6.11).

The citizens pursue a variety of activities in republics: for example, military prowess, commerce, peace (4.6, 5.6). In republics that have war as their principal aim—the characteristic form of the republic—"all work and all professions that could lead to earning silver were regarded as unworthy of a free man. . . . In the Greek republics one was, therefore, in a very awkward position. One did not want the citizens to work in commerce, agriculture, or the arts; nor did one want them to be idle" (4.8). The citizens spent their time in exercises, in gymnastic and in those exercises that were a preparation for war. Such people were tough and savage; they needed some tempering. Music, "which enters the spirit through the organs of the body" and which arouses all the passions, provides an avenue to a mean between the toughness of exercise and the savagery, or asociability, of the sciences of speculation. For men to be virtuous they must be willing both to give all to their country and to do so in concert with other men.

Sophocles' *Ajax* provides us with a clear example of the

character that, according to Montesquieu and Sophocles, presented a problem for the ancient republics. Ajax, when shamed by not having received Achilles' armor as a prize for his valor, is fooled by Athena into slaughtering sheep, as he would have slaughtered his fellow Greeks in his anger. Nothing mattered to him but the shame done to his honor; he was not deterred from the slaughter by fellow feeling for the Greeks; nor was he deterred from suicide by feeling for his wife. Some gentleness, pity, tenderness, sweet pleasure, and love is required, even in a republic of warriors. Music makes possible passions other than harshness, anger, and cruelty; in arousing gentler passions, it makes it possible for men to have a weakness for each other, to assist and be assisted. For the citizens to love their country and act together in ancient republics, some other ingredient had to be added to the warriors' passion to be recognized for their devotion to their country. It seems, then, that some sympathy for those who are not warriors and for the possibility that even warriors share something with the others and with each other, permits the development of a spirit of the country. This sympathy and common spirit contrast with the asociability of warriors and of speculation.[7] Spirit has something to do with what we can hold in common with some others, not with the universality and individuality of the passions. The passions must be shaped and limited in order to support a spirit.

In despotism, there are equality, utter dependence, punishment, and the appearance of universality. The people in a despotism are all equally under despotic rule. "In despotic states the nature of the government requires extreme obedience, and the prince's will, once known, should produce its effect as infallibly as does one ball thrown against another" (3.10). Most peoples are subjected to despotisms, because "a despotic government leaps into view, so to speak; it is uniform throughout; as only the passions are needed to establish it, everyone is good enough for that" (5.14). Despotism—that is, a government based exclusively on the passions—is the easiest to imagine and to put into effect; and it is the same everywhere. A despotism is so big that it appears to be the whole world to its inhabitants. This is a state that collects on the obligations of a people to the society in which they live; its mechanism, or principle, is fear of punishment. Only religion or the rules of the divinity can counter the prince's will in a despotism. "There is, however, one thing with which one can sometimes counter the prince's will: that is religion. . . . The laws of religion are a part of a higher precept, because they apply to the prince as well as to the subjects. But, it is not the same for natural right; the prince is not assumed to be a man" (3.10). Only with respect to the divine must the prince admit his humanity; in so doing, he must accept its despotic rule, because he knows only of despotic rule. Despotic rule, then, is altogether uniform; it is applied equally and universally; and it is based on punishments without limit for wrongs done.

Both republics and despotisms are based on a notion of equity that assumes equality among the people and the utter dependence of that people upon the government because they have received everything from it. "Men are all equal in republican government; they are equal in despotic government; in the former it is because they are everything; in the latter, it is because they are nothing" (6.2). The two governments differ in the extent to which they rely upon punishments and in the range of people who are considered to be equal. Republics do not rely primarily upon punishment; rather they rely upon their citizens' wanting to act for the whole; they limit the range of their singular union to those with whom they share some sympathy and a common spirit. A rigid equity based on retaliation is not imposed upon those within the republic, although it does reappear in their view of how those outside the republic are to be treated (10.3). Despotisms rely entirely upon punishments and do so in essentially the same way from despotism to despotism.

From the preceding, it would appear that punishment itself is an important consideration for Montesquieu. Governments must move from the principle of equity to the actual punishment of people. In book 12, Montesquieu writes that the appropriate retaliation is one that mirrors the evil done but does not go beyond it. "The penalties for these last crimes [those that attack security] are what are called punishments. They are a kind of retaliation, which causes the society to refuse to give security to a citizen who has deprived or has wanted to deprive another of it. This penalty is derived from the nature of the thing and is drawn from reason and from the sources of good and evil" (12.4). The law is enforced by punishment that is a precise retaliation. Elsewhere, Montesquieu wrote: "Despotic states which prefer simple laws, make much use of the law of retaliation; moderate states sometimes accept it. But the difference is that the former have it exercised strictly, while the others almost always temper it" (6.19). The others temper retaliation because such punishments are problematic in themselves. Harsh and cruel punishments, even if they succeed in correcting the offense, mean that "a vice produced by the harshness remains in the state; spirits are corrupted; they have become accustomed to despotism" (6.12). Punishment itself—that is, doing some physical harm to another man, however guilty he may be—accustoms the spirits of those responsible for the punishment to despotism. The ruler becomes accustomed to treating others as if they responded only to violence, to the slavish rule of slaves.

Despotism is described as the rule whose principle is fear of punishment. It has no other principle. In despotisms, fear must "beat down everyone's courage and extinguish even the slightest feeling of ambition" (3.9). Under despotisms, men are like beasts whose portion is instinct, obedience, and chastisement (3.10). Education is "reduced to putting fear in the heart and in teaching the spirit a few very simple religious principles" (4.3). Under despotisms, rulers have no recourse in punishing crimes but to turn to ever-greater punishments: "Souls that are everywhere startled and made more atrocious can be guided only by a greater atrocity" (6.13). The terror leads to greater terror, to terrorized, depraved spirits; but it does not lead to greater obedience.

Despotism is endlessly corrupted, ruined by its internal vice. It maintains itself only when "circumstances, which arise from the climate, the religion, and the situation or the genius of the people, force it to follow some order and to suffer some rule" (8.10). A rule based on punishment and fear has no stability, no limit, no regularity of its own. These latter are only provided by some external force. In book 12, where Montesquieu approaches the problem of punishment from the point of view of the security of a citizen in a free government, he begins by asserting that the punishment should be appropriate to the offense (12.4) and ends with a long consideration of those offenses that present the possibility of endless punishment. Offenses that inevitably contain an element of secrecy (e.g., magic, heresy, homosexuality, treason) present the danger that the prosecution will become so concerned with the possibility that there might be a crime behind every action that there comes to be no end to the punishment. He goes so far as to say, "Vagueness in the crime of high treason is enough to make government degenerate into despotism" (12.7).

Two other examples of endless punishment for wrongs done suggest that one purpose of government is to put an end to such punishment and to justice understood as an exact exchange of goods and punishments. These examples concern limits to the law of retaliation in international politics. First, according to Montesquieu, the members of the Amphictyon league of ancient republics took the oath "I swear that I will never destroy a town of the Amphictyons and that I will not divert its running water; if any people dare do such a thing, I shall declare war on them, and I shall destroy their towns"(29.5). This law opened the door to the destruction, rather than to the preservation, of the Greek towns. In order to preserve the towns, the Greeks needed to come to think that it was such an atrocious thing to destroy another Greek town that they would not do it even when justice required such an action. A good right of nations requires such a change. The notion that a community sets some limit to the enforcement of a strict reciprocal justice seems to be a prerequisite for any nondespotic political life.

Second, the analysis of the right of a conqueror in book 10 takes a similar course. To paraphrase Montesquieu, that right is based on the law of nature, the law of natural enlightenment, the law that forms political societies and that is drawn from the thing itself. The law of natural enlightenment "wants us to do to others what we would want to have done to us" (10.3). This appears to be the reciprocal justice of book 1, but the point of view is the "we" of the community, not what is due to the offended, to the other. Montesquieu writes here that there are four ways in which a conquered state has been treated. These vary from continuing to govern according to the laws of the conquered and taking for the conqueror only the exercise of political and civil government, on the one hand, to exterminating all of the citizens of the conquered state, on the other hand. Montesquieu assigns the first to his own times, "to contemporary reasoning, to the religion of the present day, to our philosophy, and to our mores" (10.3); the latter he assigns to the Romans. In book 21, in his consideration of Roman commerce, Montesquieu refers to the Romans' right of nations as one that assumed no common rules about ownership, with the result that any thing or man that fell into enemy hands was assumed to belong to the enemy (21.14). These limits on an equal exchange are due in large part to the opinions of a time, the opinions that create a community within which the entire force of strict, reciprocal justice is to be limited.

Christianity seems to offer the possibility that that community is all mankind. Christianity offers two entirely different motives—fear and love—for the restraint of punishment among its adherents. First, it does so through its own threat of punishment. It holds the prince accountable for his actions by threatening him with punishment. A prince who loves and fears religion is said to be like a tamed lion, but the one who fears and hates it is "like the wild beasts who gnaw the chain that keeps them from throwing themselves on passers-by" (24.2). The punishment that religion threatens the prince with has the same effect as the punishment that a prince threatens the people with: it controls, even tames, the beast in people. At the end of book 6, on the forms of judgment and kinds of punishments, Montesquieu remarks, "The Greek emperors had forgotten that they did not carry the sword in vain" (6.21).[8] But that sword is the force that controls the beast within people.[9]

One must turn to the love that Christianity engenders to find a motive for restraint that is not dehumanizing. Montesquieu says that because people are ordered to love one another, the Christian religion must promote the best political laws (24.1). It is suited to moderate rather than to despotic government because of its gentleness and because it insists on monogamy. It makes princes less separate, more human, and therefore less timid and cruel because they and the subjects can count on each other. As Montesquieu remarks elsewhere, Christianity makes people communicative (19.18) and leads to a right of nations that leaves the vanquished their "life, liberty, laws, goods, and always religion, when one does not blind oneself" (24.3). Christianity, then, demands a relation between Christians that leads to limits on punishment. This analysis of Christianity departs altogether from that relating the divinity, or primitive reason, to the particular intelligences in book 1, chapter 1; Christianity counsels that we see ourselves in everyone else in such a way that an equity based on retaliation for wrongs done appears unjust.

Montesquieu goes on, however, to say that the perfect love required of Christians should be a counsel, not a precept. Laws, or precepts, speak to the spirit, not to the heart; to the good, not to the perfect; to the general, not to the particular. Here the command to love one's neighbor is seen as a counsel to individuals for perfection of the heart. "Celibacy was a counsel of Christianity; when it was made into a law for a certain order of people, new laws had to be made every day in order to bring men to observe the first one. The legislator tired himself, he tired the society, making men execute by precept what those who love perfection would have executed by counsel" (24.7). Then, Christian love offers a new danger for the laws—that of trying to ensure its rules for perfection through command—which leads to another source of endless laws and punishments. The generality of that spiritual being's claim for worship suggests the generality of the laws or precepts that speak to the spirit. Spirit, in this instance and in that of the republics, is associated with communication and commonalty. Although Christian love counters the ruthlessness of a universal divine abstract justice between individuals with their forgiveness for each other's sins, the effort to enforce that counsel for love through political precepts or laws would produce, not political restraint or moderation, but even greater punishment and despotism.

In his analysis of the justice of the Franks, Montesquieu shows a way in which the strict justice of reciprocity between individuals has been limited. The justice of the Franks, as Montesquieu presents it, begins with a simple rule of retaliation: you killed my relative; therefore I shall kill you—then your relatives will try to kill me; and so on and so on. This sequence was only interrupted by the payment of the settlement for the injury. "The law puts itself in the place of the offended man and asks for him the satisfaction, that, in a cool moment, he himself would have demanded" (30.19). This satisfaction was the payment of a sum carefully calculated in respect to the standing of the man harmed and the character of the crime. An additional payment was made to the lord of the fief for protecting the guilty party from the injured party.[10] This was the justice of the lords, a lucrative right that was as much a consequence of holding a fief as was any other benefice. Rendering justice among these violent nations amounted to "granting to him who had committed an offense one's protection from the vengeance of him who had received it, and obliging the latter to receive the satisfaction that was his due" (30.20). Justice, then, meant establishing a limited scale on which vengeance was to be exacted and then enforcing that scale. As was the case in the ancient republics, a justice that does not lead to endless punishment requires the identification of a group within which the full strength of retaliatory justice is not exercised.

In sum, the result of viewing justice as retribution is endless punishment.[11] The equity implied by a divine law of retaliation is, Montesquieu makes clear throughout his book, not compatible with human, political justice. Christianity proposes an end to the law of retaliation by asking us to love our neighbors as ourselves, to see ourselves in the offender. In so doing, it offers a ground for forgiving injustices. But this means that it asks of us such perfection in our love for each other that any political enforcement of that love provides another, perhaps more powerful, ground for despotic government, as there is no way that such perfection, when it is expected of everyone toward everyone, can be enforced politically.[12] In his discussion of the justices of the lords, Montesquieu makes the limits on retaliation the origin of their justice. Human, political justice requires some limit to punishment, some group within which the full play of retribution is not permitted. This justice is a good, but not the best, thing; to pursue the best is to come too close to the worst.

NATURAL LAW

The concluding paragraphs of the first chapter of book 1 suggest another sort of general law that might be more applicable to political life than that of particular intelligences. What if, Montesquieu seems to ask, beasts have a nature other than the simply material one, but one that, like the material, acts in accord with general laws, although not with the same necessity? These beasts have sentiments that are effective among themselves; their general laws are called natural laws. That is, could one understand that men's common life could be arranged by taking into account the natural laws of their sentiments while leaving their intelligences to move toward reason or God, unencumbered by any direct concern with their common life and limited only by their particularity? This is an account of a liberalism that gives control of the sentiments or passions to politics so that the higher human impulses can move freely toward their own ends. To explore this last possibility, we must return to book 1 and examine chapter 2, "On the Laws of Nature," to see the limit of the natural law as Montesquieu sees it and then to move toward an understanding of the natural spirit that emerges from this analysis.

Because natural laws are those that "derive uniquely from the constitution of our being" (1.2), it is not unreasonable to look for them before all others, before those laws that are a part of society and of political life. In this search, Montesquieu says, we must consider the natural sentiments in order of increasing complexity. One cannot, as Hobbes did, ascribe to men in nature the complex ideas of men in society. This argument is virtually a précis of Rousseau's later position in his *Discourse on the Origins of Inequality;* but for Montesquieu, in contrast to Rousseau, the sentiments of natural men slip from a feeling of their weakness to that of their needs, to their pleasure at the approach of another, and to the desire to live in society. In presenting the natural sentiments in this manner, Montesquieu suggests that the natural sentiments are not limited to those that existed before and outside of society. Rather, there are natural sentiments that move people toward one another and are a part of social life. Here Montesquieu points toward David Hume and Adam Smith and theories of moral sentiments in which the sentiments of those in society are assumed to be as natural as any hypothetical sentiments of people outside of society.

According to Montesquieu, the human recognition of sentiments (of his weakness, of his needs); of mutual weakness, or of pleasure at the approach of one's own kind and the charm of the other sex; and of an ability—for example, to acquire knowledge— lead to intentions that are said to be natural laws: namely, to seek peace and nourishment, to be attentive to those of the opposite sex, and to desire to live in society. Because these laws make no distinctions among people, they assume natural equality—that everyone is equally subject to these sentiments and is equally led to these intentions. Although everyone comes to desire to live in society as a consequence of the acquisition of knowledge, each person, in fact, takes part in a particular society. This seems to suggest that the relevant knowledge is that some similarity exists with others, which would make a common life desirable. In this way, the general desire to live in society in effect divides people into separate societies, making distinctions among peoples and implying, for each society, that its way of life is preferable. Warfare follows from pursuing the advantages of individuals and of societies.

In addition, there is the natural law by which we are led to the creator by having the idea of one impressed upon us. Among laws, this is the first in importance, but not in the order of their development in men. Men come last to speculative ideas. If a natural law that leads us to our creator is impressed upon us by him, it seems reasonable to think, unless told otherwise by the creator, that the law is impressed upon all who are human. But if we come to recognize this law after the formation of societies, the particular expressions of it are likely to be quite different and a consequence of the kind of society within which it comes to be recognized.

This presentation of the natural law indicates a possible disjunction between a sentiment or an inclination and the intention to satisfy it, and also between that intention and the particular action that is to carry it out. This disjunction leaves open the possibility that political life could have purposes beyond the enforcement of natural laws. Montesquieu takes up the question of the relation between natural inclinations and the intentions that are designed to satisfy those inclinations of the natural law in his discussion of climate in books 14 through 17. To summarize, Montesquieu seems to say there that there are some natural circumstances in which the natural inclinations do not lead to forming the intentions that would satisfy the end implied in those inclinations. Only despotic force, or slavery, can establish a link between our natural inclinations or sentiments and those intentions by forcing us to put our inclinations aside. In books 18 and 19, Montesquieu moves on to the circumstances in which a variety of intentions can both satisfy the ends implied by the natural inclinations and move beyond those ends to some particular way of life.

In his discussion of women in book 16, "How the Laws of Domestic Slavery Are Related to the Nature of the Climate," Montesquieu explicitly raises the question of the conflict between our sentiments and the natural laws that express the intentions to seek peace and nourishment, to be attentive to those of the other sex, and to live in society. In chapter 12, "On Natural Modesty," Montesquieu writes that nature has spoken to all nations and that they are agreed in attaching scorn to the incontinence of women. He mentions defense and attack, mutual desires, temerity and shame, and long periods of time for preservation and brief moments for reproduction. It is, he says, "in the nature of intelligent beings to feel their imperfections; nature has then given us modesty, that is, shame for our imperfections" (16.12). Modesty, then, is natural to us as intelligent beings.

Women's modesty is a natural law, a kind of corollary of the natural law of the two sexes, which asserts their attentiveness to each other. Modesty follows from the conflict between preservation of one's being and preservation of the species, or reproduction. Intemperance, or an excess of time spent on reproduction, keeps men from work and keeps women pregnant. To understand this requires an act of intelligence in which the competing natural claims are weighed. Women are to recognize their weakness, feel shame for it, and acknowledge their greater need for care and protection. In the natural law according to which women are modest, women apply intelligence to the characteristics of their sexuality. In so doing, they come up with a variation on the natural law by which men and women seek one another. According to it, women add the knowledge of their weakness to their inclinations. This suggests that nature, in the sense of passions or inclinations, is contradictory; people must apply their intelligences to that human weakness and provide for it in society.

Montesquieu concludes this chapter by asserting that when "the physical power of certain climates violates the natural law of the two sexes and that of intelligent beings, it is for the legislator to make civil laws which forcefully oppose the nature of the climate and re-establish primitive laws" (16.12). In extreme situations, for example in very hot climates, the connection between the sentiment or inclination and the intention designed to satisfy it must be forcefully imposed. Slavery, the enclosure of women, and even despotism itself can be efforts to establish the natural law in situations wherein work, modesty, and peace are so hard to maintain that they require that every ounce of available human strength be used in their pursuit. There is no room left for any other pursuit, as there might be in other situations. But the thought remains that the enforcement of the natural law requires force.

These last two suggestions—that the movement from natural sentiments or inclinations to those intentions that Montesquieu calls natural laws is unclear because of the contradictions among the inclinations and that the enforcement of those natural laws requires force—make us suspect that Montesquieu thinks the natural law in this sense is not the only guide for political life. In other words, no single principle could be devised to satisfy the requirements of nature. Intelligence and judgment—particular solutions—were required. And the rule that is based solely on those needs is slavery; it is despotic. That is, no single standard for decent politics can be devised in response to natural needs, as proposed by Hobbes and Locke. Montesquieu sorts his way through these difficulties in books 14–19 with an investigation into the variety of those impulses that we have heretofore called sentiments or inclinations.

In beginning his discussion of climate, Montesquieu distinguishes among our inclinations; there are two different sources within our soul and two different sorts of resulting inclinations: "If it is true that the character of the spirit and the passions of the heart are extremely different in the various climates, *laws* should be relative both to the difference in these passions and to the differences in these characters" (14.1). Expressions of the spirit are characters; those of the heart are passions. Montesquieu repeats the distinction as being one between passions and between characters. Montesquieu here presents the reader with a formal division of the inclinations and with the question of the extent and manner in which each is affected by climate, by the physical environment.

The inclinations most affected by climate are those closest to
nature in the sense of a continuing physical existence. Although
Montesquieu's outdated science may seem absurd to us now, to
connect the inclinations that seem most connected to our bodies,
to our physiology, with our physical existence and its physical
causes does not seem so peculiar.[13] Heat, he says, lengthens the
fibers of the body, and cold shortens them (14.2). This affects the
strength and the sensitivity of people. The shorter fibers in the
peoples of northern climates lead to greater strength; that strength
leads to confidence, courage, and frankness. It makes people less
susceptible to the desire for vengeance, to suspiciousness, to
plotting, and to trickery. These traits result from strength itself,
from the opinion that one is strong and from the effect that both
have on the way people act toward one another. We speak of
strength of character, believing with Montesquieu that such
strength is required for admirable action. Sensitivity, on the other
hand, is a consequence of the subtlety with which sensations are
received. In the north, people are so unsubtle that they only get
pleasure from things that "can start the spirits in motion again:
hunting, travels, war, and wine" (14.2). The desire for pleasure
among northern peoples leads to sincerity and frankness. In the
south the situation is different: crimes multiply; pleasures come
easily, passively to a body relaxed in the warmth; pleasures require
no activity. Montesquieu makes this clear by finishing the chapter
with reference to a climate so hot that the body is altogether
without force. Weakness passes to the spirit itself. Inclinations
become totally passive. "Most chastisements there will be less
difficult to bear than the action of the soul, and servitude will be
less intolerable than the strength of spirit necessary to guide one's
own conduct" (14.2). The extreme passivity of these people, their
utter dependence on their passions, makes them so weak that they
have no capacity to act, no spirit.

Montesquieu divided the inclinations into active and passive
elements—the spirit and the heart. Spirit has to do with action
from within a person toward something. The passions happen to
us. Insofar as we are subject to the passions, we are subject to the
action of universal physical laws, which can only be countered and
given a specifically human shape by the forceful imposition of
natural law. People with spirit can come to have different

characters. This seems to be the result of the activity of the spirit as it comes against some barrier that requires it to choose a direction. Climate would have the most effect in hot climates; there people are so subject to its effects that their spirits are too weak to carry them off in directions that are not predictable from climate alone.

A hot climate, then, leads to a situation in which people are so subject to universal physical laws that only externally applied force will get them to do the things required for simple preservation. Slavery is required when people are so subject to their passions that they will not work, when they are so involved in sexual passion that raising children is too much trouble, and when they are so fearful and cowardly that they do not protect themselves. In each case, only externally applied force can get people to do the things required for their preservation. Because there is no internally generated activity, only punishment and the threat of punishment can move such peoples. Such slavery "may be founded on a natural reason," although it is against nature "as all men are born equal." Montesquieu here distinguishes between the natural reasons behind physical phenomena and the basis of the natural law that transforms those inclinations into human intentions. In Europe, slavery might be rejected for a natural reason—the moderate climate—by the natural law whose basis is equality, or because the people are Christian. Christianity, Montesquieu remarks, has brought back the age of Saturn in which, according to Plutarch's "Life of Numa," there was neither master nor slave (15.7). The reader is certainly led here to wonder about the implication of saying that Christianity has come to make us act as if we lived in a mythical golden age. This remark is similar to Montesquieu's observation, quoted earlier, that the Greek emperors—that is, the Christian emperors of the Eastern Roman Empire—forgot that they did not hold the sword in vain. Neither the natural reasons pointing toward slavery or despotic governance nor punishment can be wholly overcome, whatever claims to the contrary might be made by Christianity. This careful treatment of the possible need for extraordinary measures clearly differentiates Montesquieu from Machiavelli.

Thus, Montesquieu divided natural inclinations into those of the heart and those of the spirit—the passions and the intentions that form character. Our passions, those natural inclinations that are most universal and appear most natural, can be ruled only by force, because they offer no ground upon which peace can be established among the conflicting impulses. Yet there is the imperative that peace be established somehow. Rule by punishment and fear of punishment is despotism, so the rule based on the passions alone is despotic.

In book 18, Montesquieu takes up the ways of life that result from the various kinds of terrain, from whether the land is easy or difficult to cultivate, from the extent to which it is productive with and without the changes made by man, and its configuration. Montesquieu moves here from the discussion of climate (bks. 14–17), of a physical circumstance that affects us without any action of ours, to terrain, a physical circumstance to which we must respond with our own actions. Montesquieu writes that when people live by cultivating the land, their governments can be neither free nor moderate, unless they live in mountains or on islands. The peoples of the plains are subject to constant conquests because a countryside bursting with goods is a constant temptation to its neighbors. Those who have many goods value the goods so highly that they value their freedom less than do those for whom freedom is virtually their only good. Their ease in protecting themselves makes "less occasion for all the laws one makes for the people's security" (18.2). A fertile plain will lead to the armed camp of the Spartans, or to a soft despotism, and will lead most often to such constant warfare that the plain will be abandoned. In difficult terrains, people can protect themselves and must "procure for themselves what the terrain refuses them" (18.4). These peoples have scope for activity and require laws that suit their lives (18.8).

The bulk of book 18 (18.9–31), however, is concerned with peoples who do not cultivate the land, who live by hunting (savage peoples) or from their own herds (barbarian peoples). Such peoples have few civil laws, no money, considerable equality, and freedom from despotism. He ends the book with a consideration of two such peoples, the Tartars (18.19–21) and the Franks (18.22–31). Terrain, then, shapes peoples by presenting situations in which decisions must be made about the way to pursue a livelihood. Some of those situations—such as mountains, islands, hunting, herding—permit the growth of singular and free peoples, one of which was somehow the origin of the French people, as we shall see in our chapter on legislation. The question taken up in that chapter is the way a government can respond to the character of its people, shaped originally by the action in response to a terrain that formed character.

Montesquieu added this last section (18.22–31) and the final books on the French monarchy (bks. 28, 30, 31) at the end of his work on *The Spirit of the Laws*.[14] Here he offers an explanation of the Salic law, the inheritance law that settled the succession to the throne of France. It began, according to Montesquieu, as a "purely economic law which gave the house and the land around it to the males who were to live in it and for whom consequently it was best suited" (18.22). By ending book 18 with the Franks and continuing in book 19 with a description of a people who suggest the French of his own time, Montesquieu seems to propose a comparison between the former natural spirit of the Franks and the modern French spirit.

The Franks whom Montesquieu depicts are not wholly barbarian, not entirely without houses and land, in contrast to the Tartars. The Salic law, he explains, had to do with the disposal of a house and the bit of land surrounding it. The preference for males was due to the fact that women entered other houses when they married. Montesquieu denies that the arrangements had to do with "perpetuating a family, a name, or a transfer of land" (18.22); but they do resemble those that the Romans used in order to perpetuate a division of the land (27.1) and some that the ancient Greeks used and suggested (5.5). The Franks, in contrast to many barbarian peoples, each had one wife (18.24) and respected marital fidelity (18.25). Thus, for them the question arose of when and how boys became adult, left the family, and joined the men. Because the men were almost always armed and were concerned with warfare rather than property, they became adult, joined the assembly, when they were able to bear arms. This was also true for the children of kings (18.27), and adoption was accomplished when weapons were given to the man to be adopted (28.28). For one man to rule the whole, he had to kill his relatives, who had a claim to inherit some portion of the lands of the king (18.29). Princes had only moderate power in peacetime (18.30), and priests had great influence, as was the case with all barbarian peoples (18.31).

This description of the Franks gives them a remarkably structured social life for a barbarian people. The Franks were organized for warfare: the spirit of the nation was so centered on the capacity to fight that even the sons of kings were not presented to the assembly before they could fight. The Salic law only makes sense for a society of families whose members have ordered relations with each other, even if perpetuation of certain families was not the intent. That is, a Frank was clearly a boy, a warrior, a king, a girl, a wife, a brother, a cousin on the mother's or the father's side. Different things can properly be expected of each; and each is understood in terms of its relation to the warrior spirit. Montesquieu contrasts this to the unstructured horde of the Tartars, who were kept together only through fear of conquest and fear of the leader, whose rule was achieved and held by his conquering the other Tartars. A society that is ordered in respect to the spirit of warriors is not the same as the society that results from constant warfare. Here, again, we have a contrast between an intention, supported by the spirit required to perform it, and the effect of events.

In book 19, Montesquieu turns to his contemporaries in France, who present an altogether different case. Here is a nation "which had a sociable humor, an openness of heart; a joy in life, a taste, an ease in communicating its thoughts; which was lively, pleasant, playful, sometimes imprudent, often indiscreet; and which had with all that, courage, generosity, frankness, and a certain point of honor" (19.5). These people watch one another, copy one another, communicate so actively that what emerges is the singularities of individuals. They do not relate to one another in a pattern structured to bring out a particular spirit. Rather, the absence of such a structure brings out a spirit that seems to consist in the general sociability of individuals. Montesquieu puts this succinctly by saying that "the more communicative peoples are, the more easily they change their manners because each man is more a spectacle for another; one sees the singularities of individuals better" (19.8). In this discussion of the French, the ranks and orders of their monarchy do not serve to distinguish people in terms of a spirit, as did the choice of a citizenry in a republic. These individualized Frenchmen remind us, not of our usual notion of France before the Revolution, but of Alexis de Tocqueville's description of American individualism. This book ends with another description of such a people (19.27), the contemporary English, which I consider in chapter 6. I shall consider the reasons for those similarities in chapter 8, on Tocqueville's democracy.

The contrast between the Franks and the French is not that between a society of warriors and one of *honnêtes hommes*. Rather, the contrast is between a society that is organized to support some intent, some spirit, that could never be the activity of everyone and a society in which everyone is involved in the same pursuit. The first kind of spirit is natural insofar as it grows out of a way of life developed in response to a terrain, which in turn is organized into a society whose spirit is typified by those who best pursue its end. They require support—customarily of servants and women—so that the other tasks required for survival and those required by perpetuation will get done. The second is predicated upon the absence of such structure. Montesquieu brings the Chinese into his discussion at this point because their society is ordered by the structure of the family—age, sex, servant, and served. There is no communication between families or between the ranks within each family. It is almost impossible for the Chinese to become Christian because "the Christian religion, by the establishment of charity, by a public worship, and by participation in the same sacraments, seems to require that everything be united" (19.18). The clearest distinction is between the utter separation of the Chinese and the communication of the Christians, but the separation of a body of citizens dedicated to the same activity, with the same spirit, also runs into conflict with the Christian assumption of communication. The societies that are based upon the limited natural spirit are, then, problematic in the Christian era. The problem is to imagine some form of government that gives its due to the generality of the Christian spirit, and of the passions, without becoming a despotism. As we shall see, the notion of personal law—that each person could carry his law with him as he traveled, hunting and herding—and the notion that different people could have sovereignty over different activities made possible the development of a new embodiment of justice and of constitutional order that was both general and particular.

In sum, spirit again refers to an element of commonalty—to something shared with others. In my consideration of Montesquieu's criticism of divine law, it became clear that justice as punishment was endless and that only justice that established an end to punishment based on some ground for a life in common was compatible with decent, nondespotic, political life. The Christian spirit could provide a ground for limiting punishment, but joined to it is a demand for total love and total control of the passions. Here, as in my analysis of Montesquieu's criticism of the divine law, the spirit also emerges as the ground on which some accommodation can be reached. The passions are altogether individual, subjecting men either to the force of nature or of one another. This view of passions is also expressed in *The Federalist,* as we shall notice in chapter 7. Only the spirit—the intention to act for some end that can be held in common—permits a shared and moderate resolution to the conflicts among the natural ends. The limited spirit that is expressed in a common way of life is in conflict with the universality of the Christian spirit as well as with the universality of despotism. As we shall see in the next section, the order of the kinds of human law reflects the relation between these two forms of the spirit.

POLITICS

Returning to Montesquieu's account of positive political laws in book 1, we shall pursue his account of those laws and then the content he gives them in the remainder of his work. Men change sufficiently upon entering society that the positive laws—that is, those made for men in society—must have some organizing principle of their own. "As soon as men are in society, they lose the feeling of their weakness; the equality among them ceases, and the state of war begins" (1.3). Particular societies and the individuals within those societies have particular strengths, feel those strengths, and turn them to their advantage. This results in two sorts of states of war: war between societies and war between individuals in a society. Laws that bear on the relations between peoples, between the governors and the governed, and between the citizens are the international, the political, and the civil rights. Montesquieu goes on to say that these rights apply to all of the various nations as inhabitants of a planet, to the political state that is formed by the union of all the individual strengths, and to the civil state that is the union of the individual wills. For each nation, the purpose of international right is to do itself the most good in peace and the least harm in war. In order to know what that might be, one must know the political right. But that political right has its source in the political state, which formed by the union of individual strengths. Those strengths cannot unite without the will to do so. This latter unity is the civil state. This description of the three rights emphasizes their interdependence, but it offers no view as to which is primary and gives no intent or content to the rights. This makes possible a change in the relations between the three rights, as well as a comparative politics based on such transformations. Montesquieu, in contrast to Rousseau, does not think that the definition of political life as the unification of wills moves one very far forward; rather, it may be the content with which the wills are filled that gives them form and shapes the relationship between the kinds of laws and rights.

In the course of *The Spirit of the Laws* a number of "revolutions" are described. In each case there is a change in the relationship between these three rights. In these cases a particular topic over which rule is exercised changes jurisdictions, so to speak. International right, for example, could change from not disturbing the property and familial arrangements of a people to taking the property of the conquered and making slaves of the people. Inheritances could move from being a direct consequence of political right to being treated as if they were indistinguishable from other contracts and a part of the civil right. These changes are revolutionary because, it seems to me, they indicate an underlying change in the spirit of the regime. They indicate a fundamental change in spirit, in the shape of the spirit. We have already seen a contrast between the particularity of the natural spirit, as groups develop a spirit in conjunction with a way of life, and the universality of the Christian spirit. A particular spirit requires an organization of the population in respect to the capacity to act in accordance with that spirit and to provide support for that action. We have even seen that Montesquieu suggests that separation between people—men, women, children, and citizens—is assumed in societies based on some particular spirit and that communication among all persons is assumed in societies of Christians. These very different organizations of the population may well require very different relations between the laws. In the succeeding pages, we shall look at three examples of revolutions and at the implicit typology of spirit they suggest: in commerce (bk. 21), in Roman inheritance law (bk. 27), and in the French monarchy (bks. 28, 30, 31).

In book 21, "On Laws in Relation to Commerce Considered in Its Revolutions in the World," revolutions in commerce are the result of changes in the political right of the peoples of the world and in their relations with each other—that is, in international right. Among the ancients, the steps in the direction of a broad international trade were halted by a notion of political right that gave military activity and political glory the first importance. Economic activity was to be in its service. The spirit of Roman political right made the activity required for a broad commerce unattractive. The Roman political right took no interest in commerce, and its right of nations was repugnant to commerce.

The international right of the barbarians, by contrast, left the conquered peoples, once they had been conquered, their former laws and their right to property and protection; this made a much-broader commerce conceivable (21.18). This is all taken up in detail in book 28, and we shall consider it further in chapter 6. However, the Christian scholastics condemned lending at interest indiscriminately and in every case; they applied the divine law, as they understood it, as if it were a political law (21.20). The commerce that developed, then, after the decline of the Roman Empire became the enterprise not merely of the low people but also of dishonest people, "for whenever one prohibits a thing that is naturally permitted or necessary, one only makes dishonest the people who do it" (21.20). Commerce passed to the Jews, because they were not bound by the religious laws against usury. Commerce was dishonest and was indistinguishable from usury in this situation. The Jews were in turn pillaged by the princes. However, the Jews found a means of saving their effects. "They invented letters of exchange, and in this way, commerce was able to avoid violence and maintain itself everywhere, for the richest trader had only invisible goods, which could be sent everywhere and leave no trace anywhere" (21.20). Commerce escaped from the realm of political right into a realm where it was primarily shaped by its own laws, rather than by those of political life.

This transformation or revolution took place, according to Montesquieu, over a great length of time—from the disintegration of the Roman Empire in the West to the beginning of commercial growth in feudal Europe. In Rome, as in the ancient Greek republics, commerce and economic life in general were subject to political law. Although there were efforts during those early times to expand commerce, to let it have a course of its own separate from the political law of particular countries, the efforts faltered each time on the limits set by those same particular political laws. The mélange of individuals who were subject to different laws and who made up western Europe as the barbarians extended their power might have created a condition for commerce had it not been for the Christian objection to lending at interest. Only when commerce escaped from the control of religious law could it begin to develop. The presumption here seems to be that the political law of the feudal monarchies did not control and limit commerce nearly as effectively as did that of the ancient republics.

In book 27, "On the Origin and Revolutions of the Roman Laws on Inheritance," Montesquieu describes, as we have already seen, the dissolution of Roman control of inheritances by political law. Romulus, he says, divided the land among the families and designed inheritance laws so as to keep one plot for each family. This political law disintegrated under a variety of pressures, leaving inheritance law to the civil rather than the political law. The Roman belief in the absolute power of fathers over their children seemed logically to extend to their being able to control, by their own wills and contracts under the civil law, each child's share of the family's goods. In addition, the first laws did not sufficiently restrict the wealth of women; the citizenry was decimated by wars, and its repopulation was encouraged by giving women with children the right to inherit; and finally, the wealth of all nations inundated Rome. The political division of land that created equal families had virtually disappeared. Montesquieu remarks that under Justinian, Roman civil law tried to follow nature itself, as if political right had no proper interest in the shape of families or the relation among families.

Christianity in the Roman Empire destroyed the link between the political need for citizens and laws about marriages. Montesquieu offers two remarks about the characteristics of Christianity which led to this result. In the first place, Christianity fixed the speculative ideas of the philosophic sects into "an idea of perfection attached to all that leads to a speculative life; . . . of distance from the causes and embarrassments of a family" (23.21). The Christian religion, which came after philosophy, fixed some ideas that the latter had proposed. In the second place, "in order to spread a new religion, one must take away the extreme dependence of children, who are always less concerned with what is established" (23.21). That is, Christianity separated out the individuals from their families in order to get them to face an idea of perfection that had no relation to the care of a family. In order to promote a new belief, it encouraged its adherents to separate from their families and the old beliefs. The family that Christianity encouraged, which Montesquieu describes in books 24–26, does not have as its purposes producing citizens for the polity and producing the goods required to support the activities of those citizens. Rather, it has as its purpose the control of sexual and acquisitive passions in the service of people's dedication to God and in the service of their spirituality. It has, as a consequence, no qualms about promoting universal rules about marriages and commerce, which lead to great political problems: for example, over- or underpopulation, bastards who cannot be integrated into society, and usurious rates of interest. A universal religious law replaced the particular political law; a universal spirit replaced the variety of human spirits.

Another shift in the domain of each right took place as the barbarians overran the Roman Empire; this made possible a new kind of political law. New laws appeared "in a moment in all of Europe without any connection with those known previously," in "an event that happened once in the world and which will perhaps never happen again" (30.1). These laws "left right when domain was ceded" and, "by giving several people various kinds of lordship over the same thing or the same persons, diminished the weight of the whole lordship" (30.1). Rule itself, over any person or thing, was shared. This is altogether different from either previous situation, in which different laws were applied to different groups within the population or in which the same religious law was applied to everyone. Here, different people and different laws rule various aspects of people's lives; a kind of compromise between the universality and the particularity of previous law and spirit was effected.

The story of that transformation is contained in book 28, "On the Origin and Revolutions of the Civil Laws among the Franks"; in book 30, "The Theory of the Feudal Laws among the Franks in Their Relation with the Establishment of the Monarchy"; and in book 31, "The Theory of the Feudal Laws among the Franks in Their Relation to the Revolutions of Their Monarchy." The plot of this story follows the transformation of political into feudal law, the dissolution of civil law, and the rise of a new kind of civil law, based on the establishment of a judicial process supported by and supporting the monarchy, and a new kind of political law. To get a clear picture of this transformation as Montesquieu understood it, these three books must be considered together.

The history of the French monarchy, whether in respect to the civil laws or the feudal laws, begins with the defeat of the universal Roman Empire by the barbarian invaders. The condition of a defeated country depends upon the right of nations of the conqueror. "When the Franks, Burgundians, and Goths invaded, they took all the gold, silver, furniture, clothing, men, women, and boys that the army could carry; everything was put together and the army divided it. The entire body of history proves that after the first establishment, that is, after the first ravages, they reached a settlement with the inhabitants and left them all their political and civil rights. This was the right of nations in those times; everything was taken in war, everything was granted in peace" (30.11). These conquerors did not impose their civil law on a conquered people. They thought of laws as something attached to individuals, as what Montesquieu called personal laws (28.2). After a conquest, each person was judged according to his own law.[15] Consequently, if a particular barbarian law distinguished between those under barbarian law and those under Roman law to the disadvantage of the Romans, the Romans tended to put themselves under the barbarian law. If the barbarians and the Romans were treated similarly, Roman law prevailed (28.4). By the time of Pepin, customs were preferred to laws, even to the Roman law. This decline of law into custom coincided with fiefs becoming hereditary and with the extension of underfiefs (28.9). It also coincided with the decline of the political law of the Frankish monarchy.

To summarize, the political law of the Frankish monarchy distinguished the nobility from the rest of the Franks; the kings distributed goods—fiscal goods, benefices, honors, fiefs—to the nobles; those who held the goods from the king were owed, and owed in return, services and payments for services rendered. That is, the king farmed out these goods to chosen nobles. Justice, for example, was a right of the nobles; it was also a source of revenue for the nobles who rendered the justice. The king's revenue came from his own domain. Taxation was no longer, as it had been among the Romans, a political right.

The free men had largely disappeared, leaving only serfs and lords by the beginning of the reign of the Capetians. Constant warfare, which led to taking booty and prisoners and distributing both among the conquerors according to their right of nations, caused this. The distinction between nobility and holding a fief disappeared. That is, the fiefs and other goods that the king had distributed according to his political right came to be inherited according to a civil law of inheritance. Although fiefs were increasingly held as a consequence of civil law in regard to inheritances, those who held fiefs were still expected to take the places that the old political law had allotted to those who held fiefs.

Two parallel transformations took place throughout the entire period of the rule of both the Merovingians and the Carolingians. In the first place, fiefs and underfiefs came to be inherited, and freeholds were converted into fiefs. Fiefs were advantageous because those who held them were given larger settlements and because the judicial penalties that were imposed were limited (31.8). Second, the civil law in the codes of laws of the barbarians was lost, and justice came to depend on usage and on combat. By the beginning of the reign of the Capetians, jurisprudence lay entirely in procedures based on the point of honor (28.19), and the multiplication of underfiefs was the despair of the great vassals. Even the counties were inherited, and the counts had their own vassals (31.28).

Montesquieu describes some efforts to halt this transformation, all of which were not merely unsuccessful but also furthered parts of this great transformation. During the reign of the Merovingians, Queen Brunhilda was punished with unusual brutality, even for that time, because she tried to return to treating fiefs as revocable. Clotaire redressed the grievances of the vassals. Montesquieu remarks that even in this ferocious, barbarous, murderous, unjust, and cruel nation, civil government required some assurance of regularity (31.2). When this regularity was a result of inherited fiefs, the question of where the king would get fiefs to reward his followers became acute. When the Romans were conquered and the fiefs came to be inherited, kings no longer had goods available to distribute to their followers. The kings had nothing other than a few remaining offices in the counties to distribute, so they turned to the wealth of the clergy.

The constitutional balance betweeen the king, the clergy, and the nobility dissolved under Charlemagne's successors. The king and the clergy continued to weaken each other. Finally, the kingdom was given to the most powerful lord and was inherited in the same way as a fief would be. There was, in effect, no political law left, unless the rule of inheritance that determined the choice of the king could be understood as a political law.

There was a parallel dissolution of the civil law. The civil law of the barbarians was based on settlements, paid for wrongs done, and on penalties, or *freda,* paid to the lord for his enforcement of the settlement. When no settlements were established by law, there were only quarreling families who pursued their vendettas to the end unless the lord provided justice, a settlement, and enforcement of that settlement. Lacking any canons of evidence, there was no way of telling the innocent from the guilty. Ordeals, of which combat was the chief example, were a way to leave the judgment to God, to the divine law. They also had the curious merit of solving the problem of appropriate penalties. The guilty were dead, and the innocent survived. There was no possible appeal. The process came to be regularized, because the outcome was not in human hands. The jurisprudence of combat was executed with a certain prudence (28.23–25). There was less injustice done than the laws were unjust (28.17).

The reestablishment of the civil law began under Saint Louis, who reigned about three hundred years after Hugh Capet. Saint Louis did this by extending the regular process of judging, not by setting up a civil law of crimes and punishments. He abolished judicial combat altogether in his domain, and in the baronies he abolished combat in the case of a challenge for false judgment (28.29). One could appeal, not the judgment of one's lord, but that of the peers in his court, to higher lords and eventually to the king. There were also appeals for default of justice, for not holding court, and for bearing false witness. This all made possible the next series of changes, in which the process of challenging a judgment and of bringing an appeal were regularized. Proceedings had become secret rather than public by 1539 with the advent of written records; costs came to be awarded; and a public party or prosecutor was added to the proceedings.

These changes were the indirect rather than the direct cause of the development of the French civil law. They did not establish a code; rather, they set an example of a new way of judging, which in turn formed a distaste for the old way. As decisions came to be the product of judgments in courts rather than a result of combat, the importance of a general rule to guide the decisions became increasingly clear. As more parlements were created to take care of the new business (28.39), their decrees were collected. The continuing recovery of the king's jurisdiction is the subject of the end of book 28. "The knowledge of Roman right, of the decisions of the courts, of that body of recently recorded customs, required a study of which the nobles and the illiterate were not capable" (28.43). The collection and the increasing generalization of custom into the written law that was to guide the judicial process continued through Charles VII.

In sum, in his account of commerce, of the Roman inheritance law, and of the French monarchy, Montesquieu repeated, with variations, the story of the decline of political right. It seems no longer to have the capacity to impose a shape on society, on its economic life, or on its family structure. The revival of the political after Saint Louis took place indirectly and outside the old nobility—that is, outside the feudal structure. Once a combat no longer determined the guilt and the penalty for a crime, there was room to truly regularize the process of judging, whose results came to depend on custom, written law, and written evidence. The rules that established the process of judging led to and formed the law. Political and civil jurisdiction, as they were revived, took an altogether new form.

Looking back, it seems that these patterns of priority of international, political, and civil law fall into three distinct groups. In the first, there is no distinction between the three kinds of law; they are all reduced to international law, to the rule of force, unrestrained by political and civil law. We recognize this rule as despotic. In the second, some portion of the population is detached from its private interests, both familial and economic, and its members become attached to one another through a political law that shapes those interests to the political intention. Here political law is paramount. The international law envisions no commonalty between societies and therefore no international law other than that of retribution. The civil law is simply a consequence of political arrangements, as was the case with the inheritance law of the first Romans. These are republics. Third, there is an international law that recognizes the legitimacy of the civil arrangements of conquered societies. Toleration of such variation and the individuality that it assumes leads to a situation wherein the civil law seems to be primary. Political law seems elusive, hard to locate. In the next chapter, we shall pursue Montesquieu's effort to understand how these monarchies can be said to be ordered politically.

When we look back at the results of our inquiry into the comments on the topics in book 1 as they are reexamined throughout *The Spirit of the Laws,* we can see the emergence of both spirit and moderation, rather than law and right, as categories for understanding and assessing political life. The divine law— understood as the law of particular intelligent beings—bears an unmistakable resemblance to despotic rule. When people are taken as equal, as subject to retaliatory punishment, and as infinitely obliged to the ruler, there is little difference between rule grounded in the equality before God and that based on the similarity of the passions. Some intermediate position, some limit to such law, some moderation, is required for decent rule over men. Such a moderate rule has its source in the spirit, rather than in the intellect or the passions. The natural spirit that appears in a variety of forms as a way of life is formed in response to the demands of a terrain; particular choices must be made, which in turn give a direction to the people's lives. But Christianity came to generalize that spirit to everyone—to make a universal community before God. This dual possibility has made the varieties of positive, political law change places and jurisdictions in the revolutions that Montesquieu observed. In the next chapter, we shall turn to the kinds of governments and to their assessment; again we shall move from the presentation early in book 2 to the amplifications throughout the book. Looking back upon these two examinations of the whole book, we shall be able to put together the typologies of the spirit and of the governments. Thus, we shall have begun to be able to lay out the structure that underlies Montesquieu's book. We shall then be in a position to inquire into the English government and into modern free governments and to finish my suggestion as to the structure of the book.

4

MODERATION

After this exploration of the relation between law and spirit suggested in book 1, we must return to the beginning of the book, that is to the forms of government first outlined in book 2. Montesquieu presents us with three forms of government—republics, monarchies, and despotisms—and with a continuum from moderation to despotism along which they are to be judged. Here we shall proceed with an introductory consideration of the governments to which he refers and then to a first look at the notion of moderation and of despotism that he suggests as a way of assessing all governments. Then we shall turn to each government in turn, taking up its structure and then Montesquieu's assessment of it in terms of its moderation and despotism as his exposition continues throughout the book. We then shall be in a position to see the connection between the forms of spirit and the three governments. Each government is based upon a view of the relation between the spirit and political life.

Montesquieu begins his second book by classifying governments into republics, monarchies, and despotisms. Montesquieu claims no theoretical ground for his classification; rather, he says that he assumes three definitions, or facts. Republican governments are those in which the people or a part of the people have sovereign power. Monarchies are those governments in which one man rules by fixed and established laws, while despotisms are those in which one alone, "without law and without rule, draws everything along by his will and his caprices" (2.1). These definitions are in terms of the nature of each government, its rule, although Montesquieu has made clear by excluding the word *rule* from his description of despotisms that the rule therein is in a way not a rule; it is not regular. Each government has its own peculiar identifying characteristic; no classificatory principle is clearly stated.

Upon examination, one can see that two classificatory principles are at work in these descriptions: (1) who rules and (2) whether that rule is exercised according to the law or according to the ruler's will and caprice. The old classification in terms of who rules—the one, the few, or the many—has been reduced to the alternatives of one or some group. Government by one is divided into government that is either under or not under the law by its nature. Nothing is said here about whether government by the people or a part of the people is or is not according to the law by its nature, or whether that government too can be divided into one sort of government that is and one that is not according to the law by its nature.

Montesquieu has taken the two great classificatory principles for political life and has used them both, rather than making a choice between them. Aristotle says that regimes are distinguished by the character of the ruler and, coincidentally, by whether those rulers are one, few, or many. Inherent in the claim of any group to rule is the claim that theirs is the best way of life, the way of life that is so good that those who do not exemplify it in their own lives could properly be expected to support it with their subordinate activities. Those who are not citizens are ordered in respect to their capacity to support the life of the citizenry. The assumption is that groups can be identified and divided according to that principle and that such a division ensures the virtue peculiar to each group. "For nature makes nothing in an economizing spirit, as smiths make the Delphic knife, but one thing with a view to one thing; and each instrument would perform most finely if it served one task rather than many."[1] In addition, that way of life is exemplified and supported by the distribution of offices, or constitution, and by the laws, both of which are properly its partisans.

By contrast, Locke and Hobbes began with individuals, who have a right to the preservation of that individuality, to self-preservation. From this point of view, everyone is equal, and everyone asks the same thing—a situation or a law—under which each of them can live out his life in safety from other men and can pursue his individual activities as long as they do not threaten that safety. The status of this law is something of a problem. If it is a natural law, it is one that men do not naturally, necessarily, obey.

Only by asserting that men are naturally a certain kind of animal was Rousseau later able to claim that they could once preserve themselves without recourse to human law. It is, then, a natural law whose purpose is achieved only under a government. Montesquieu, as we have seen, followed something of this pattern when he distinguished between natural inclinations and the intentions that made up that natural law. Here, the government is judged by whether or not it sees to it that the natural law is followed; the government is judged by its adherence to that law as the principle of its actions. But the question remains of how the government adheres to that law. It can threaten or kill those who threaten or kill others, acting simply as a superior power—like the despotic rule that enforces the natural law in Montesquieu. Hobbes's Leviathan bears a remarkable resemblance to Montesquieu's despot. Or a law can be established that the government, too, obeys, so that self-preservation is a result of the law that the government enforces and obeys. Even under such a law there remain instances in which preservation and that law are not identical; here one recognizes the Lockian prerogative. Everyone is held to the same law; the rulers are expected to know better how to administer it, but not to have some way of life that sets them and their virtue apart and deserves the support of the rest of the population.

By combining these two understandings of the relation of law and nature in one classification and by offering each in effect as the alternatives on a grid, Montesquieu suggests that neither offers a principle that includes all governments and that some governments could embody both. Once they are combined, the principles of three governments emerge; these principles—the passions that move the governments—also suggest a pattern of relations between governments and the people who animate the governments and are governed by them. That each government has its own principle, that its people relate to it in a distinctive way, suggests that this combining of views about the nature of governments is plausible.

Montesquieu, however, does suggest a criterion for all governments: all governments can be ranged along a line from moderate to despotic. Moderation is Montesquieu's clearest aim for political life. It is spread across the book, as we shall see in the discussion of moderation as a standard for each of Montesquieu's governments. This is not to say that he does not admit expansion, war, religion, commerce, public tranquility, navigation, natural liberty, the delights of the prince, the glory of the prince and the state, the independence of each individual (11.5), and all the other goods that are the ends of political action; rather, it says that the standard he applies to each is the moderation or the despotism inherent in it or with which it is pursued.

Moderation appears in two quite different contexts in the beginning of *The Spirit of the Laws*. It is mentioned first as the principle of aristocracies (2.4). Aristocracies, Montesquieu says, have the advantages over democracies that result from a body that can repress others; their problem is the repression of the aristocrats themselves. The virtue of aristocrats need not be so great; they need only to be able to keep themselves from attacking one another; they need only be moderate, so that they will remain equal among themselves. The other possibility—a great virtue that makes the nobles equal to the people—forms a great republic, but Montesquieu does not seem to regard this virtue as essential to an aristocracy. Moderation is a limit to the ambition of aristocrats; they give themselves only what is required by their nobility and their rule, but no more. Then, moderation in the context of republican government is, in effect, having the rulers take only what is required to maintain their distinctive characteristic.

Moderation is next mentioned when Montesquieu discusses the need in despotisms for fear to be applied constantly and to the smallest things. Moderate governments, he says, can relax their springs, or loosen their control; but despotic governments cannot. A moderate government maintains itself by its laws and by its force (3.9). Moderate governments have some strength apart from that of the rulers; the power of monarchical and moderate governments is limited by that which is the spring, by honor in monarchies (3.10). That the government has some strength apart from the rulers seems to be connected to its having a spring that acts on both the rulers and the ruled and to the government's moderation. Moderation itself seems to be a characteristic of aristocrats and a characteristic of the structure of some governments. The link between the moderation of aristocrats and that of monarchies may be that monarchies have a kind of self-control which limits the activities of its rulers and which is built into its structure, rather than into the character of the nobles.

Moderation is a curious standard for political or moral action, because it seems to have no stability, nothing to offer as a guide for action other than not going too far. As a guide, it is dependent upon the excesses beyond which one is not to go. A direction that results from a balancing or a tempering of extremes is an ambiguous thing. It appears to be more a consequence of circumstance, of habit, or of history than of principle and therefore to be a standard whose sensibleness and attractiveness must be measured against its slipperiness and its unreliability.

It seems to me that a counsel of moderation that does not fall into one of merely going along must be based upon the inevitability of at least two possibilities in political life—neither of which can be denied some legitimacy and neither of which can be accepted entirely without bad consequences. Among the ancients, politics was thought always to arouse a conflict between the few or the one who claimed it was proper for them to rule because they knew best how to rule, whether as a result of education, character, birth, or even wealth, and those who claimed rule because they were free—that is, it was they who were in effect the city. They were its guardians, its soldiers, and they were essential to the city. But if we are all equal—citizens, aristocrats, women, slaves— before God or by nature, there are no inevitable groups whose recognition produces moderation in the actions of the rulers. Only one standard follows—namely, adherence to that equality. However, there are various grounds for equality—for example, before God as intelligences, as spirits moving toward God, or in the needs and passions given by nature. Even the satisfaction of those needs requires a particular solution, because they are not necessarily congruent. Not only are there two positions, but the weakness of each position points toward the other, giving moderation a ground in nature. Then, moderate governments are not unstable compromises or balances of opposites; rather, they are firmly set upon the diversity inherent in human nature, at some relatively stable middle, mixing particularity and universality into a specific way of life.

To further pursue the question of the meaning and basis for

moderation in Montesquieu, let us look into the three forms of
government, asking the relation of those forms to the alternative
between moderation and despotism. We shall do so by taking the
division of governments into despotisms, republics, and monarchies, which pervades the first eight books, and trying to
understand what kind of a typology this is. Then, we shall move
through Montesquieu's book, trying to understand the relation of
each type to the alternation between despotism and moderation.[2]
We shall take up despotism first, because its standing both as a
government and as a standard for all governments needs to be
sorted out.

DESPOTISMS

In considering despotisms here, the chief difficulty will be to
disentangle despotisms as kinds of governments from the despotic
as a tendency or possibility within any government. Here we shall
offer a more orderly treatment of the governments, although the
rule of republics and despotisms has already been compared to
that of the limited intelligences of book 1. Each chapter or section
in *The Spirit of the Laws* can be seen as a card in a deck of cards,
each with its own pattern and with a variety of relations to the
whole. One must take it up a number of times to begin to
understand its relation to the whole. Here, we shall begin by
examining Montesquieu's description of despotisms in books
2–8, where he takes up the kinds of governments. Then, we shall
look at his treatment of China, a government that can be described,
he says, as a despotism in spite of elements of regularity and control
that make it appear moderate, or "enlightened." Despotisms, in
order to exist, must be moderated, but they are moderated in a
way that remains despotic—namely, from the outside.
      Despotisms are states in which rule is exercised by one person
alone, without constraints.[3] A result of this is "that the one man
who exercises it has it likewise exercised by another. . . . In this
state, the establishment of a vizier is a fundamental law" (2.5).
This is because the despot "whose five senses constantly tell him
that he is everything and that others are nothing is naturally lazy,
ignorant, and voluptuous." He shuns the problems of govern-

ment, cannot even adjudicate between ministers, and abandons his administration to a vizier (2.5), to a eunuch whose passion has been curbed by force. Power passes "intact to those to whom he [the prince] entrusts it" (3.9). People who are capable of any self-esteem would be in a position to revolt, so rule must be through fear alone. The king's will must have its effect "as infallibly as does one ball thrown against another" (3.10). Montesquieu continues, remarking that "man is a creature that obeys a creature that wants" and that "there, men's portion, like beasts', is instinct, obedience and chastisement" (3.10). Here there is no currency but force—the perfectly despotic despotism.

Montesquieu identifies acting without constraints with acting perfectly willfully and with following the passion of the moment. Any principle of action would, in effect, be a constraint; that is, any consistency in action implies a restraint on action and thus some basis for action other than perfect willfulness. Such perfect willfulness produces fear in the subjects, and that same fear can result from the demands of nature or of the divinity. Beause they are inhuman, they, even if we believe them to be consistent, are not experienced as consistent. There are no fundamental laws in despotisms, not even ones that establish the succession to the throne. Preservation of the state is reduced to preservation of the despot or of the palace in which he is enclosed. As we have seen, there is a certain universality to despotisms, both in the way they rule and in their appeal. Most peoples are subject to such governments, despite their love of liberty and hatred of violence, because moderate governments are complicated structures, masterpieces of legislation. "On the contrary, a despotic government leaps into view, so to speak; it is uniform throughout; as only passions are needed to establish it, everyone is good for that" (5.14). This simplicity is reflected in the laws. There is no need for civil laws because land, inheritance, and trade are not separate from the power of the prince, and marriage is with slaves (6.1). "Each household is a separate empire" (4.3). Women and their luxury are not public questions in despotisms; women "do not introduce luxury, but they are themselves an object of luxury" (7.9). They are enclosed, and their virtue is ensured by force.

There are no formalities of justice, and justice is swift, simple, and violent. That very violence is corrupting both of the people and of whatever laws there are. Therefore, "atrocity in the laws prevents their execution. When the penalty is excessive, often one is obliged to prefer impunity" (6.13). It is hard to believe that this perfectly despotic despotism could continue to exist, and Montesquieu, in his formal description of despotisms as governments, offers some sources of regularity and limits on the violence of the government and the will of the prince. Montesquieu suggests that only religious belief can counter the will of the prince. "The laws of religion are part of a higher precept, because they apply to the prince as well as to the subjects. But it is not the same for natural right; the prince is not assumed to be a man" (3.10). Nature, in addition, can affect despotisms and create a certain order. In China the climate and the terrain, he says, lead to a constant threat of overpopulation and famine unless the people and the monarch are disciplined and frugal. When they are not, famine and revolution occur, permitting a new, disciplined, and frugal monarch to take the throne (8.21). Education in a despotism is quite limited; "it is reduced to putting fear in the heart and in teaching the spirit a few very simple religious principles" (4.3).

Rule that is despotic is willful or arbitrary; it has no source of regularity or dependability; and it is based exclusively on force. But any state, any rule, implies some regularity. Force and will alone are a ground for rule because they inescapably produce fear; but they are not a source of order. Montesquieu has offered religious practice as the source of direct control in a despotism, the source of regularity in such a state. Religion in this instance seems to offer the fear of a god's displeasure if his rules are not obeyed, but the god also offers rules about the conduct of everyday life. This divinity differs from human despots by having rules; it is similar in basing its rule on fear. This suggests that despotisms could have an order imposed from without, by forces that are not human. Despotisms could have an order and yet be based exclusively on force and its resulting fear. In this sense they could, paradoxically, be moderated and still remain despotisms.

Montesquieu's chief example of a moderated despotism is China. Montesquieu's concern is to explain that the sources of China's moderation are despotic, not human; they are not due to the enlightenment of its rulers. China, he says, is under great pressure because its climate leads to extraordinary fertility in the women. Such fertility puts a constant pressure on their capacity to produce food, however fertile the land. As in all countries that are primarily dependent upon rice, famine is a frequent possibility (8.21). Much of the land is, in effect, made by men, as in Holland (18.6). In this situation, there is not merely a premium on order and hard work to moderate arbitrary power there (18.6), but the consequences of disorder are immediate and dire. "Disorder is born suddenly when this prodigious number of people lacks subsistence" (8.21). The prince is necessarily alerted promptly about the disorder and fears, not for his well-being in this life or the next, but for his empire and his life (8.21). Nature, in the guise of climate, the fertility of women, and the terrain's compatibility with cultivating rice, forces the prince to promote hard work and regularity (7.6, 7.7, 19.20).

The aim of the Chinese government is public tranquility (11.5), but tranquility alone is the end of all despotisms (5.14). This public tranquility is produced by a civility that combines religion, laws, mores, and manners into what the Chinese called rites (19.17). These rites are extremely complicated rules for writing and living that "are in no way spiritual but are simply rules of a common practice; it is easier to convince and to stamp spirits with them than with something intellectual" (19.17). These rites establish subordination in order to ensure tranquility by inspiring respect for fathers and, by extension, old men, teachers, magistrates, the emperor. "This empire is formed on the idea of family government" (19.19). As we have seen, this separation of families and emphasis on family government ensure the isolation of women and their subjection to the family rules, making it impossible for Christianity ever to be established in China. "The vows of virginity, the assembly of women in churches, their necessary communication with the ministers of the religion, their participation in the sacraments, the auricular confession, extreme unction, marriage to a single woman, all this overthrows the mores and manners of the country and strikes against the religion and laws at the same time" (19.18). China, then, like all despotisms, is divided into families, each of which is ruled separately. Subordination, the principle of that family rule, is also the principle of all other rule, making an orderly society based on the rites of family life.

China, then, is moderate insofar as circumstances force it to maintain order. At the same time it is a despotism because force and fear of force, both human and natural or physical, maintain order in a society based exclusively upon private and familial needs and structures. The spirit is stamped with common practices, rather than being related to some common expression of spirit. There is nothing that takes people out of those structures; they are so firmly bound into them that they cannot relate to God as individuals and become Christian. Public tranquility, or peace, as an end for political life, provides no ground for a life or spirit in common; rather, it is a basis for dividing the society into separate families, each of which follows a standard for orderly family life which provides them with their sole relation to each other.

Even the regularity, then, of despotisms is despotic.[4] Its functioning is due to the passions, particularly the fear, of all those concerned, both the ruler and the ruled. Despotism is imposed from the outside. Its only rule or regularity, from the divine or from nature, is felt as arbitrary violence, just as is the rule of the despot himself. Here we have an extreme of political life against which other governments can be measured. Its universality, which is grounded in the passions and in nature understood as the source of the passions, implies that less-bad governments will be more particular, based on some intentionality, some spirit, some good, which limits a government and defines its end. Moderate governments, then, are those whose laws are particular, not universal. With this notion in mind, let us turn to the most particular or singular of governments—namely, republics.

REPUBLICS

Because republics are governments "in which the people as a body, or only a part of the people, have sovereign power" (2.1), the laws that derive from the nature of the government are those that define the people, that establish those whose wills are to rule through their votes (2.2). If a portion of the people is to rule, as in an aristocracy, the aristocracy is more nearly perfect as it approaches democracy and less perfect as it approaches monarchy

(2.3). This seems to be because of the conflicts inherent in aristocracy, "a government that has already established the most grievous distinctions" (2.3). The principle that sustains democracy is virtue. Democratic peoples must be willing to pass laws to which they will be subject and whose weight they will bear. Without that virtue, "ambition enters those hearts that can admit it, and avarice enters them all. Desires change their objects: that which one used to love, one loves no longer. One was free under the laws, one wants to be free against them. Each citizen is like a slave who has escaped from his master's house. What was a *maxim* is now called *severity*: what was a *rule* is now called *constraint*: what was *vigilance* is now called *fear*" (3.3). Virtue, then, is an internal constraint on the passions. Without virtue, a democratic people is no better than a gathering of slaves, each following his own will; the government is, then, a democratic despotism.[5] That which keeps a democracy from being a despotism is not the form of rule, but is those institutions that maintain virtue in the citizens.

In aristocracies, the people are constrained because they are subject to the laws made by the aristocrats. The difficulty is in constraining the aristocrats. They can either have great virtue, becoming in effect a part of the people, or they can have a moderation, which keeps them equal among themselves (3.4). The aristocrats must, somehow, not take undue advantage of not being constrained by the laws made for the people; otherwise they would become as simply willful as despots, forming an aristocratic despotism, as in Poland (2.3). In each case, Montesquieu has asked the source of the constraints on those who are both rulers and ruled.

To support virtue, republics rely upon the full power of education and upon laws that a legislator has given to settle the inheritance of property. Political virtue is "a renunciation of oneself, which is always a very painful thing"; that virtue can also be defined as "the love of the laws and the homeland," which requires "a continuous preference of the public interest over one's own" (4.5). The public education that best achieved this end was that of Sparta, where personal sentiments were totally detached from their usual individual aims. "He [Lycurgus] seemed to remove all its resources, arts, commerce, silver, walls:

one had ambition there without the expectation of bettering oneself; one had natural feelings but was neither child, husband, nor father; modesty itself was removed from chastity" (4.6). Montesquieu suggests that the institutions of Plato's republic are an extension of this notion. To the extent that such men are separated from family, from the private realm, their ambition and their devotion to their country is without limits. These are not moderate men, even though their passions and activities are constrained and directed by their devotion to the republic. Montesquieu suggests, as we have seen, that the Greeks added music to their education in order to give the citizens some gentler spirit in common, encouraging some softness for each other without promoting activities that would contradict the other institutions of the state that promoted the virtue of the citizens.

This care to establish a consistent way of life for the citizens, which both educates them and maintains that education, distinguishes republics. When Montesquieu takes up his next question—namely, the laws the legislator gives that are relative to the principle of the government—he returns to the same question, the relation between the private passions and public virtue. Virtue, he says, is love of the republic, love of equality, and love of frugality. In this section (5.2–5), he suggests an original property settlement that divides the land into equal small parcels, one for each family, and he proposes inheritance laws that maintain such a division. The image here is of an agricultural, family-based republic. The private concerns of the rulers are not entirely reshaped as in Lycurgus's Sparta and Plato's *Republic*; rather, they are carefully circumscribed, more on the model of Plato's *Laws*.[6] The republic provides the avenue for the expression of virtue, for ambition, and for the use of any luxury. Montesquieu does suggest two other ways of maintaining frugality, if not equality: first, in a commercial republic, "the spirit of commerce brings with it the spirit of frugality, economy, moderation, work, wisdom, tranquility, order, and rule" (5.6); and second, in republics whose established inequalities are dangerous to overthrow, a senate can provide both an example and an enforcement of old severe mores, as can respect for the old, for magistrates, and for paternal authority. Each institution takes a person away from concern with private goods; commerce in effect moves the private desire to have more into the public arena, controlling it with public, common standards.

The population, as in a despotism, is divided into a number of households. Within the household there are women, children, servants, and slaves. The households relate to one another through the head of the household, the father. In a despotism, each head of a household relates to the despot or his vizier, but they have no direct relations with one another, and there is no stable number or relative wealth of households. In a republic, a law establishes the number and relative wealth of the households. Within those households, as in a despotism, the women, children, servants, and slaves have no public role. The heads of the households make up the people, the citizenry of a republic. They, in effect, replace the despot. In both despotisms and republics, the sovereign rules according to his will or their wills; the difference is that republics rely upon educated, formed, and directed wills.[7]

The first lesson of book 6, in which Montesquieu takes up the questions of the forms of judgments and the severity of penalties, is that republics and monarchies are alike in that they give importance "to the honor, fortune, life, and liberty of the citizens" (6.2). This makes possible a variety of punishments—for example, those that shame, reduce fortunes, and take away liberty. The government is not reduced, as in a despotism, to torture and death as punishments. In monarchies, spirits need not be corrupted by becoming accustomed to harsh punishments.

However, there are the similarities between republics and despotisms in respect to the form of judgments that we noticed earlier. Men are equal in both governments, even if they are everything in one and nothing in the other (6.2). No distinctions in respect to the persons of the accused are possible. However, the manner of judging came to be fixed in republics. This was a reform of the arbitrariness of the Lacedaemonian ephors and the Roman consuls who judged without laws (6.2). The decemvirs, who first wrote down Roman law and then became despots, illustrate how close the arbitrariness of republics is to that of despotisms. Montesquieu says that the decemvir Appius illustrates the danger of the lawgiver who interprets his own law (6.7). But that danger continues to exist in any republic.[8] Even when the laws established both the crime and the punishments, the problem remained of framing the definition of the crime, the "formulae for actions at law," so that in the course of a case the question that the people were supposed to decide would not change continually and become unrecognizable (6.4). Otherwise, a single magistrate, or the people acting as a single magistrate, could decide the issue according to irrelevant, wrong, or malicious criteria. Montesquieu uses Appius's judgment of Virginia as his example of a single magistrate's judging according to malicious criteria (6.7). There is no mention here of Virginius's having murdered his daughter in order to save her from Appius and the ensuing public outcry against the decemvirs. The end of the story would have illustrated a recourse to mores, to the prelegal standards. Rather, Montesquieu raises the issue of the similarity between republican and despotic judgments. Even republican virtue must be guided in judgments by a legal tradition that poses the question that the people—or the jury, or even the magistrate—is to answer. Republics must be more like monarchies; they must rely on the limits that are a result of the form of judgment, if they are to be reliably moderate.

If a republic succeeds in establishing equality, there is no luxury; in establishing frugality, there is no need for sumptuary laws; and in establishing virtue, there is no need for special officers or courts to see to the morals of women. But the same family structure that limits the excesses of the society of warriors offers a great temptation to the citizen to try to accumulate some extra, or luxury, and to expend it on his family. "So far as luxury is established in a republic, so far does the spirit turn to the interest of the individual. . . . But a soul corrupted by luxury has many other desires; soon it becomes an enemy of the laws that hamper it" (7.2). Not only do men's desires become corrupt, but so do those of women. These women, legally under the guardianship of the closest male relative or the authority of their husband, became so debased, debauched, and dissolute that laws were made to control them (7.13). Laws, as Montesquieu often notes, imply the crimes they punish; but they also mean that the actions under the law are legitimate concerns of the government. Here women are held publicly responsible for their acts. In republics, in contrast to despotisms, the regime has a proper interest in the conduct of families: the virtue of women, as well as of men, is finally enforced by public institutions.

The moderation of republics is problematic. The citizenry is constrained by virtue, which in turn is shaped by the education and is maintained by the laws that see to the equal distribution of property. That constraint produces a regularity that can be moderate. But the structure of republics implies certain despotic qualities. At first the citizenry, or its magistrates, ruled simply according to their wills, without reference to a written law. The laws according to which they judged were the principles of virtue, to which they had been educated. If the education failed, the judgments could be terrible. Written law serves to remind and make clear any breaches in that education on the part of the magistrates or the citizenry. Procedures can be devised to guide the judgment of a case; nevertheless, judgment remains in the end in the hands of the rulers, the lawmakers, and the citizenry. This republican moderation is hard-won and precarious.[9]

The family structure of republics presents an avenue for the growth of private interests, as well as the possibility of controlling both public and private passions. Families in republics are curiously ambiguous institutions. When Montesquieu suggests that a senate can enforce early severe mores, such as respect for the old, the magistrates, and paternal authority, we are reminded of his description of China. But his discussion of Roman efforts to ensure the virtue of women through magistracies and courts reminds us that the members of families—women, servants, and children—were treated as private by arrangement, rather than thought to be altogether so by nature. The city has only delegated its interest in their virtue and can take it back up again. Then, Christianity's insistence on some public role for these people will not preclude its acceptance, as it would in China. This suggests that the structure that underlies the different governments can be separate families; a body of people, separated out from families, which shares a certain character; or, finally, everyone.

Moderation and an orderly republic are the same thing. That is, a republic in which each kind of person does the thing it is supposed to do is also a moderate republic. The virtue of the citizenry and the work of the rest of the population are, in effect, coordinated toward the favored activity. This moderation resembles that of the aristocrats. In each case the question is the self-control of the rulers in respect to the ruled—that they continue to do what they are supposed to do, not turning to use their subjects and goods for other purposes.

Another possiblity for moderation in a republic follows from its very disorder—from the claims of both the democrats and the aristocrats that they are each the real expression of the activities proper to that country. Their virtues are in conflict, controlling each other and thus enforcing the virtue of each. We need to examine this possibility for moderation in republics, a mixed government that balances the people and the aristocrats. Montesquieu's major discussion of mixed governments takes place in the context of his discussion of the balance of power in Rome (11.11–20). It follows his description of the English balance of power, whose purpose was political liberty (11.6) and which is the topic for our next chapter. Rome, according to Montesquieu, began as an elective monarchy sustained by a powerful aristocracy. When such a monarchy fails, it changes into a tyranny or into a popular government in which patricians are superfluous. "Therefore, the situation required that Rome be a democracy, but nevertheless it was not one. The power of the principal men had yet to be tempered, and the laws had yet to be inclined toward democracy" (11.13). The history of Rome from the expulsion of the kings to the time of the Gracchi is the story of this change, of "the imperceptible shift from one constitution to another" in which "states are often more flourishing" than under either of these constitutions (11.13). In this situation, "there is a noble rivalry between those who defend the declining constitution and those who put forth the one that prevails" (11.13). The Roman balance that kept both aristocratic and democratic virtue from abuse was not precisely a constitutional balance; rather, it was a state in a prolonged transition from one constitution to another.

The balance was between the people and the senate, or the patricians. Each held a certain portion of the legislative, executive, and judicial power; the two governments faced each other. "In Rome, as the people had the greater part of the legislative power, part of the executive power, and part of the power of judging, they were a great power that had to be counter-balanced by another" (11.18). When the judges were no longer chosen from among the senators, the constitution was tipped in favor of the people. "Therefore, they ran counter to the liberty of the constitution in order to favor the liberty of the citizen, but the latter was lost along with the former" (11.18). In this situation, such great power had to counter great power to ensure the liberty of the constitution that there was no room to change the arrangements in the courts to favor the liberty of individual citizens.

The Romans could not move from the liberty of the constitution, which was guaranteed by balancing the offices held by democrats or aristocrats, to one in which the liberty of each individual citizen was protected in the courts. To suggest that there might be some aspect in which the citizens were undifferentiated was, in effect, to tip the scale to the democrats. In an introductory chapter in book 11 on the liberty of the constitution, Montesquieu wrote: "Democracy and aristocracy are not free states by their nature. Political liberty is found only in moderate governments. But it is not always in moderate states. It is present only when power is not abused; but it has eternally been observed that any man who has power is led to abuse it; he continues until he finds limits. Who would think: Even virtue has need of limits" (11.4). In moderate states, democracies and aristocracies, there is an ongoing danger that power will be abused; virtue is no guarantee against that possibility. Nor, as we have just seen, does a mixed state in which aristocratic and democratic institutions are pitted against one another provide such a guarantee. The moderation of the arrangement is essentially precarious, and the state cannot be called free by its nature, although it was in large part for hundreds of years free in practice. The moderation and the freedom of republics and aristocracies, even when balanced against one another in a mixed government, are not essential; they are not part of their nature.

Democracies decline as a result not only of losing the spirit of equality itself but also of acquiring a spirit of extreme equality. If the democrats refuse to entrust power to others, if they insist on doing everything themselves—on deliberating, executing, and judging—there can be no virtue. The end of respect for magistrates or for senators, implies the end of respect for elders, for husbands, for masters. "Everyone will come to love this license; the restraint of commanding will be as tiresome as that of obeying had been. Women, children, and slaves will submit to no one. There will no longer be mores or love of order, and finally, there will no longer be virtue" (8.2). We have seen that republics are built on separated, complex families, whose heads are the equal citizens. When those distinctions dissolve, the republic resembles a despotism in which there are no stable distinctions: everyone is a slave of some kind. The suggestion here is that republics harbor a conflict between the equality of their citizens and the inequalities inherent in the underlying family structure.

Equality is an economic and social condition that encourages virtue by removing men who are heads of households from private and familial concerns and by limiting the sphere of those concerns. This makes it easier for them to devote themselves to their country. Their virtue is something else, a willingness to accept constraint on their actions for the good of the country. That devotion is also a competition in virtue, in service to one's country, which reveals inequalities that come to be expressed in the democratic delegation of some tasks to the more able. But this last notion of a graduated ability to be virtuous raises the possibility that the familial structure is arbitrary. What about the servants and slaves who are taken in war but were once citizens of another republic? When are children adults, and what about children for whom there is no estate to inherit and who are thus without an authorized share, family, and children? What about the women whose virtue keeps the families separate, maintains their frugality, and is the basis of the early education of the children? Earlier we noticed that Montesquieu remarks that Spartan institutions and Plato's republic took the notion of political virtue to its extreme, abandoning family structure to direct everyone's attention to the country. Of course, Sparta still relied on the helots, on some portion of the population that was not measured by any potentiality for virtue.

Montesquieu later suggests a similarity in the relation between philosophy and political life and that between Christianity and political life; he does this in the context of the end of a discussion about Roman laws that encouraged marriages and families. He remarks, of the decline of such laws during the empire, that "sects of philosophy had already introduced into the empire a spirit of distance from public business which could not have reached this point at the time of the republic, when everyone was busy with the arts of war and peace. From it came an idea of perfection attached to all that leads to a speculative life; from it came the distance from the cares and encumbrance of a family. The Christian religion, succeeding philosophy, fixed, so to speak, ideas for which the former had only cleared the way" (23.21). Notions of perfection, both human and divine, can make the inequalities of families or of citizens seem unimportant; this leads to an insistence upon treating people as altogether equal, so that they are equally available for the most important things. This notion of equality resembles the natural, asocial equality of men who lack societies. In regard to Justinian and his revision of Roman law for the Christian Roman empire, Montesquieu says: "He believed he followed nature itself, when he set aside what he called the encumbrances of the old jurisprudence" (27.1). The limited equality of the citizens of a republic seems vulnerable to dissolution in the face of the criticism inherent in the separation of the philosophic sects and in the universality of equality before God and of natural equality, once those notions are abroad in the world. Republican equality of the citizens in their common pursuit of political virtue is vulnerable to becoming transformed into their equality as mere humans, as slaves to their passions and to one another, or into their equality as souls before God.

In sum, by directing the passions of the citizenry to the service of their country, republics acquire the regularity that is a prerequisite for moderation. In so doing, they give form to the shapeless willfullness of despots and of the people in despotisms. That shape, regularity, or direction is not, however, necessarily moderate. Montesquieu points this out very early when he discusses the need for music in the education of virtuous republicans. Their virtue has no inherent limits. Their passions are directed and regularized, but they remain passions, individual and infinite. Music arouses the spirit, another impulse within people that expresses a commonalty and offers a limit to the political passion. Insofar as republican government is seen as a middle between the natural, or familial, and the universal of the gods, of god, or of philosophy, its moderation in the sense of limits to its aspirations is implied. But this moderation is threatened by the possibility of identifying the universality of natural equality,

that before the Christian god, and political equality. The other
source of moderation in the balance between the aristocrats and
the democrats within a republic—a balance between conflicting
understandings of political virtue—was, according to Montesquieu, a source of tension leading to activity, but not necessarily a
source of moderation. Rome, after all, became a universal
despotism.

MONARCHY

Although republics and despotisms could be considered governments of another time or another place, monarchy raises the issue
of France, of the government under which Montesquieu lived and
in which he had served as a member of the Parlement of
Bordeaux.[10] He lived under a monarchy that claimed to rule by
divine right, in which rule was the private business of the king and
his servants. In the seventeenth century, that monarchy had
successfully put down a revolt by the nobility, both military and
parlementary, called the Fronde, in which the prerogatives of the
nobility were claimed to have as much standing as those of the
king.[11] Montesquieu has often been identified with the "thèse
nobiliaire"—that is, with the Fronde—both because he was a
noble and member of the Parlement of Bordeaux and because his
description of monarchy clearly includes the old orders as well as
the king.[12] In his later historical books, Montesquieu threads his
way between the Abbé Dubos, who claimed that the French king
took the place of the Roman emperors, ruling the whole population legitimately and alone and creating the nobility as he needed
it, and Henri de Boulainvilliers, for whom the old military
nobility, equals among themselves, were the conquerors of Roman
France and should have ruled it together since that time. Montesquieu argues that the Romans were defeated and that among the
Germans there was always a king who distributed goods among his
followers, an aristocracy, and a people. Montesquieu clearly
wished to fall into neither camp, but more importantly he wished,
it seems to me, to establish a new understanding of monarchy, if
not of the French monarchy in the middle of the eighteenth
century, which would make of monarchy a form of government

that was in itself moderate. In so doing, he lays the groundwork for understanding a government that was in itself both moderate and free—the English.

Montesquieu begins his discussion of the nature of monarchy by asserting: "Intermediate, subordinate, and dependent powers constitute the nature of monarchical government, that is of the government in which one alone governs by fundamental laws. . . ."[13] These fundamental laws necessarily assumed mediate channels through which power flows; for if in the state there is only the temporary and capricious will of one alone, nothing can be fixed and consequently there is no fundamental law" (2.4). If there is to be moderation, the king must act in accordance with the law, rather than his temporary and capricious will; but here he is not taught, asked, or persuaded to follow the laws. What is shaped is, not his will, but the way it can act. The shape is a consequence of the channels through which his will must flow, of the intermediate, subordinate, and dependent powers of the monarchy. Therefore, the nature of a monarchical government is the result of the intermediate powers because they distinguish it from the despotism of one alone by providing the regularity necessary for moderate government. They do so, not by directly affecting the will or character of the prince, but by making certain actions easier or more difficult for him. The king, to use the image of an earlier theorist of the French monarch, is not reined in; rather, he tends to follow the easiest road through rough terrain.[14]

To put the matter somewhat more straightforwardly, monarchical government is made up of intermediate powers, and its nature is set by the shape of those powers. Without intermediate powers to channel the flow of power from the monarch, there would only be the temporary and capricious will of one alone: nothing would be fixed, and there would be no fundamental law. Without "the prerogatives of the lords, clergy, nobility, and towns, in a monarchy, you will soon have a popular state or else a despotic state" (2.4). Without privilege, the state will be despotic if it is ruled by one person; otherwise it will become a popular state. Montesquieu suggests the possibility of another moderate government in which rule is mediated and shaped through intermediate institutions, but one that has a popular rather than a monarchical basis.

In this same chapter, Montesquieu uses water to present another image about the effects of intermediate powers. "Just as the sea, which seems to want to cover the whole earth, is checked by the grasses and the smallest bits of gravel on the shore, so monarchs, whose power seems unlimited, are checked by the slightest obstacles and submit their natural pride to supplication and prayer" (2.4). The issue here is the power of the clergy in monarchies, "especially in those tending to despotism," such as Spain and Portugal. "Ever a good barrier, when no other exists, because, as despotism causes appalling evils to human nature, the very ill that limits it is a good" (2.4). This clergy is that of the Inquisition, whose evil pushes Montesquieu to one of the most dramatic and ironic chapters in his book (25.13). Religion here moderates despotism, not through the despot's fear of God, however, but because of the existence of the clergy as one of the intermediate powers.

In the first image, the power of the monarchy, like water, seeks to spread over everything, unless it is stopped by something higher. However, one might as easily see the power of the nobility or the clergy in action and that of the king as a riverbank or shore that stops them from spreading over everything. The view of the terrain changes as the kind of lordship—the topics and kinds of rule—varies. This expansion and contraction of the power of the monarch, the nobility, and the clergy is tracked in book 31. Twice the kings of France virtually disappeared and were replaced by a new line: the Merovingians were replaced by the mayors of the palace; the Carolingians were replaced when the kings no longer led the nobles to war, losing the incentives with which they controlled the nobles (31.5); the Carolingians were replaced by the Capetians when virtually all fiefs became inherited, leaving the reigning house so stripped of domains that it could not support the king (31.30), and the crown had to be conferred upon the holder of a great fief who could defend the country (31.32). Similarly, "the clergy have always acquired, they have always returned, and they still acquire" (31.10). The goods of the clergy can accumulate endlessly because "the clergy is a family which cannot perish; therefore, goods are attached to it forever and cannot pass out of it" (25.5). These endless acquisitions of the clergy "seem so unreasonable to the peoples that anyone who would want to speak in their favor would be regarded as an imbecile" (25.5). During the reigns of the Merovingians, Carolingians, and Capetians, the clergy received so much that "they must have been given the whole of the goods of the kingdom several times" (31.10). The nobility and the clergy, as well as the king, sought to expand their domain or power until they were halted.

The last element in the nature of a monarchy is what Montesquieu calls a "depository of the laws." Here we reach what Montesquieu is later to call the power to punish crimes or judge disputes between individuals (11.6). He goes on to say that in most kingdoms of Europe, the government is moderate because that power is left to the subjects. In a monarchy the question arises, Which subjects? At the begining of the chapter on the laws in their relation to the nature of the monarchy (2.4), Montesquieu defends the justice of the lords and the clergy as being a part of their prerogatives, whose abolition will lead to the end of monarchy. But later in the book, he traces the dissolution of those forms of justice and the rise of what was to become the parlements. The justices of the lords were established before the end of the reign of the Carolingians (30.22). But separation of justice from the fief began in France with the beginning of appeals during the reign of the Capetian kings in the thirteenth century, particularly with appeals to the court of an overlord, because "an infinity of men with fiefs had no men under them, they were not in a position to hold their own court" (28.27). That separation led to what Montesquieu calls a "depository of the laws," to the customs being written down, becoming more general, and receiving the stamp of royal authority (28.45), and then, to add the implied remaining step, being held, interpreted, and rewritten by a judicial body, by some people defined by the political task they perform rather than by their birth. "It is not enough to have intermediate ranks in a monarchy; there must also be a depository of laws. This depository can only be in the political bodies, which announce the laws when they are made and recall them when they are forgotten. The ignorance natural to the nobility, its laxity, and its scorn for civil government require a body that constantly brings the laws out of the dust in which they would be buried" (2.4). In France, the body of law that has become the law of the country is preserved and enforced in the parlements.[15] If monarchies rest on the prerogatives of the nobility, they also require judicial institutions which are formed by the task to be done.

As we noticed earlier, the law of republics and despotisms was relatively simple. Judges were not required to consider circumstances or to distinguish among the people and goods before them, although there had come to be an effort to distinguish kinds of actions before courts, as well as the evidence and the course of judgment appropriate to them. "The differences in rank, origin, and condition that are established in monarchical government often carry with them distinctions in the nature of men's goods, and the laws regarding the constitution of this state can increase the number of these distinctions. . . . Each sort of goods is subject to particular rules; these must be followed in order to make disposition of the goods, which further removes simplicity" (6.1). Monarchies are also altogether different in respect to judgment. Judges are to deliberate with each other and to take into account a great variety of circumstances.[16] "In monarchies judges assume the manner of arbiters; they deliberate together, they share their thoughts, they come to an agreement; one modifies his opinion to make it like another's; opinions with the least support are incorporated into the two more widely held" (6.4). One cannot help but notice that Montesquieu has put deliberation—that is, the capacity to consider the best action in a set of circumstances— in the hands of people who have not been selected simply by their birth or by their service to the king.[17]

As we have seen, the great change in the French monarchy centered around the change in the status of fiefs, which began as revocable or for life and later became permanent or inherited. The fiefs themselves were rights over some aspect of government—for example, justice, taxation, or military service. Jurisdiction over the same person was divided into a number of fiefdoms and among a number of persons. The great invention of Gothic government was that rule over the same good or person could be shared, so that no person or group need be sovereign over any good or man (30.1). Monarchies, then, have no citizenry; they have no distinctive group that could express political virtue itself. This leaves open the possibility of a great variety of change within this kind of government. In his history of the French monarchy,

Montesquieu distinguishes between two aspects of monarchies: the division and separation of powers so that each had some jurisdiction over the same person, and the way the persons who were to fill those offices were chosen. In the beginning of the Germanic monarchy, the king gave the fiefs to the noblemen of his choice, but gradually those fiefs came to be inherited and to be inherited according to rules of inheritance that kept the wealth and the fief or office in the hands of one member of a great family. Montesquieu calls this the change from political to feudal rule. Here we can see some of the variability within monarchy and the possibilities for change again in the way the offices are to be filled.

After this extended inquiry into the nature of monarchical government, we must turn to its principle. Montesquieu begins by asserting that virtue has never been a characteristic of the courtiers or of the people in a monarchy. It is awkward, he claims, to expect the people to be decent when the principal men of the state are dishonest (3.5). "HONOR, that is the prejudice of each person and each condition takes the place of the political virtue of which I have spoken and represents it everywhere" (3.6). Monarchies have a variety of preeminences and ranks; "the nature of *honor* is to demand preferences and distinctions, therefore honor has, in and of itself, a place in this government" (3.7). Honor, then, is based upon an opinion that one's own rank is preferable to that of others (at least some others) and that one belongs in such a place. By using the word *prejudice (préjuge),* Montesquieu intends us to know that the opinion is unexamined; it is the result either of laziness or of deference to received opinion. But it should be noticed that when the honor of each person is identified with a place in the monarchy, the constitution of the monarchy—that is, the array of intermediate powers—is represented by the sum of the honor.

What is clear in this regard is that honor and the grand actions that accompany it are not dependent upon any match between the person and the rank. It suffices for one to believe that the rank is appropriate and to act as if one properly belonged to that rank. Max Weber, in *The Protestant Ethic and the Spirit of Capitalism,* attributes this same trick of mind to the Calvinist elect; he adds a touch of anxiety in regard to the reliability of one's belief that one is really one of the elect, which Montesquieu only hints at here with his notion that great activity results from this sense of honor. People are always trying to demonstrate by their actions that they belong in their place. This restless desire to prove that one belongs in one's place implies either a distrust that one truly does belong in such a place or a distrust of inequality itself.

Education to honor does not take place within those public institutions where children are instructed; rather, it begins when one enters the world. In contrast to what pertains in republics, a child's family life—his life before entering the public realm—is not shaped by the interest of the public in having a particular kind of citizen. Rather, the society itself shapes people as they enter it. "The world is the school of what is called *honor*, the universal master that should everywhere guide us" (4.2). In the first place, the virtues in a monarchy are "not so much what calls us to our fellow citizens as what distinguishes us from them." Second, in respect to mores, men speak the truth because they want to appear to be daring and free, to seem "dependent only on things and not on the way another receives them." Third, "we are polite from arrogance; we flatter ourselves that our manners prove that we are not common and that we have not lived with the sort of people who have been neglected through the ages" (4.2). In sum, nobility in the virtues, frankness in mores, and politeness in manners are each designed to express a distinction. Thus, honor and its accompanying characteristics are shaped by the ranks and orders of the monarchy.

Montesquieu suggests, however, that those same ranks and orders make a situation in which the greatest of the moral virtues—magnanimity—can exist. "In monarchies one sees the subjects around the prince receive his light; there, as each one has, so to speak, a larger space, he can exercise those virtues that give the soul not independence, but greatness" (5.12). Those who are either unable or not in a position to be magnanimous may be vain or arrogant. The difference is a consequence of the extent to which the orders of the monarchy are stable and clear.

In book 19, Montesquieu describes a people characterized by its sociability and vanity, which sounds remarkably like the French. "If there were in the world a nation which had a sociable humor, an openness of heart; a joy in life, a taste, an ease in communicating its thoughts; which was lively, pleasant, playful, sometimes imprudent, often indiscreet; and which had with all that, courage, generosity, frankness, and a certain point of honor, one should avoid disturbing its manners by laws, in order not to disturb its virtues" (19.5). This sociability has the effect of showing up the singularities of individuals. "The more communicative peoples are, the more easily they change their manners because each man is more a spectacle for another; one sees the singularities of individuals better" (19.8). This communication, observation, and imitation can take place only if the ranks and orders are not so definitive as to make sociability unlikely and vanity, whose ground is fundamental equality, impossible. That is, here Montesquieu seems to make clear not only the arbitrariness of the orders of the monarchies but also that those who are a part of the monarchy suspect, or believe, them to be arbitrary.

A clear separation between the ranks and orders leads to arrogance, the improvement in morals is not clear, and the loss in economic activity is predictable. To turn monarchies toward republican virtue, to try to get the public men to identify their good with that of the country and to act seriously and virtuously, leads to arrogance and laziness. To suggest this, Montesquieu compares this vain and sociable people with the arrogance and isolation of the Spanish. A correction of the excesses of vanity in a monarchy, Montesquieu implies, leads to pedantry and loss of taste and to a society in which "gravity, arrogance, and laziness go hand in hand" (19.9). Tocqueville moves this criticism to the French monarchy, arguing that the French nobility had become in effect a caste. Monarchies seem to thrive on a lack of clarity and definition—in contrast to republics, which require clarity as to who is a citizen and how they are to act toward each other.

Monarchies, like republics, are supported by an inheritance law. But rather than ensuring a number of equal families, the inheritance law of monarchies sustains the privileges of the noble families. "Noble lands, like noble persons, will have privileges. One cannot separate the dignity of the monarch from that of the kingdom; one can scarcely separate the dignity of the noble from that of his fief" (5.9). The monarchical inheritance law is designed to keep together a great estate and to give it a single head, so that a noble family remains a privileged political body. It is very difficult, if not impossible, to sort out the public and the private in these great families. In a way, the noble families are the actors, the citizens, in a monarchy. Then, the wives, the servants, the younger sons, and the daughters—all lead a public life. They cannot be kept private when the household itself, as at court, is where political life takes place. Montesquieu writes: "In monarchies, women have so little restraint because, called to court by the distinction of ranks, they there take up the spirit of liberty that is almost the only one tolerated. Each man uses their charms and their passions to advance his fortune; and as their weakness allows them not arrogance but vanity, luxury always reigns there with them" (7.9). The sociability of the court, where all these people from many noble families along with their retainers meet and jostle for position, is the environment for sociability, communication, and vanity. In order to support the inequality of monarchies, there must be luxury, so that the rich will spend and, by so doing, will pay the poor for the work that sustains the luxury of the wealthy (7.4). Families and economic activity are in the public domain; monarchies blur the sharp distinctions between public and private which are maintained by republics.

The law-abidingness and moderation of republics are the same thing. The king rules in accordance with the kind of monarchy it is, because he rules through the intermediate powers of that monarchy. Therefore the law that the king obeys is the one that sets the order of the monarchy. The depository of the laws—the judiciary—is essential; its job is to maintain the distinctions—to treat people according to their ranks and goods according to their place. The moderation of monarchies, like that of aristocracies, limits and directs the actions of the rulers. But in monarchies, the limit on the actions of the ruler, the king, is a result of his having to rule through subjects who were not chosen by him. When slavery or serfdom came to an end in the monarchies (11.8), the entire population had some, however small, political or civil role. Those roles were, as we have seen, partial. This made for the curious combination of universality and distinctiveness that typified monarchies. Everyone was involved, but with different ranks and in various ways. This distinguishes monarchy from any previous government.

Montesquieu repeatedly objects to John Law's financial manipulations because they dissolved the orders of the monarchy and treated the population equally badly. The English were said to have risked everything, in effect, by dissolving their nobility and settling upon a government whose end was political liberty. Their moderation was not the condition for their liberty; rather, it was coextensive with it. Tocqueville said that the king, in fact, tried to move around what he saw as disorder to form his own administration and to treat his subjects—the population as a whole—as equally subject to his rule. This mixture of universal and particular makes both the moderation of monarchies and the danger of despotism. That the rule of the monarchy must be filtered through the activities of those whose claim to their position is as legitimate as the prince's because it has the same source—namely, the nobles—leads to moderation through what Tocqueville was, in the American context, to call decentralized administration. The king, like the American democracy, has every claim to rule but has no way to exercise that rule directly. If either he or it did find a way, the result would be despotism.

CONCLUSION

We are now in a position to put together the notions of law and spirit with those of the three kinds of government and of moderation. We can see that Montesquieu's principles of governments are representations of the characteristic human interactions, or spirits, that typify and distinguish these governments. The moderation or the despotism of a government follows from this structure.[18]

Despotisms are altogether without spirit, without any intention or purpose that might unite the people. They are based only upon the passions; thus, they are universal and recognize only force and its response, fear. The only justice is based on punishment, reciprocity, and the equality of everyone. There is no internal principle or spirit within a despotism that would propel people toward the actions that would satisfy the natural law. They have to be forced to preserve themselves, to work to take care of their children. Even the force that keeps them together and keeps them regular is a product of having some external circumstance exert the same fear upon the ruler that he imposes upon his people—

whether that circumstance be fear of god or of the climate and circumstance. We have noticed the formal similarity between this rule and that of the divine over the individual intelligences. In each case the ruler holds the subject absolutely accountable, no quarter is given, and the subjects are each individually subject to the ruler. Montesquieu seems to say that the divine rule over intelligences will, if applied to ordinary human politics, be a despotism. Human justice, or moderation, requires some limit on reciprocity, some groups within which the full power of neither the passions nor the divine intelligence has effect.

Republics are distinctive societies, based on a particular spirit. The various spirits that result as people bestir themselves to satisfy their needs in certain terrains are given form in the distinctive spirits of the citizens of a republic. In this natural, pre-Christian situation the varieties of human spirit are exemplified by different societies. Each society was based on and supported a certain kind of human activity, a form of the human spirit. In so doing, it ordered itself so that those who exemplified the particular spirit were favored and the others supplied the goods necessary for its practice. The premise of such a regime is that the population can be divided into those who express its spirit and those who do not, or who do so to a lesser extent. These latter have to be controlled, or ruled, in a manner appropriate to their limitations. They are not educated to be the citizens; rather, they are to supply the materials needed by the citizens. Thus, in effect, each citizen is supported by a family that supplies his needs and educates the citizens to come. The passions of the citizenry are contained by their virtue, their dedication to the whole, and are directed to the ends of the regime, to the actions encompassed in its spirit. The citizenry itself is an egalitarian body, ruled in ways that are analogous to the despotic rule and the rule of intelligences: they are, after all, equal individuals.

But the punishments are moderated because the spirit of the citizenry offers a number of punishments that were not available before—namely, those based on shame before the principles of action of the other citizens. The punishments are also moderated by the beginnings of legal process, of institutions that point the decision making and the punishments of the republic toward the ends or spirit of the regime with a regularity that is not dependent upon the character of the particular ruler at hand. Conversely, dangers to the moderation of republics are to be found in the collapse of their particularity, of their spirit. These exist, first, in a tendency toward extreme equality, in a tendency to collapse the institutions of the republic itself that are designed to maintain its principle. Along this same line are the tendencies to elevate private life to an importance comparable to that of political life, thus giving familial and economic purposes comparable importance. Second, the spirit of the republic itself can point to a kind of universality, whether in the Roman progress toward conquering the world or in the ambition of the Greek philosophers to put the spiritedness of the republics underneath the generality of the ambitions of the philosophic sects. In each case the republic becomes a part or an example of universal rule, not a particular good or spirit in action.

Monarchies are based on an international law that does not make ordered distinctions between peoples. Christianity presumes that everyone has a spirit of which the highest demands on the spirit can properly be made. If so, there can be no natural slaves because no one is thought to be without spirit, so that he could properly be ruled despotically. Women are held to the same standards as men and must be admitted to the sacraments of the church; thus, they cannot be kept entirely private. Sociability, or communication, is universal.[19] The divine reasserts itself here as a universal spirit, but not as a universal law based on the justice of retaliation. In the context of the world after the conquest of the Roman Empire, in which peoples from different tribes and countries lived side by side, the law was reduced to "personal law"; such personal law refuses to make distinctions among the laws, and thus among men. The relations between these individuals could only be settled through a process of judging, whether by combat or by judges who adhered to a code of law that was to emerge out of that very process.

What emerged from this process was, as we have noticed, a rule that was divided both in its source and in its application. That is, by and large, different aspects of one's life were ruled by different people. This unique event in history presented an altogether new pattern for political life. The shape of political life became a result of the changing jurisdictions and the changing sources of rule.

Moderation is to be found in the regularity that results from the balance between these varying rules and sources of rule.[20] Although reasons—based on the divinity, on history and birth, or on choice and election—could be given for any particular arrangement, there remained within it the suspicion of arbitrariness. That suspicion is the source both of the honor of monarchies and of its vulnerability. For this politics not to fall into the despotism implied by its universality, it must both give some shape to the variety of spirits and even some liberty to pursue one's own ends within that shape. Here we have entered into the topic of the next chapter, the notion of political liberty in *The Spirit of the Laws*. Both this free government and monarchies fall within the same category; in each a division of power leads to a particular way of life and moderation built upon a notion of equality, before god or by nature.[21]

5

LIBERTY

We have been taught that political liberty, as the end of political life, is a result of the view that men are by nature equal and that this equality gives them the same rights to life, to liberty, and to the pursuit of the ends implied by liberty, whether those ends are expressed in terms of property or of happiness. Governments are instituted to keep these human entities from bumping into each other unduly—to protect each person's liberty. But we also believe that efforts which the legislature, the executive, or the judiciary make in order to ignore, by-pass, or corrupt the other two powers are signs of despotism and tyranny. Liberty here is understood as the result of a process in which government is divided, shared, and balanced, in which governmental power is not exercised directly by one agent or political body. The relation between these two views of liberty vexes American politics. Here we are in a position to look at a relatively pure case of the argument for liberty as a consequence of divided and balanced governmental arrangements: namely, Montesquieu's discussion of the English government and of its advantages and disadvantages. Montesquieu offers us, not a variation on the argument from natural right, but an example of a government whose end, he says, is political liberty alone, a government that does not identify liberty with the liberty to pursue some particular end, such as expansion, war, religion, the laws, commerce, public tranquility, navigation, natural liberty, the delights of the prince, the glory of the prince, or the independence of each individual (11.5).

Before proceeding to examine his discussion of a free government (11.6) and of the kind of people who result from a life within such a government (19.27), we should examine briefly the differences between Hobbes and Locke and Montesquieu in their treatment of natural right. First we shall collect Montesquieu's views on natural law and natural right as they bear directly on the question of liberty in order to understand why he frames his discussion of political liberty around a government, rather than the rights of individuals. Then we shall be able to examine Montesquieu's objections to the way in which Hobbes and Locke proceeded.

Montesquieu remarks that "as all men are born equal, one must say that slavery is against nature" (15.7). He did not remark directly upon that equality in his discussion of natural law in book 1 (1.2). The generality he implies for the natural sentiments and capacities implies equality in that these impulses are within everyone. But the recognition of those sentiments and the development of an intention that would satisfy them do not imply similarity and equality. If natural conditions are hard enough, men may need to be slaves (bk. 15), women enclosed (bk. 16), and populations subjected to despotic rule (bk. 17) in order to satisfy the conditions of their continued existence—to satisfy the natural law. But those despotic solutions use the least preferable, if most obvious and easy, solution to the needs given to people by nature. Despotism is the consequence, in Montesquieu's opinion, of measuring political life by natural equality and natural liberty.

Hobbes thought that the movement from natural to political life did not entail a new standard; rather, it entailed an organization that would better guarantee that the demands of nature would be met without moving beyond the natural purposes. According to Hobbes, men are equal in respect to their capacity to preserve themselves in nature; each has the liberty "to use his own power as he will himself, for the preservation of his own nature; that is to say, of his own life; and consequently, of doing any thing, which in his own judgment, and reason, he shall conceive to be the aptest means thereunto."[1] The natural law, then, is a precept that sets the conditions under which that life can in fact be preserved. The peace that is the chief precept of the natural law is a consequence of the existence of a sovereign invested with the rights of all. Two clever human inventions—the natural law and the representative sovereign—serve as a machine to redirect the passions of men so that they in fact act to further their own ends. Through his analysis of despotism Montesquieu seems to say to Hobbes that he cannot see how the transition from the domain of natural right to that of natural law can be made. Cleverness is not a characteristic of natural or despotic life; despots are products of the mindless order in which they live, and they will act like everyone else, leading to lives filled with fear, want, and early death for all. The chances for preservation may be improved under despotism, but the result is a deadly peace.

Montesquieu measures political life by something other than natural equality and the liberty it implies. In book 1, chapter 2, Montesquieu moves from the ability to acquire knowledge to the desire to live in society. Social life is, then, linked to a capacity that people do not share equally. But it is in the movement from sentiments or abilities to the intentions to satisfy them that one finds the movement from the passions to Montesquieu's natural spirit, which, as we saw in chapter 3, embodies the capacity to do something, to have an intention, to act toward some end. That capacity is ordinarily expressed through a common way of life that supports and encourages a preferred activity. We have come around to the natural groupings that result from differences in terrain (bk. 18) and the ancient republics that embodied, formalized, shaped, those natural spirits. These governments were not moderate by nature. Their very virtues were in danger of being taken to excess. But there is no doubt about one's—or Montesquieu's—choice when the alternatives are either despotisms or republics. Rather, one should move to temper the particularity and ferocity of republics with some sense of common vulnerability and common life.

Another situation altogether appears if all men are thought to have the capacity to move toward God—that is, if all men are thought to have the divine spirit within themselves. Like the citizens of a republic, they must discipline their passions, but in doing so, they altogether remove themselves from any particular attachments, whether familial or political. This thought gives vitality to natural equality. The equal entities subject to natural passions in their natural liberty are also the equal subjects of a universal God. Their passions are limited to the love of God, to His image in the love of all, and their spirits are pointed toward God. And where, one might plausibly ask, is everyday political life? What has happened to the natural spirits that suggest the variety of family and political life, the particular groups within which virtually all lead their lives? If the ancients did not easily envision a common humanity, the modern Christian does not easily give way to the particularity of the political life within which our human lives are led. Unless that particularity and the limits that it implies for the ends of any government, however Christian, is acknowledged, there is a persistent danger of having governments identify their ends and spirit with that of God; this leads to the modern despotism.

Locke's difference from Hobbes has often been thought to be in the content that Locke gives to the human soul. The view is that Locke's references to Hooker and Locke's connection to the Thomistic tradition, which saw men's nature as pointing toward God, must be taken seriously. Men are not simply atoms in search of self-preservation; they are souls in search of God. Governments were to assure self-preservation and the conditions under which men could pursue the Divinity. Montesquieu, it seems to me, takes this view of Locke's intention seriously, but he suggests that Locke could move simultaneously toward both ends of men because they both imply equality and because neither of them even suggests any human ends between nature and God that political life itself might have. Then politics remains a facilitating, clever mechanism for ends beyond itself.

In Montesquieu, political liberty is not a consequence of natural right, of the autonomy of individuals in nature. Rather, the natural law that emerges as a solution to natural human sentiments and capacities implies both equality and inequality. Although all men have the sentiments and capacities, they must either be forced by despots to do the things required, or they must move toward particular solutions in particular social situations from their own spirits, which are shared by only a part of the population. In either case, the social solution is not liberty for all. When the divine law forces a greater attention to the equal right to liberty of all men because they are all equal before God, it gives, by implication, greater importance to natural equality. The importance Montesquieu gives to the egalitarian, universal characteristics of natural right is a result of circumstance—the advent of Christianity—and of the egalitarian aspects of natural right that circumstance brings to the fore. In the text he introduces his discussion of political liberty in books 11 and 12 with a discussion of international law in books 9 and 10. There, as we have previously noticed, he examines the change in international law to one in which all things that are regarded as property among men—civil liberty, goods, women, children, temples, and even sepulchers—are somehow independent of the government and are defensible even when the government loses a war. This was not true at all under the ancient republics (9.1).

Monarchies were the first governments to emerge in this new situation. They were a curious mix. They began with the rule established by barbaric tribes, which relied upon herding and warfare for their subsistence. These tribes were governed by an aristocracy of warriors, one of whom was the king. In contrast to the more settled rule and, perhaps, to the southern temperaments of the Greek and Roman republics, they did not follow an international law that denied to the defeated the potentiality for citizenship. Rather, these tribes distinguished between the spoils of war and the peace settlement. They seemed, in effect, to recognize each other's natural liberty once the warfare had come to an end. They gave no one the entire rule over another; instead, they invented overlapping jurisdictions. This also, perhaps, was a response to their natural liberty, their discomfort with being ruled by someone else. With time, a number of transformations took place in this government. When feudalism was established, the posts were given, in effect, to families, rather than to some member of the nobility. Political bodies that judged and were not simply inherited then developed. Servitude was first expanded as serfdom and then was contracted. The suggestion is that the unremitting pressure of Christian belief was against such servitude. The consequence is a government in which the offices are held by families—a feudal rather than a political government, to use Montesquieu's expressions. The end of such a government is the glory of certain individuals and families; it acts using the sense of honor, however false, of all. There is a tension between the notion of nobility and the arbitrariness of its inheritance. Honor becomes vanity as inheritance seems to mean less, and everyone has some hope of being well regarded. Rule and reputation come from above and are somehow filtered through these intermediate institutions to everyone.

Moderation is intrinsic to such governments, but their liberty is what Tocqueville was later to call aristocratic liberty. Some men have the space—the liberty—to become quite extraordinary and magnanimous, to become true gentlemen (5.12). Liberty in this context is the liberty of some, chosen by inheritance, or chance, to fill this space or to appear to fill it. These activities fill the intermediate spaces and institutions with a variety of specific, possible, yet Christian lives in government, which makes it difficult to imagine the despotism that results from identifying the Christian best, the natural, and political virtue. This despotism required a collapse of the plausibility of those noble, Christian lives—a point that Montesquieu only suggests in his discussion of vanity in France. The paths left for human action by the intermediate powers of a monarchy come to form, give shape, even give a purpose, to those actions as people move to take advantage of the possibilities that are open to them. The intermediate institutions in political life act analogously to the terrain in nature: they lead to particular political, rather than natural, lives.

Montesquieu begins his explicit discussion of liberty by asserting that liberty is ordinarily identified with the government that is consistent with one's customs or inclinations (11.2). As republics and democracies appear to follow the inclinations of their people, they have been identified with liberty, thus confusing the power of the people with their liberty. Rather, "in a state, that is, in a society where there are laws, liberty can consist only in having the power to do what one should want to do and in no way being constrained to do what one should not want to do" (11.3). That is, political liberty takes place only within laws, and those laws both indicate preferred actions and prohibit others. Liberty can also be defined as having the right to do everything that the law permits and as not having others free to do what it prohibits.[2] By assuming that in practice a government that prohibits also, by implication, encourages, Montesquieu denies the possibility of a government that only prohibits actions—that is, a liberal government in the strictest sense.[3] What, then, is he to think of a government that has liberty as its sole end? What are to be the boundaries, the shapes, the lives of men in a government that is not directed by any end other than their liberty? England, he says, presents him with an example to examine. There are two long chapters on England—chapter 6 of book 11 and chapter 27 of book 19—and two short chapters—chapter 13 of book 14 and chapter 8 of book

20. The first long chapter takes up the governmental institutions that create and sustain English liberty; the second, the kinds of men that result from such institutions. There is a parallel here between the first and second parts of Tocqueville's *Democracy in America*. The short chapters take up the natural English character and English commerce. We shall now examine these chapters on England, keeping in mind that liberty, as the end for politics, raises for Montesquieu the question of exactly what the people in such a state will do with themselves and of what they will be like as a result of that activity. In the course of this examination, in order to amplify Montesquieu's understanding of English liberty, we shall also look briefly at book 12, on liberty in respect to individuals, and book 13, on taxation.

Montesquieu's understanding of English political life as a result of balanced powers of government has been both criticized and defended in respect to its historical accuracy.[4] Montesquieu himself says that looking for liberty in England is like looking in a mirror (11.5), and he claims to speak not of English practice, but of the principles of the government. In fact, although England is mentioned in the titles of the chapters about it, England and its history are not mentioned directly. Rather, the language is abstract and is even somewhat peculiarly and awkwardly put into the conditional tense: for example, "It would be" or "It could happen that . . . ."

Montesquieu begins by saying that "in each state there are three sorts of powers: legislative power, executive power over the things depending on the right of nations, and executive power over the things depending on civil right" (11.6). The first is the power to make laws; the second, to conduct foreign policy; and the third, or judicial, to punish crimes and judge disputes between individuals. Any rulers would have to do these things, and their acts could be considered under these headings. Montesquieu makes explicit the variety of possible sources of rulers by referring in each case to "the prince or the magistrate" (11.6).

John Locke divides political power into the legislative, the executive, and the federative. The differences between Locke's and Montesquieu's divisions of power center on the executive. Montesquieu's executive power over the civil right is judicial power because it is seen from the point of view of the punishment of individual offenders rather than from the point of view of the need to set out regulations, send out tax forms, and establish criteria for prosecution. These last tasks are those of Locke's executive. "But because the Laws, that are at once, and in a short time made, have a constant and lasting force and need a *perpetual execution*, or an attendance thereunto: Therefore, 'tis necessary there should be a *Power always in being* which should see to the *Execution* of the laws that are made and remain in force."[5] But as Montesquieu continues, his executive power seems to include Locke's executive power. For example, he calls executive power the power of "executing public resolutions"; he worries that the power to make and execute the laws should not be in the same hands; and he calls legislative power the "general will of the state" and executive power "the execution of that general will" when he asserts that they can be held by magistrates or political bodies (11.6).

Because political right varies altogether from republics to monarchies in respect to the question of its capacity to act directly upon private lives, it is very difficult to speak of its execution. However, Montesquieu has some reasons to subsume the execution of the political right under that of the right of nations. The purpose of all states (11.5) is to maintain themselves. Insofar as a prince or a magistrate serves this purpose, he can be spoken of as executing the right of nations. If the preservation of the regime is the task of the executive, then his task differs with each government. The executive whose job is to establish safety can be expected to protect both the lives and the way of life of the people.

Montesquieu's skittishness about executive power may be due to his unwillingness to explicitly promote that power for the French king. He does say here that "thus princes who have wanted to make themselves despotic have always begun by uniting in their person all the magistracies, and many kings of Europe have begun by uniting all the great posts of their state" (11.6). Tocqueville also takes up that point in his investigation of the development of the French administrative structure, which, he says, tended toward despotism because it used commoners, who had no independence from the king, and because it was linked to a king who legislated.

In a government that is directed toward political liberty, whose political right is arranged toward the end of political liberty itself, the offenses that the executive prosecutes are limited chiefly to those against the civil law, to those in which someone's private well-being is threatened. Such a regime has two typically difficult executive problems. First there is the question of offenses against its purpose—that is, of treason. As principles, liberty and safety offer few guides for prudential action against those who violate them (bk. 12). Second is the question of taxation, of the extent to which a state can take the goods, the guarantee of individual safety, from a person for its own use when it has no purpose other than that safety (bk. 13). In other governments one would be left with the question of magistrates who are concerned with education, family structure, sumptuary laws, or religious establishments; but not in the government with liberty alone for its end.

The shape of executive, legislative, and judicial power in a particular government is a result of the kind of government. That is, the jobs of these powers and thus the relations between them change as the ends of the government change. A divison of powers that is protected by balancing through some shared tasks must be peculiar to each kind of government and must lead to governmental action appropriate to that government. We shall see a balanced government with a somewhat different intention when we examine the development of the United States Constitution in our chapter 7. Montesquieu writes of the English government: "The form of these three powers should be rest or inaction. But as they are constrained to move by the necessary motion of things, they will be forced to move in concert" (11.6). The powers of government, balanced perfectly so that their aim can be only liberty, would not move without an impulse from the outside— that is, from external circumstances. They can move together because they are the parts of a particular government—here, one aimed exclusively toward liberty.

There is neither liberty nor moderation when the three powers are united. Both can exist if the judicial power is separate. The citizens fear neither that one another's acts nor that those of the state are directly aimed at them personally. Here the issue is whether the people have the liberty to pursue in safety the ends that are either permitted or encouraged by a government. Without that safety there can be no liberty. This points the reader to book 12, where Montesquieu looks at the crimes whose punishment is particularly dangerous to a citizen's feeling of security, his liberty, even with a separate judiciary. Montesquieu here identifies the separate judiciary in England with the jury. Its advantage is that it is never a "political body," to use Montesquieu's term. "In this fashion the power of judging, so terrible among men, being attached neither to a certain state nor to a certain profession, becomes, so to speak, invisible and null. Jurors are not continually in view; one fears the magistracy, not the magistrates" (11.6). This suggests that moderation and liberty are linked to a separate judiciary, but that for liberty to be the purpose of the government, the judicial power must dissolve out of sight into juries, so that this fearsome power cannot be exercised either for some end of its own or in conjunction with the other two powers.[6]

Judges in republics follow the letter of the law. They have no discretion because discretion would mean that they could interpret the law to the detriment of a citizen. In both Rome and England, after the decision as to guilt or innocence has been given, "the judge pronounces the penalty imposed by the law for this deed; and he needs only his eyes for that" (6.3). The unanimity required of juries to condemn a man to death is, Montesquieu believes, a result of the need, when judgments were moving from the battlefield to the court, for the judges to stand together so that the accused would not challenge any one of them to combat because of his decision (28.27). Some group of one's peers makes the decision, which it stands by as a group. This group serves, in effect, as a representative of the people—the sovereign in a republic—but as a representative body that has such a brief existence that one would not expect it to be able to develop any interest of its own or to respond to political pressures.

The difficulty arises when even the anonymity of the jurors and the brief duration of juries do not protect them from pressures. The pressure that is most likely to overwhelm juries is the passion aroused by the suspicion and accusation of treason. In book 6, Montesquieu agrees with Machiavelli's concern that a few can be corrupted by a few in great cases involving the accusation of crimes against the state, and that those cases will somehow have to be judged by the whole. In his discussion of England, Montesquieu promotes an explicit procedure for trials of crimes against the state within the legislative body, as we shall notice shortly.

But that same passion—the suspicion of secret actions and beliefs that are subversive to the general order—is a more general problem for the security of individuals. This is the topic of book 12, where Montesquieu takes up the question of how to treat heresy, magic, homosexuality, and treason. These offenses share the characteristics of secrecy and of alien rule, whether by another god, the devil, another nature, or another sovereign. Montesquieu here suggests a set of rules to guide and control prosecutions; these are rather like the Romans' formulae for actions or the American Bill of Rights. In the context of discussing crimes against religion, he distinguishes between offenses against religion itelf, against the mores, against tranquility, and, finally, against the security of the citizens. The first cannot be punished by men because they have no way of knowing about and no appropriate penalties for crimes against God. The second should be subject to deprivation of the advantages that society accords to those who have good mores. The third should receive penalties that hope for correction. Only the fourth is punished by retribution for the wrong done, whether economic or capital. In the remainder of book 12, Montesquieu concentrates on the dangers of prosecution for things unseen but suspected. Neither speech nor writing, he says, should be the primary evidence for treason. Montesquieu continues this book with an array of topics: the violation of modesty in punishing; the requirement that conspiracies be revealed; the excessive punishment for treason in republics; bills of attainder; the cruelty of laws against debtors in republics; judgments by commissioners; spies; anonymous letters; and the dictum that a king should be polite to his subjects. These topics follow from the principles of proportion and attention to deeds and of reluctance to search for a hidden motive; the best analogy to all this in our political experience is the array of interpretations that have followed upon the Bill of Rights.

Only two separate powers are left to be balanced. In a free state the people as a body should have legislative power because "every man, considered to have a free soul, should be governed by himself" (11.6). Self-government is, in effect, the appropriate kind of rule for those thought to be free. This remark contains the same ambiguity—in regard to both the truth of the claim and the extent of free souls—as does the remark in *The Federalist* that republican government rests on the "honorable determination which animates every votary of freedom to rest all our experiments on the capacity of mankind for self-government" (*Fed.* no. 39). In a large state it is impossible for the people as a whole to rule; such rule is subject to many drawbacks even in small states. The primary drawback is that the people cannot discuss public business. Montesquieu seems to presume that a large people's inappropriateness for such discussion is obvious.[7] The representatives improve upon any assembly of the people because they can discuss business; therefore they should be chosen and instructed in a way that will permit such discussion: they should be chosen from districts so that the choice will be informed by neighborliness and the representatives' actions will be limited by that same neighborliness; but they should not be given specific instructions.

The characteristic of representatives is that they discuss affairs, deliberate, and that they do it for others. That is, they act for someone else in an arena where the person cannot act for himself. A representative is necessarily something other than what he represents. The consequence Montesquieu draws from this difference is, not that it should be minimized, but that in order to understand any representative we must have clearly in mind the respect in which he is different from that which he represents. That is, a representative differs from the people because he has the possibility of deliberation—like the judges in a monarchy.[8] Then, the institutions that shape representation could be judged by the extent to which they facilitate the expression of this activity which is proper to the representatives but not to the people who elect them.

The executive power "should be in the hands of a monarch, because the part of the government that almost always needs immediate action is better administered by one than by many, whereas what depends on legislative power is often better ordered by many than by one" (11.6). This means that the monarch is defined by its singularity, by its number; this is a way of thought that is also characteristic of *The Federalist*, as we shall see. Montesquieu proceeds to argue that the executive power should not be given to a "certain number of persons drawn from the legislative body." There would no longer be liberty because the two powers would be united: that is, there should not be any cabinet government. The virtue of inheritance, then, is that it provides an independent source of executive power, not that inheritance itself is the source of some good. This leaves open the possibility of coming up with another device for choosing the executive and ensuring its independence.

At the end of book 13, on taxation in relation to liberty, Montesquieu ends by asserting with great clarity and definitiveness that taxes should be collected by agents of the government, by bureaucrats, and not by independent agents, or tax farmers, whose pay is some portion of the taxes collected. Even in monarchies, where tax collecting is a separate order, if the profession comes to be honored, honor itself "loses all its esteem there" (13.20), as money alone should be enough reward for the tax collectors. Tax collection is, then, explicitly the concern of the executive in a moderate government.

Book 13 consists largely of a discussion of how and what should be taxed. The conclusions and alternatives are some of the platitudes of our political life: namely, that freedom and commercial vitality offer the possibility of larger taxes, but that excessive taxation could destroy both; that taxes are least objectionable if they are proportional to the value of the thing taxed, if they leave room for necessity and tax luxury at a higher rate, if they are hidden in taxes on commodities, or in some other way. Book 13 begins by making a distinction between countries in which a part of the peoples are slaves to the land and those in which "all the individuals are citizens and each one of them possesses by his domain that which the prince possesses by his empire" (13.7). That is, free citizens and modern alienable property are the conditions under which the preceeding considerations are relevant. Otherwise, in a monarchy the king should depend on the revenues of his domain and on the military service of his nobles, and a republic should take a fixed proportion and never increase the tax (13.4). Montesquieu's distrust of the means that the monarchy has used in collecting taxes—the tax farmers—points toward having the taxes collected by the executive even in a monarchy. But this means that the monarch would both make the rules for taxation and collect the taxes himself—a situation with great potential for despotism, even if there is a separate judiciary. This points toward the need in the modern situation, where taxes must be collected from the population at large, for a division between the legislation that establishes taxation and the executive who is to collect them. The suggestion, again, is that the monarchy has moved too far away from its division into orders for that division to guarantee moderation, much less liberty.

A balance between two powers has little capacity for correction once some circumstance has shifted the balance to one side or another. Once a weight has shifted, something has to be able to move from one side or the other or to move either side away from or toward the center of balance in order to restore the balance. The image is that of a seesaw or a scale. Montesquieu suggests that a second legislative body, composed of nobles, can make adjustment possible in a government that aims toward liberty. The other possibility is for people to shift their allegiance from one branch to the other, as Montesquieu points out in chapter 27 of book 19. Balance is possible both from the point of view of the institutions and from that of their support.

This second legislative body also protects those "people who are distinguished by birth, wealth, or honors" (11.6). Those people would be enslaved if they were simply subject to a legislature formed from the people, for most of the resolutions of the legislature would be against them. This group of notables is not the nobility of a feudal monarchy. There is considerable evidence that Montesquieu thought there was no longer a feudal nobility in England. He wrote earlier in the book that "in order to favor liberty, the English have removed all the intermediate powers that formed their monarchy" (2.4). He remarks later that "in a nation where the republic hides under the form of monarchy, observe how a particular estate for fighting men is feared and how the warrior still remains a citizen or even a magistrate, so that these titles serve as a pledge to the homeland so that it is never forgotten" (5.19). This is not a state in which the nobility can protect the moderation and freedom of the government by its existence as a separate order. Rather, the notables must be protected from the envy of the majority. To do so is sufficiently difficult that they need to be hereditary; this gives them enough interest in defending themselves and is, he says, natural (11.6).

Why protect this minority? The existence of notables of a variety of kinds must add something important to the government other than the moderation that their existence supported in a feudal monarchy. The grander ways of life of the notables must be protected from the envy of the people. Liberty, the purpose of this government, did not point toward a particular way of life. However, the protection of the notables does seem to point the state toward ways of life of some distinction, if not toward a choice among them. One cannot help but be reminded of Tocqueville, of both his worry about democractic individualism and his admiration for aristocratic liberty.

The mechanisms that balance this government have two purposes: first, they maintain the division of power by protecting each part of the government from the encroachments of the others; and second, they promote what perhaps can best be called good government—that is, they make it easier, or possible, for the parts of the government to perform their tasks well. Each mechanism is a breach of the principle of separation of powers, because each involves the action of one branch in what is properly the domain of another branch. This balancing is only possible if the whole is thought of as something whose parts can be identified but cannot be taken altogether apart—a machine or body, not a collection of discrete parts.

In this division of powers, Montesquieu has divided up rule itself. Ruling is to be regularized and limited, not from the outside, as in a monarchy, by the intermediate powers—by the honor identified with their particular tasks and lives—but from within itself. In that way, liberty will be the end; the government will have no aim other than regular, limited rule. Rule has to be taken apart to guarantee regularity, but it is hard to conceive of it apart; one is always looking around for sovereignty. In addition, it must be taken apart in a way that permits or encourages it to proceed competently, or the government will not last. Hence, there is a need for forceful mechanisms to protect the institutions from their tendency to incorporate all of rule within their purview, and there is a need to do so in a way that will encourage good government. Let us look at the mechanisms of each kind in each of the three branches of the government in Montesquieu's description of the English government.

The judicial branch's most important protection against the incursions of the other two branches of government is its invisibility. The jurors disappear as they finish judging each case; this makes consistent corruption virtually impossible.[9] The executive, in turn, is protected from the judiciary by his immunity from their judgment, although his ministers are not. To ensure fair judgment, Montesquieu requires that the judges be of the same status as the judged; the juries for the people are taken from the people, and the nobles are to be judged by the noble branch of the legislature. To ensure consistency in judgment, the punishments must be according to the precise text of the law. But the noble branch of the legislature can moderate judgments to meliorate the harshness of that consistency. Impeachment—that is, judgment for political crimes—must be brought by the house of the legislature of the people before that of the nobles. In these last considerations, Montesquieu limits judging and moves aspects of it to nonjudicial institutions in order to improve the judgments rendered, not to protect the independence of the judiciary.

The executive is protected from the legislative branch both by the fact that he is the monarch and by his veto over legislation. He is not to propose laws; this limits his involvement in legislation, thus protecting the division of powers. Then, Montesquieu says that the executive is to set the times for the meeting of the legislature. The legislature needs an outsider to convene and to prorogue it in order for it to be simply one body in the government and for it to reemerge after each election as another body. In addition, the executive is to supervise the army. The army would never respect the legislature, because the army's way of life is in opposition to the legislature's. Again the executive takes over a task to protect the legislature from an enterprise that would make it impossible for it to do its job.

The legislature protects itself from the executive by its capacity to oversee, but not to veto, the actions of the executive. The executive power, Montesquieu says, is limited by its own nature; it cannot work properly if it cannot act immediately in particular instances—that is, in accordance with its nature. The suggestion is, then, that the particularity limits the executive action. In addition, the legislature is both to originate taxation and to do so on a year-to-year basis in order to protect itself from the executive.

The actions of the legislature itself are limited to those that will not do active harm to the notables by the existence of a branch made up of those notables. As a hereditary body, they could easily follow their particular interests and forget those of the people, so they must only be able to veto in those matters in which "one has a sovereign interest in corrupting" (11.6)—for example, taxation. Rather, the people's house must originate tax bills. Montesquieu puts the need for two branches of the legislature in terms of a substantive issue—namely, the tendency of the many to threaten the liberty of the few in a government whose purpose is the liberty of all—not in terms of the need to limit the generally excessive activism of legislatures.

The result of all this balancing is rest or inaction. Only inevitable changes in circumstances can force the government to move, but it is so constructed that the parts will be forced to move together. The government favors no group or purpose, but it is sufficiently well constructed that its parts will move together to produce coherent rule. Then, it seems to follow that the character of the people will not be affected by the government. It will simply facilitate purposes and characters that are developed in some other realm—natural, economic, religious, or historical. Montesquieu's other great chapter on England provides an explicit rejection of this conclusion. At the end of book 19, whose general point is the importance of having government respect the preexisting character of a people, he puts a chapter titled "How Laws Can Contribute to Forming the Mores, Manners, and Character of a Nation" (19.27). He refers to writing about the principles of the constitution of a free people in book 11; but here we are to "see the effects that had to follow, the character that was formed from it, and the manners that result from it" (19.27). That is, living under such a constitution does, in fact, form the character of the people, even if it does not intend to do so.

This is not to say that climate does not have its prior effect. Whatever character people have as a result of the way of life imposed on them by nature cannot be discounted. In a brief earlier chapter on the English character and climate, Montesquieu typifies the English character insofar as it is due to climate (14.13). The English are a people to whom everything can be intolerable and who are both impatient and courageous. Therefore, they require a government in which no one person can be blamed for anything, and their constant agitation not only disorganizes the projects of tyranny but also makes difficult the politics that requires patience and persistence.

For liberty alone to be the end of the government, the institutions of government have to embody parts of rule itself, rather than any particular kind of rule. Then, Montesquieu says in book 19, chapter 27, although parties form around the legislative and the executive branch, depending upon whether people do or do not hope for places in the executive branch, there would be no allegiance to either party. This is because people would be motivated by all the passions, as the passions would all be free there, and because they would act as independent individuals, each following his own caprice and fantasies. Even the monarch would have to put his trust in those who had been his enemies, because he would have no reliable allies. A free society, then, is made up of individuals who are following their particular passions and fantasies, without having any coherent or reliable allegiances or groupings within the society. They form and reform groupings around the separate powers of the government, as the interests, real or imagined, of the individuals indicate at any moment.

These people do not feel secure. Montesquieu describes them as uneasy, filled with terror. They are, it seems, principally afraid of losing their liberty. The existence of the legislative branch keeps them from visiting those terrors upon the executive, and they ordinarily would "produce only empty clamors and insults and would even have the good effect of stretching all the springs of the government and making all the citizens attentive" (19.27). But they can be turned against anyone who overthrows the fundamental laws or against foreign threats.

The nation's attachment to its liberty is such that it would sacrifice its goods, its ease, and its interests such that it would take on burdens that no absolute prince would dare ask of his subjects. Its credit would be secure, it would be safe, and yet it would not conquer abroad. It would not become a conquering nation because it is difficult and unsafe for island nations to conquer, because the nation did not need to go to war to prosper, and because "no citizen would depend on another citizen, each would make more of his liberty than of the glory of a few citizens, or of a single one" (19.27). Military men, then, would be regarded as useful, engaged in a dangerous and arduous occupation; but civil status would be more highly esteemed.

The result of peace, liberty, and freedom from destructive prejudices is, according to Montesquieu, that the nation would be inclined to become commercial. Insofar as this list of causes is a summary of the preceeding discussion, then it seems that freedom from destructive prejudices is to be identified with the individualism and the absence of any fixed order or ranks in the population that Montesquieu describes in the beginning of the chapter. The conditions for commerce have all been met in England, and no other direction has been set for the people, thus making commerce the most likely avenue for their restless activity. This commercial people would trade with the south, often emigrate in search of wealth, be petty and jealous over trade advantage, have rigid laws about commerce, and send colonies abroad for commerce more than domination. Its colonies would also prosper because they would be given its form of government, but its rule over a neighboring state would crush any political independence out of jealousy for that nation's wealth, while permitting civil liberties to all of its people. The commerce would make possible a great navy, which is also the most acceptable defense of a free government on an island. This would lead to great power, as other nations have to finance a land army as well. This nation would have the pride that results from impunity and from the capacity to insult others everywhere, and it could have great influence on its neighbors. In negotiations it would be a bit more honest than others because it could not be as secretive.

Having completed his picture of the way of life that results from this government, Montesquieu turns to the manners of its people and their character. Neither the nobility nor religion sets the standards in this society. The nobility once had an immoderate power and ruled arbitrarily; although its style is preserved, what one sees is the "form of an absolute government over the foundation of a free government" (19.27). In these comments, Montesquieu warns the reader against paying undue attention to the monarchical forms in England. Religion in such a state will be a result of the enlightenment or the fantasies of individuals. If they were generally indifferent, they would all embrace the dominant religion, but if they were serious about religion, sects would multiply. No one would take kindly, however indifferently they felt about religion, to a demand to change religion; and any religion that had a history of such attempts would remain odious, although the laws against it would not be bloodthirsty. (One can only presume that Montesquieu is discussing the fate of Catholicism in England.) Members of the clergy would not be highly enough regarded to seek a separate rank; rather, they would bear the same burdens as lay people do and would try to distinguish themselves by the quality of their lives. The only ranks, then, would be those belonging to the fundamental constitution. They would be more fixed than ranks elsewhere, but those who held the ranks would be closer to the people than elsewhere. Men who hold ranks and govern would have regard for those who would be useful to them, not those who could divert them. "Men would scarcely be judged there by frivolous talents or attributes, but by real qualities, and of these there are only two, wealth and personal merit" (19.27). Their politeness is that of people who must deal with one another regularly and not cause displeasure, not that of the court, which is founded on idleness and arbitrary power. Women are scarcely to be seen among men in this society of confederates who share the administration of the state. These men talk about politics continuously, calculating about things that depend upon fortune. "In a free nation it often does not matter whether individuals reason well or badly; it suffices that they reason; from that comes the liberty that protects them from the effects of these same reasonings" (19.27).

He proceeds to conclude with a description of the malaise that results from this situation—from there being no generally accepted standards. Montesquieu writes that although many do not worry and abandon themselves to their own humors, most of those with wit, or spirit, are tormented by that same wit, disdaining everything. Their pride is founded on their independence, on living on their own, so in an unfamiliar society they demonstrate a strange mixture of bashfulness and pride. Their solitary, withdrawn way of life and thought inclines them to feel individual vices and to resort to satire, rather than to the ridicule that society teaches us. Their party spirit makes their historians as much the slaves of the prejudices of their own party as they would be of any despot. Their poets show more the original bluntness of invention than any delicacy or grace.

Montesquieu here presents a social scheme that is familiar to us today. The ranks of the constitutional governments are faced with a population in which there are no settled groupings, only individuals willing to change allegiances for the passions or interests of the moment. There are no distinct orders in the society—no nobility, no clergy, no military; only the rank given by the constitution is reliable, and the adherents of each division of power change continuously. The people have nothing beyond their individual interests, passions, and terrors. The people are uneasy, frightened, moved by the passions of the moment. They turn their attention to commerce, and its pursuit is a source of strict rule. But Montesquieu does not suggest that commerce offers a reliable social order. There is not even an allegiance to one another among the people beyond the consideration that is due to confederates or allies. The various positions that might be expected to give the individuals a sense of accomplishment and stability do so in such a way as to produce anxiety as well. Those who hold the ranks established in the constitution cannot expect recognition beyond their own circle, and they demonstrate a curious mixture of pride and bashfulness. The men of wit, or spirit, express disdain for the others in the society. Those who are prone to humor settle on the satire of individual vices rather than the gentler ridicule of social life. The arts are limited to rough invention; there is no context for acquiring grace or style. In each case, the individuality and the flux within which they live their lives limit their accomplishments and give them a certain unfinished, uneasy quality. Here, Montesquieu begins to sketch the analysis and criticism of modern democratic man that Madison implied in *The Federalist* and that Tocqueville amplified later.

From another point of view, the English government, which was aimed exclusively toward liberty and not toward forming character, in fact did not form character; rather, it confined the passions by pitting them against each other. In so doing, it created separated, limited inidividuals whose passions were limited by their positions and by the habits that those positions engendered, but whose spirits seemed to fly off in any direction.[10]

With this in mind, one is pushed to return to inquire into the conditions of English lives—to the economic, religious, and historical conditions that might give direction and can be directed. The question has become, How are these things to be thought about and acted upon? They are no longer intrinsic to the political life and to the political law of the country, as in a republic; but they are not irrelevant. They are not topics about which a government can properly have no opinions and to which it ought to give way as far as possible without countermanding the force of political liberty. Here we turn to the topics of parts 4, 5, and 6 of *The Spirit of the Laws,* the latter half of the book. We have already looked at these topics in the preceding chapters, asking the question of how they came to be loosened from political law and of the consequences of that loosening in the development of monarchies and modern republics. Here, rather, we are turning to the question of how they are to be understood once they have been loosened, whether they have a shape and direction of their own, and if so, what and how they can, under these latter circumstances, be brought under some political law—that is, how they can be legislated about.

6

LEGISLATION

Of the English, Montesquieu writes: "This is the people in the world who have best known how to take advantage of each of these three great things at the same time: religion, commerce, and liberty" (20.7). To take advantage of, to make use of, these three great things, they must first of all be understood to be things. They must have some activity, purpose, shape, and even history of their own. That is, commerce must be distinguished from wealth, luxury, or greed; religion, from God, belief, and sin; and liberty, from natural right.[1] Although we have already examined Montesquieu's suggestions that political law has lost its grip on and its jurisdiction over these topics, we have not asked whether they can be thought of as things, as phenomena with shapes and lives of their own once they are not directly subordinate to political purpose. These are the questions of the modern social sciences, of economics, sociology, and history. Here we can see Montesquieu moving toward an understanding of the way economic and social things work when they are thought to be and are permitted to be things on their own. However, for Montesquieu these remain the material for legislation, for political action. The question is to understand them and then to understand how they are to be controlled and dealt with in the modern circumstances of political life.

According to Montesquieu, religion, commerce, and liberty are the great topics of modern legislation, and he takes each one up in turn in the second half of *The Spirit of the Laws:* commerce in books 20–23; religion in books 24–26; and in books 27–31, liberty in the history of the Germanic institutions that were the source of modern liberty. In this chapter we shall take up these three in turn, examining Montesquieu's efforts to see what kinds of things they are and to see how they can be used to best effect when, as in our times, they must be treated as distinct things.[2] In each of the three, the relations between separated individuals are mediated. In economics, individuals relate to one another through the market; in religion, through their god and his rules; and in the history of the Germanic tribes, they carried their own law with them and came to settle their quarrels through formalized battles. Governments must devise ways of affecting these systems so that they will fit into a particular government and spirit. The goods, men, and money in trade can be managed; the civil law can be expanded to increase the distance between political and religious crimes and punishments; the liberty of the Germanic tribes can be transformed into the institutions of a free government. In each case, a government can nudge the system into a shape, give it a form that is appropriate to that government, if it takes into account both its own nature and that of the system to be shaped.

COMMERCE

In books 2–8, in which Montesquieu first takes up his three governments, those things that are the subjects of commerce are in the jurisdiction of political life and choice. His treatment of the distribution of goods in book 5 and of luxury in book 7 make both a function of a legislator's choices; this is particularly true in republics. He claims that it is best to divide the land into parcels just large enough to support a family and to allot one parcel to each family; inheritance laws are devised to maintain the division. There is no luxury in such a society; its members are "poor only because they have disdained or because they did not know the comforts of life, and these last can do great things because this poverty is a part of their liberty" (20.3). The legislator—with Solon, Lycurgus, and even the decemvirs in mind—is spoken of as having a choice, of creating property settlements that will shape and direct the passions so as to produce political virtue, devotion to the country, and a capacity and willingness to engage in the activities that characterize that people.

If there is to be luxury, something beyond the necessary, either the society must be divided into classes of increasing luxury, as in Solon's Athens or Plato's republic, or each family may have just a bit more than necessary. Although there is no clear-cut source of the luxury in an agrarian republic, conquest and slavery—which reduce others to less than what is necessary for citizenship—are the most obvious. Montesquieu remarks that the "total absence of commerce produces, on the other hand, the banditry that Aristotle puts among the ways of acquiring" (20.2). He hastens to add that such peoples have virtues—for example, hospitality—that are not found among commercial peoples. The luxury of republics, however secured, must be spent on the republic itself, on festivals, and on religion (7.3); otherwise, individual wealth and interest might become important.

By contrast, the inequality of monarchies requires commerce. In his consideration of luxury, Montesquieu makes it clear that there must be luxury in a monarchy, because there must be trade and the circulation of wealth back to the poor if such a society is to continue. "Individual wealth has increased only because it has removed physical necessities from a part of the citizens; these must, therefore, be returned to them" (7.4). Women in monarchies are not the primary exemplars of private interest and the private use of wealth; rather, they are most importantly a part of a family of a certain rank. "In monarchies women have so little restraint because, called to court by the distinction of ranks, they there take up the spirit of liberty that is the only one tolerated. Each man uses their charms and their passions to advance his fortunes; and as their weakness allows them not arrogance but vanity, luxury always reigns there with them" (7.9). Sumptuary laws—that is, direct controls on the use of wealth—are not simply unnecessary, as they are in a good republic; they are a distinctly bad idea, because they would cut off the circulation of wealth that makes it possible for such a country to flourish.

If there is to be commerce, according to Montesquieu, there must be the independent use of one's own goods. Commerce is shaped by the number and kinds of goods whose use is not directly under political law; by the people who possess such goods, whether few or many, men or women (bks. 20 and 21); by the medium of exchange (bk. 22); and by the sheer numbers of people who have both the excess and the possibility of trading (bk. 23). To put the matter another way, those who trade, the goods they trade, and the trade they engage in are all, at least originally, the result of the people, the goods, and the kinds of trade permitted or encouraged by the different governments. Here we shall follow Montesquieu's order in our discussion of these topics.

Commerce is trade. Trade between countries requires some tolerance for various ways of life and peace. Trade, therefore, according to Montesquieu, encourages peace between peoples and helps to cure destructive prejudices; but it also corrupts the pure mores of singular, isolated peoples. The spirit of commerce unites nations, but within a nation it separates people, because "there is traffic in all human activities and all moral virtues; the smallest things, those required by humanity, are done or given for money" (20.2). Thus, commerce offers a way—universal and individual, but mediated by money rather than punishment—of getting along with other people that is an alternative to the political, both between countries and within a country.

The first shape given to commerce is a result of the government of the country. In a government by one person, there is a demand for luxury, for the things that serve "its arrogance, its delights, and its fancies" (20.4). In a government by many, commerce is founded on economy, "on gaining little and even of gaining less than any other nation and of being compensated only by gaining continually" (20.4). One cannot imagine an economic commerce in a monarchy, wherein the reigning intention is to do great deeds and to acquire great honor; the men in a monarchy are not going to put their minds to small profits on everyday items. In addition, Montesquieu suggests that the great enterprises that arise out of economic commerce are necessarily mixed with public affairs, which makes it difficult to pursue these enterprises in a monarchy where traders are always wary of such involvement. Banks and trading companies are not suited to monarchies, wherein power and money rarely stay separate for long; they will be appropriated by the prince. Although we have been taught since Adam Smith that trade, or commerce, is all one thing, following the same rules, we can understand the two types to which Montesquieu refers. In one a luxury good is made by a number of workers, each of whom is paid only enough to keep working and to buy food and shelter. In the other a good is made by an equal or greater number of workers cheaply enough that they can buy it themselves. The first commerce is static and needs protection; the second seems to be able to take care of itself.

This brings us to book 21, on commerce. "Commerce," Montesquieu writes, "sometimes destroyed by conquerors, sometimes hampered by monarchs, wanders across the earth, flees from where it is oppressed, and remains where it is left to breathe: it reigns today where one used to see only deserted places, seas, and rocks; there where it used to reign are now only deserted places" (21.5). Montesquieu follows commerce throughout the world, commenting on the things that blocked and those that encouraged it. That commerce was limited to the Mediterranean, that Athens depended more on power and honor than on trade, that Alexander's conquest was a one-time event, that the Romans distrusted seafaring and trade, that the destruction of the Roman empire ended what trade there was, that feudal Europe adopted an ill-conceived rule against any interest charges, that the kings harassed the Jews who were the chief traders—all contributed to slowing and diverting the growth of commerce. That banking and letters of credit were devised and freed the wealth of the Jews and others from the rapacity of feudal kings, that exploration and trade came to go on the sea rather than over land, that trade expanded to include more diverse climates—all contributed to the growth of commerce in his time. Commerce has become truly international; no single country can directly halt it any longer.

Banks and letters of exchange and credit have loosened commerce from the direct political constraints imposed by the feudal monarchies. Montesquieu's final example is Spain, where trade was understood to be the accumulation of the signs of wealth (gold) and where trade led to poverty, not wealth. In other words, to misunderstand the nature of commerce now leads to disaster. Then, if kings or any rulers want to control and direct economic activity, they must turn their attention to this kind of money—that is, to money that is only a medium of exchange.

Trade beyond mere barter requires money; there must be money for any particular trade to be based on the greatest, rather than the least needy, of the trading partners. In a trade, money can make up the difference between the needs for particular goods by offering the possibility of procuring other goods with the surplus. Montesquieu defines money as "a sign representing the value of all commodities" (22.2). Silver and precious metals are a convenient sign, but paper is a possibility. Montesquieu here turns his attention to the question of the characteristics of this representation, and this remains the underlying concern of book 22. Here he says that the representation should be reciprocal, that there should be no limits to the things money can represent. "Just as silver is the sign of a thing and represents it, each thing is a sign of silver and represents it; and a state is prosperous insofar as, on the one hand, the silver indeed represents all things, and on the other, all things indeed represent silver, and they are signs of one another; that is, their relative value is such that one can have the first as soon as one has the other" (22.2). Montesquieu proceeds to disapprove of laws that favor an unjust debtor, to approve of Magna Carta's assumption that all the goods of an Englishman represent silver in payment of a debt, even if movable goods, rather than land, are to be taken first, and to remark upon circumstances in which the reciprocal characteristic of money as a sign has made it possible to treat goods as money when there was not enough silver. Having every good be in trade and measurable by the same standard—money—runs directly counter to the ranks and orders of the feudal monarchy, in which there were as many kinds of goods as there were ranks of men and in which lands as well as men could be called noble.

Montesquieu turns his attention to the other source of variability in the representation of goods by money—namely, that the amount of money, whether silver or ideal, can be and may inherently be changeable. Rulers have converted real into ideal monies by withdrawing some of the metal from each coin, while still calling it by the same name. Montesquieu disapproves of such actions (22.3), but then he goes on to remark upon the effect of the great increase in silver that resulted from the Spanish rule of South America. Therefore, it appears that an inescapable variability can enter into the realm of money. Montesquieu proceeds to discuss a number of topics based on that variability: the change in the price of renting money, or interest; the increase in the price of everything in proportion to the increase in the total amount of money; and the fact that that increase is affected by any change in the total number of goods in trade. This all is processed through the exchange. For Montesquieu the exchange is both, and alternately, a place and a process. He describes a number of monetary maneuvers extensively in chapter 9, but the lesson is that governmental interference will be compensated for by the actions of individuals who have letters of exchange and by foreign bankers in such a way that the balance between goods and money is reestablished. Then, it seems that great variability is inherent in the economy; to know how to manage it for stability is the question at hand, not how to hold on to a preexisting standard. Montesquieu proceeds to discuss the usefulness of paper that is a sign of a debt, the payment of national debts, and the importance of a low interest rate if commerce is to proceed. He finishes with a history of Roman efforts to control interest rates, noting how and when that effort was successful. The point is not that rulers should not attend to the economy but that they should attend, not to particular enterprises, but to controlling the general relationship between the goods in trade and the money or sign used to represent those goods so that it is as stable as is possible in any particular circumstance.

Montesquieu's next topic, in book 23, is population. This book is the last in part 4 on economic matters, and the topic serves as a kind of bridge between the consideration of commerce and that of religion in part 5. The number of people has an effect on economic life; but it is affected in turn by economic life and by religious practice. He begins by saying that the fertility of humans is not consistent, as that of animals is; rather, it is affected by character and the opinions of people. Later, he quotes an ecclesiastical historian, who said: "Those laws were established as if the multiplication of mankind could be a result of our cares, instead of seeing that this number grows larger or smaller according to the order of providence" (23.21). Montesquieu answers by saying simply that "the principles of religion have greatly influenced the propagation of the human species" and by listing some that encouraged and some that ran counter to it, including "the Romans who became Christians" (23.21). Not providence, but religious opinion, like other opinions, affects the size of the population; but how is not yet clear. Rules and opinions may not have the intended effect.

Population, Montesquieu seems to say, is a result of family structure and of the willingness of each family to produce and raise children. This last is affected by some physical circumstances, by the government, and by the economy. These can all be affected and manipulated, if not transformed, by our care. The question of what we can do with our religion, with Christianity, is left open for consideration in books 24–26, but Montesquieu is remarkably frank about the problems that Christianity poses for a government interested in a stable family structure and in increasing population. Here, we shall first examine his account of the problems posed by Christianity, and then we shall look at his discussions of population problems in his own time.

Christianity, according to Montesquieu, followed a path begun by the philosophic sects of the ancients, although it goes further than they went. The Romans, as their size and wealth grew, tried to maintain the population with laws favoring families, but exceptions increased until Constantine revoked these laws. The Christian laws, with Christian perfection and spirituality as their purpose, went so far as to encourage celibacy and to remove honor from marriage. These laws were established by the emperor Constantine and his successors, not for the sect of a small people, but for the Roman Empire. The laws became actively hostile to families; they encouraged spirituality and otherworldliness. In this situation, direct laws that encouraged families were not a plausible way to stabilize families and to increase the population; they would run counter to the church. Indirect action became the only way.

When Montesquieu considers the causes of population growth and the decline of monarchies, he considers the wealth and division of goods of the society. If land is unequally distributed, as it is in a monarchy, the country will not be populated without the arts. Those who own the land must have some way to use the excess they can produce, and the arts provide that opportunity. "In a word, these states need many people to grow more than is necessary for themselves; for that, they must be given the desire to have the superfluous, but only artisans can give that" (23.15). In book 15, Montesquieu expresses the hope that all employment could be done by free men in a well-organized state (15.8). Here, Montesquieu is suspicious of labor-saving machines because he worries that they will reduce the number of jobs. In sum, a population of any size in a monarchy requires trade between the landowners who farm their own land, and the artisans, who make the goods the landowners want.

Without that commerce there is no easy remedy for depopulation. "An almost incurable ill is seen when depopulation is of long standing because of an internal vice and a bad government. . . . Those countries desolated by despotism or by the excessive advantages of the clergy over laity are great examples of this. . . . The clergy, the prince, the towns, the important men, and some principal citizens have gradually become owners of the whole region; it is uncultivated but the ruined families have left their pastures to them, and the working man has nothing" (23.28). Here Montesquieu makes clear that he considers the monarchy of his time a harsh, if not despotic, government. Poor people, he says earlier in this book, either have many children because they are so poor, or are beggars, that the children cost them nothing and may even bring in something; or they have very few children because of the difficulty they face in providing for them (23.11). These beleaguered poor populate the countryside. The solution Montesquieu offers is to "distribute the lands to all of the families who have nothing, provide for them the means of clearing them and cultivating them. This distribution should be made until the last man gets a share, so that not a moment for work is lost" (23.28). The arts are not enough to keep these few owners farming; more people must work the land if there is to be a demand for goods in trade. One cannot help but think of the French Revolution and other revolutions in which the redistribution of land has been a primary issue.[3]

Montesquieu finishes this book with a consideration of poorhouses, or of welfare as we would now put it. The argument is that in a society in which the arts are extensively practiced, as they must be in a monarchy, there must be assistance from the "state, which owes all the citizens an assured sustenance, nourishment, suitable clothing, and a kind of life which is not contrary to health" (23.29). This is so because, unlike agriculture, the arts leave the worker who is unable to work, the old, the sick, and the orphaned, with no means of support. In addition, in a rich state with much commerce, some branches of that commerce always suffer from some temporary difficulty, so the wealth of a state itself is never a solution to the need. Montesquieu quotes the Mogul emperor Aurangzeb, who said he did not build poorhouses because "I shall make my empire so rich that it will not need poorhouses." Montesquieu says Aurangzeb should have said, "I shall begin by making my empire rich, and I shall build poorhouses" (23.29). The notion, Montesquieu hastens to say, is to provide temporary relief, not to encourage laziness.

By this point—the end of the books on commerce—Montesquieu's discussion of the alternatives before the lawmaker, whoever he may be, sound remarkably like our public-policy discussions today. Economic activity has become the enterprise, not of particular individuals, families, or ranks, but of the whole society; and its movements have to be understood in the whole in that context, as do remedies for its ills. That is, economic activity is not settled, contained, or given a shape as the society is structured into families and ranks with particular jobs. Rather, its structure must be affected through indirect actions—on the goods, people, and money traded—that are designed to keep economic activity moving forward as evenly as possible, given the inevitable changes in circumstances.

RELIGION

In the case of religion, as in that of commerce, one is confronted with a phenomenon to be managed. However, Montesquieu treats commerce and religion differently. If commerce has always had the possibility of being independent of direct political control, its steps in that direction have been halting and easily sidetracked. It offers a relationship between people that is mediated by trade, and by money, in which men's relation to one another is measured by the advantages they give to one another in commerce. Commerce seemed to be shaped and limited by governments; even after developing considerable independence in Montesquieu's own time, commerce needs tending not to be harmful, as in Spain, or to be useful, as in Holland and England. Religion, however, offers a system of rewards and punishments and a way of life that is potentially in direct competition with the government. The question here is how to fit religion in, to make use of it, and, particularly, to ascertain the peculiar demands and problems raised by Christianity.

The birth of Christianity coincided with the establishment of the Roman Empire under Augustus; its growth coincided with the decline of that empire. Under Augustus, unceasing warfare was replaced by universal peace as the maxim of Roman government. "In the days of the republic, the principle was to make war continually; under the emperors, the maxim was to maintain the peace."[4] Roman universality was a consequence of the fact that the singularity of the Romans was the perfection of the art of warfare; they kept conquering until they had conquered the world. The singularity of the Greek cities was not expressed in warfare alone. Montesquieu remarks that they blocked the effect of their ferocity with music in order to moderate the souls of their citizens. Rome ignored that balance, and the Greek cities lost their independence, first to Alexander and then to Rome. The philosophic sects that paved the way for Christianity had their origins in the Greek cities. As we have seen, Montesquieu remarks upon the presence of these philosophic sects in the Roman Empire and says that they paved the way for Christianity—that is, for a religion based upon a notion of a perfect life, apart from family and country, which would be applicable to every individual in the universe, to the Roman Empire. In his *Pensées,* he remarks: "This could not be entered into *the religion*: Julian took pains that were surely useless. The traits of enlightenment had appeared in the universe. Philosophy had been established, and if he had overturned Christianity, he would have surely been able to establish a third religion, but not to reestablish paganism."[5] Paganism, with its particularity, was, Montesquieu suggests, impossible to maintain once philosophy had suggested that the best was not particular to any one group, but, instead, was universally available.

Montesquieu wrote the *Défense de "l'Esprit des lois"* in response to objections to his book on the part of a Jansenist. There he asserts that his book is about laws, not about theology. Speaking of himself in the third person, he writes: "When he examined, as a writer about politics, any practice whatsoever, it was said to him: you should have included such and such a dogma of Christian theology. You say that you are a jurist, and I shall make of you a theologian in spite of yourself."[6] But from the point of view of a believer, there is no room for political reasons that are made without reference to the higher religious truths. To assert the separate topic and to subject politics and then religion itself to purely human reasons, however respectfully the religion is treated, is to run counter to the belief in a universal god who offers universal principles for human life.[7] In this section on religion, Montesquieu retains just this tone of respect and the deferential sentences that he quotes in his *Défense,* but he proceeds to treat religion as an institution, as a part of political life, not as the guide to human life.

Books 24, 25, and 26 make up Montesquieu's fifth part. In book 24, religions are treated in respect to the structure and subject of their rule. In book 25, they are treated as institutions that require motives for people to be attached to them. This is parallel to the discussion of the nature of governments in book 2 and of their principles in book 3. This permits Montesquieu to make clear, if not explicit, the conflicts between religion and politics. In book 26, Montesquieu places religious law into the context supplied by political and civil law, particularly the law about families, while it suggests the problems raised by Christianity.

Montesquieu's clearest political advice in this part is that religious and political activity must be separated from each other; but, unlike Locke, he does not move in this direction through the assertion that religion and politics do not have similar concerns. Montesquieu presents himself as an opponent of Bayle's views that atheism is preferable to idolatry (24.2) and that a society of perfect Christians is impossible (24.6). By so doing, he allies himself with Catholics against Protestants, with religion against atheism, and with religions that are concerned with life in this world against a purely speculative view of God. A Christianity that had been transformed into a purely speculative religion, as Bayle seemed to propose, would have no use for the spirit, for that aspect of Christian thought which somehow links the human characteristic identified with social and political life with the divine. Bayle's divinity would resemble the supreme reason of book 1. Rather, Montesquieu begins with an assertion that Christianity is gentle, that this gentleness removes it from pure despotism, and that its insistence on monogamy means that the princes are less confined, less distant from their wives, and thus more human (24.3).

In book 24, Montesquieu offers an understanding of the way Christianity rules: it demands total devotion, it forgives sins, and it asks for further devotion. "Human laws made to speak to the spirit should give precepts and not counsels at all; religion, made to speak to the heart, should give many counsels and few precepts" (24.7). The rules of religion are not for the good but are for the better and the best: "It is suitable for these to be counsels and not laws, for perfection does not concern men or things universally" (24.7). Religion, then, demands the best of everyone's heart; no limit is put on the demand. But Montesquieu suggests that the enforcement of such demands by law can only tire the legislator and his subject with endless, hopeless laws. When a religion is "no more jealous of acts than of desires and thoughts" and "leaves human justice behind to begin another justice," it acts by moving "constantly from repentance to love and from love to repentance," by putting "a great mediator between the judge and the criminal, a great judge between the just man and the mediator" (24.13). The rule of religion concentrates on morality in the sense of control of the passions, or the heart. In so doing, it can help, or even substitute for politics, particularly for the civil law—that is, in the control of the passions that the civil law also requires—as long as it does not move toward too much control or too little respect for local differences (24.24–26).

At the beginning of book 25, Montesquieu remarks upon two different motives for attachment to religion, saying: "We are exceedingly drawn to idolatry, and nevertheless we are not strongly attached to idolatrous religions; we are scarcely inclined to spiritual ideas, and nevertheless we are very attached to religions that have us worship a spiritual being" (25.2). An altogether spiritual religion cannot attach the people to itself through their attachment to physical, sensible objects. If people are attached to a religion through things, there is some suspicion that they are attached to the things themselves, that their devotion to god is not complete. There is a certain satisfaction in thinking well of oneself for choosing a higher divinity: "The spirit of religion is to lead us to exert effort to perform great and difficult things" (26.14). In book 25, Montesquieu takes up the problems caused for the country by the religion's capacity to acquire wealth forever and by having those who were raised by a religion think that its spirituality is altogether preferable and should be enforced by the government.

As is the case with the religious, the Stoics scorned pleasures and pains and considered "wealth, human greatness, suffering, sorrows, and pleasures to be vain things" (24.10). The Stoics occupied themselves with the duties of society; "they were occupied only in working for men's happiness and in exercising the sacred spirit which they believed to be within themselves as a kind of favorable providence watching over mankind" (24.10). Christianity, Montesquieu suggests, has transformed both aspects of the sects of the ancients. It expanded the distrust for the human passions, and its spirituality is directed toward God and to everyone else, but only through him; in effect, both the control and the spirituality are generalized, or universalized. Although the ancient republics did not disdain the passions generally, they did construct their institutions in such a way that the citizens' love was concentrated on the city and on their fellow citizens. These three can be summarized by noticing that (1) the ancient republics reshaped the passions by structuring family life so that the republic itself was the object of the citizens' love, (2) the Stoics disdained the things of this world and turned their spirits to their civic duty, and (3) the Christians disdained the things of this world, demanding that everyone turn his spirit to God.

One cannot envision a truce between Christianity and the ancient republics—their common concern with the passions but their altogether different uses for those same passions would always produce great conflict if they were to exist together in the same state. Early in the book, Montesquieu sketches the alignment of religious and political concerns that he gives a formal shape to in book 26. "Today we receive three different or opposing educations: that of our fathers, that of our schoolmaster, and that of the world. What we are told by the last upsets all the ideas of the first two. This comes partly from the opposition there is for us between the ties of religion and those of the world, a thing unknown among the ancients" (4.4; see also 4.2). Here, in book 26, Montesquieu moves to give space for and shape to a civil law that could serve political rather than religious ends—that is, to a civil law that encourages families and economic activity. Such a civil law serves some of the purposes of the political law of the ancient republics, while, perhaps, serving as a buffer between the religious and the political law. Taking into account that school-masters were members of the religious orders, the education of the family and its administration and its goods could stand between the individuality of the religious education and the public seeking of honor in a monarchy.

Montesquieu begins by reminding us that the civil laws and religion ought not run counter to simple self-preservation (26.3–5), that inheritance is a political or a civil law (26.6), and that divorce is a concern of the civil law that seeks to maintain families (26.8). That is, Montesquieu begins by suggesting the limits of the realm within which the civil law is to act; it is to attend to the multiplicity of goods in a variety of circumstances; it should avoid incorporating or running directly against the absolutes of the natural and the divine law.

This point is repeated as Montesquieu formally introduces the distinction between civil and religious laws. Religious laws are sublime, of perfection, and have as their object the goodness of the man who observes them; civil laws are extensive and have as an object the moral goodness of men in general (26.9). These laws come into conflict if the generality of humankind cannot achieve the perfection of some individuals. Montesquieu uses as his example the laws on divorce. The Roman family laws were political under the republic and civil under the monarchy; but Constantine and Justinian put such stock in the Christian princi-ple of the indissolubility of marriages and in the desire of religious people to enter religious orders that the effect was to reduce the number of families to the detriment of the society at large. Montesquieu's solution is to try to limit the religious interest in marriage to sanctifying it, but to leave the arrangement of property and family to the civil law (26.13).[8]

Similarly, Montesquieu distinguishes between the natural and the civil law as to who can marry; he does this by seeing the natural law as setting conditions—for example, those who are members of the same household are not to marry, because courtship cannot be permitted within a household—and the civil law as defining who constitute the members of a household (26.14). Although the political law should cede to the civil in the way it takes the property of individuals (26.15), the domain and succession of kings (26.16) and ostracism (26.17) are matters for the political law, while internal domestic relations should be the concern of domestic, not civil, law. The right of nations, which is grounded in the independence rather than the freedom of princes (26.20), should regulate treaties, ambassadors, and finally, the rules of succession to a crown when the political law fails to protect the independence of the country. There are, however, particular circumstances that require their own particular rules (26.24–25). Montesquieu has suggested that the range of the civil law must be increased at the expense both of the religious law and of the political law; in that way, religious and economic things can be shaped to political purpose without the appearance of direct political action.

LIBERTY AND HISTORY

It is hard to understand what Montesquieu meant when he suggested that the English knew how to take advantage of liberty in the same way they took advantage of commerce and religion. Liberty was, after all, the aim of the English government. Let us recall, however, that Montesquieu has already said that the spirited action that makes moderation and liberty possible exists in the northern peoples by nature. This liberty was embedded in the institutions of the Germanic peoples who conquered the Roman empire, and it has been transformed in a variety of ways as that rule became feudal and monarchical, or even representative and republican. Of the project of trying to understand this historical process, he says, "I have tried to give a clear idea of these things which are so confused and obscure in the authors of those times that, in truth, drawing them out of their chaos is to discover them" (28.28). Similarly, the project of taking advantage of liberty requires, as we shall see, finding that liberty in the historical life of the country, understanding its possibilities, and bringing it forward and giving it reliable form in legislation.

Montesquieu asserts that these Germanic peoples were each

free and independent; they were separated from each other; and they preferred that separation.⁹ When they had banded together to fight the Romans, they had kept their independence. In these federations, each person retained the law of his tribe, thus remaining in effect a citizen of that republic. The laws were personal rather than territorial. Each man carried his rule with him as he traveled—hunting, herding, and conquering. Over time the law became somewhat territorial, because people put themselves under the law that treated them most advantageously or at least did not treat them disadvantageously. However, all these laws, both Roman and barbarian, were virtually unused by the time the Capetians became kings of France. "Thus just as in the establishment of the monarchy, German usages passed into written law, some centuries later written laws returned to unwritten usages" (28.11). This left room for history, in the sense of undirected social interaction, to take over.

At the same time, combat was extended as a way of proving guilt or innocence. The Germans had modified the custom of families' warring over infractions by putting that warfare under the control of the magistrate (28.17). The Germans' idea of proof encouraged trial by combat. Montesquieu distinguishes between negative and positive proofs, between the accused's being able to deny the accusation and the accused's being required to prove his innocence. In the first case—that of negative proof—the accused demonstrated his innocence by swearing to it with an oath, an oath that often was backed by the oaths of his friends and relatives. This latter system of proof led to trial by combat because the accuser could only deny the truth of the oath. The church was inclined to prefer oaths, and the nobility was inclined to distrust them as being an incentive to lie and to commit sacrilege (28.17). In nations concerned almost exclusively with war, in which cowardice was the most serious vice, there was a kind of sense to trial by combat, for the winners tended to be those who shared the warrior spirit. Montesquieu remarks that "there was such an agreement between these laws and the mores that the laws less produced injustice than they were unjust, that the effects were more innocent than the causes, that they more ran counter to fairness than they violated rights, that they were more unreasonable than tyrannical" (28.17). The spread of trial by combat was a further cause of the decline of the laws (28.19). There were no laws and no judges to decide whether the laws had been obeyed or not.

Trial by combat developed into a system for resolving disputes as a set of rules came to govern its operation (28.20–28). The mores of the barbarian warriors slowly gave way to gallantry, which was born "when one imagined extraordinary men who, upon seeing virtue joined to beauty and weakness in the same person, were led to expose themselves to danger for her sake and to please her in all the ordinary actions of life" (28.22). Christian chivalry came to rule these encounters. This combat was reduced to following rules that were in effect the jurisprudence of those times. "Men who are fundamentally reasonable place even their prejudices under rules" (28.23). The rules, however, established a process of judging but not law in the sense of a list of crimes and punishments. Montesquieu remarks that the best source of information about this process is in the accounts of its correction (28.23). There were rules about setting up a combat; it was limited to certain crimes and certain people (28.24–25). But the problems with combat as a judicial process arose over challenges to combat of witnesses, challenges for false judgment, and challenges for default of right. In each case, someone other than the two opposing parties was involved—the witness, the judge, or the lord who was to hold the court. Difficulties with these people—that is, with the tribunal—are what bring about appeals to higher courts. Appeals were not possible; it was the nature of decision by combat to terminate the business forever (28.27), because one party to the dispute died.

In his discussion of the challenge for false judgment, Montesquieu indicates the point at which French and English practice parted. When peers judged in a lord's court, they could protect one another from a challenge to combat for false judgment by declaring the judgment together, so that the party to be punished could not challenge the peers one by one. The English practice of requiring unanimous juries in capital cases arises from this (28.27). France, however, had already gone in another direction. Fiefs were so divided that many who held fiefs had no men under them and so could hold no court; they carried their business to the court of their overlord, and the overlords put their courts into the king's court to protect themselves from appeals. Thus, justice was separated from the fief—from judgment by one's peers, as the English would say—and its recourse was "the king, who was ever the source from which all the rivers flowed and the sea to which they returned" (28.27). Here, the channels through which power flows in a monarchy clearly can come together into the sea—that is, into despotism.

Saint Louis introduced the practice of appeals without challenges to combat. His was, according to Montesquieu, a model for legislation; the king introduced into his own domains a new process whose advantages were seen by others and which, therefore, spread to the rest of the kingdom without the exercise of tyrannical power. What he introduced was a better process, as well as some mechanisms for developing a legal code out of an amalgam of custom and Roman law. Taking advantage of the process that had developed, he regularized the punishments of these independent warriors and gave it an orderly, peaceful form. When this happened, however, proceedings became secret rather than public, and judging passed out of the hands of the lords. The parlements took up the judicial forms of canonical right and reformed them in some instances (28.40, 41). Montesquieu remarks upon the importance of the checks between ecclesiastical and lay jurisdiction: "By a misfortune attached to the human condition, great men who are moderate are rare; and, as it is always easier to follow one's strength than to check it, perhaps, in the class of superior people, it is easier to find extremely virtuous people than extremely wise men" (28.41). The movement toward secret and private process was further encouraged as Roman written law was revived (28.42) and as customary law was written and organized (28.45). Judging by peers diminished, while judging by bailiffs—by men learned in the laws—increased; this happened gradually and by the force of the thing itself (28.43). Montesquieu notes in this respect that "peers and chivalrous men were no longer in a position to judge; peers began to withdraw from the tribunals of the lord; lords were little inclined to convoke them, the more so because judgments, instead of being a striking action pleasing to the nobility, and interesting to warriors, had become only a practice they neither knew nor wanted to know" (28.42). This warrior nobility was not becoming domesticated;

judging, in the sense both of rendering judgment about a circumstance and of knowing the law, became the province of a new rank—of the *noblesse de robe.*

Montesquieu offers a formal comparison between English and French practice in respect to witnesses in book 29, *On the Way to Compose the Laws,* in chapter 11, "In What Way Two Different Laws Can Be Compared." In France, false witness is a capital offense: criminals are put to the question (tortured), and the accused does not produce his own witnesses to swear for him; rather, the prosecutor, or the party for the public, produces all the witnesses. This system still relies on positive proofs (proofs that one did not do the crime), but now the judges must exert great force on the parties and witnesses to produce the truth. In England, there is no capital punishment or torture for false witness, and witnesses are produced by both sides. The prosecutor and the judges are removed from the actual judging of the dispute. The English judicial process, like the English constitution, incorporates a balance and a competition, while it provides great stability to the offices. The French system is more like the Roman one, in which a great power had to be counterbalanced by another (11.18), in which the offices themselves are in competition.

Some reflection on the analogy between Rome and France, as Montesquieu draws it, may illustrate the way he thought about the French monarchy. Of Rome's long transition from monarchy to democracy, or despotism, Montesquieu writes: "States are often more flourishing during the imperceptible shift from one constitution to another than they are under either constitution. At that time all the springs of the government are stretched; all the citizens have claims; one is attacked or flattered; and there is a noble rivalry between those who defend the declining constitution and those who put forward the one that prevails (11.13). Earlier, Montesquieu has made an explicit comparison between the intermediate orders of the monarchy and the tribunes in the Roman republic. In a monarchy, but not in a despotism, the intermediate orders blunt the tendencies of the people who, "led by themselves, always carry things as far as they can go; all the disorder they commit is extreme; whereas, in monarchies, things are rarely carried to excess." When the king depends upon these orders of the state to blunt and lead the discontent, "people of

wisdom and authority intervene; temperings are proposed, agree-
ments are reached, corrections are made; the laws become
vigorous again and make themselves heard." That is, the terrible
force of the people who have no leader, as Cicero put it according
to Montesquieu, does not happen in a monarchy in which "the
people do, in a way, have tribunes" (5.11). In Rome, Montesquieu
says, it was when the people were given all of judging to ensure the
liberty of the citizens at the expense of the liberty of the
constitution that both were lost (11.18). If Montesquieu sees the
French monarchy in a transition between monarchy and democracy, then his attention to the fate of the intermediate institutions
can be understood as an effort to maintain overlapping intermediate institutions—to paraphrase his remark about England, to keep
the forms of the monarchy while the republic develops. The
danger lies in a Cromwell or a Robespierre. As we shall see, the
question for Tocqueville became whether, after Robespierre, these
monarchical institutions could be revived or whether some other
institutions would have to be sought.

The principal message of books 30 and 31 is that the French
monarchy is a thoroughly understandable human creation that has
undergone a number of extensive changes.[10] In this respect, these
books serve the same purpose as Locke's *First Treatise*—that is,
they remove the divine from the monarchy. Characteristically,
Locke takes up the general question of whether kings can trace
their origins to some divine source, and Montesquieu takes up the
specific question of the historical origin of the arrangements of the
French monarchy, including its rule of succession to the throne.
But in both cases the exercise leaves open for public discussion the
defects, the advantages, and possible improvements in the existing monarchy.

As we have seen, Montesquieu has an additional, an allied,
analysis of the change in the monarchy from political to feudal
government; and he has a suggestion about the possibilities for the
revival of the political. In the beginning, the king and the nobles
ruled, and the nobles filled the offices of the government. These
nobles were the king's men: they fought with him; they were given
spoils of war, fiefs to run, and offices to hold—all at the discretion
of the king; and they elected the new king from the family, or race,
of the kings. The king ruled through the nobles, but by the

beginning of the rule of the Capetians, the kingdom had been divided into inherited fiefs. The offices became the possessions of the noble families. The king was left with only his own fief, or domain, as a resource. In this context, one can see, not Montesquieu's agreement with the "thèse nobiliaire," but his agreement with the Abbé Dubos that the king must somehow rule if there is to be government at all. A king, he seems to suggest, needs some officers who, in some way, act for him. In spite of Montesquieu's preference for nobles as such officers because they hold principles of personal honor that can keep them from doing dishonorable things that the king orders, one must remember his suggestion here and in book 28 that the warrior nobles could not bring themselves to do the ordinary work of ruling, judging, or even thinking about ruling. The balance is between the ruler's need for officers and the country's need for those officers to hold principles of action more dear than the momentary will of the sovereign. Although Montesquieu offers no clear suggestions, one can see the need for and the distrust of direct administrative rule, whether it be by one or by many. Something must be done to give the administrators character and purpose of their own. These observations are the basis for many of Madison's concerns about giving the representatives a sense of place and even honor, as well as Tocqueville's worry about administrative officers who serve either the king or the people.

In these last books, more than in the first eight books, the clergy undergoes a more explicit discussion as an order in the monarchy. Its goods, too, are fiefs, which it accumulates steadily in times of relative order. Those goods have served a number of times as plunder for conquerors and for those who wanted new fiefs or a redistribution of the fiefs. "He [Charles Martel] took for himself and his captains the goods of the churches and even the churches, and put an end to an abuse which, unlike ordinary ills, was the easier to cure for being so extreme" (31.9). The Merovingians, the Normans, and later the Calvinists took the goods of the clergy. That the Calvinists were not altogether successful and that the redistribution needs to be made again in his own time becomes clear when one recalls the remarks we have noticed in book 23: "The clergy, the prince, the towns, the important men, and some principal citizens have gradually become owners of the whole region; it is uncultivated, but the ruined families have left their pastures to them, and the working man has nothing" (23.28). His solution, as we have noticed before, is to distribute the lands to the families who have nothing.

That the laws of the Germanic tribes were personal—that is, that each member of a tribe was subject to his own law wherever he happened to be—left each person independent, separate, and free. He was ruled more by law than by a person. As the Germanic tribes settled down and became monarchies, that liberty came to be embedded in the institutions of the monarchy. The relations between these free subjects and the monarch were never decided according to his will; rather they were decided through a series of historical adjustments. To have done anything else would have been to risk becoming a despotism.[11] At each juncture, a variety of possibilities, and of monarchies, became possible. To take advantage of liberty is to manipulate these institutions, to keep them in balance, and to try to avoid the simple call to natural right inherent in the belief in natural equality, which would destroy the monarchical, or noble, establishment without replacing it with another, a representative, institution that could serve the same intermediary purpose of indirectly inculcating political, particular ends. This job was the task, not of a single legislator, but of a series of legislative acts or understandings by kings, nobles, parlementarians, and even historians. Montesquieu himself, insofar as he is a legislator for his times, must act as he recommends that they should do, making use of the institutions and character of the people and not arousing the despotic possibilities inherent in a call to natural law.

Commerce, religion, and liberty—all exist apart from political life but in different fashions. Commerce and religion can occupy very much the same space as politics. They use and direct the passions, while encouraging a way that people can relate to one another. If there is to be no commerce, the wealth held within families must be strictly limited, and the excess, or luxury, must be controlled by the polity. Men's attention must be turned to the public realm. This can all work quite well; commerce never succeeded in really getting started in the ancient world. To keep commerce going and yet in the direction that is politically desirable requires some care; commerce can be stopped by direct actions and must be controlled by indirect actions based on some understanding of its processes. Religion can run either directly counter to or along the same lines as political life. Religion demands a control of the passions that can, but does not have to, match that of the government. The difficulty arises when the religion's spirituality is universal, thus demanding things of the passions of man that no government can enforce. The jurisdiction of such a religion must be defined carefully so as to leave some room for political life. By contrast, once liberty has become the foundation of political life, one must believe that politics cannot directly produce liberty—that is, free and independent action. This modern politics can create the space for free, spirited action, but it cannot get people to move of their own accord. To try to do so is to be despotic, to move toward the universality of nature and of God. Politics needs to nurture and give institutional structure to the preexisting tendencies to act freely wherever they are to be found. In each case, the rulers and the legislators must treat each of these things as if it were independent, although the quality of that independence varies greatly—from the precariousness of liberty, to the chameleonlike quality of commerce, to the virtual immovability of religion.

CONCLUSION

Let us work our way back through the whole of Montesquieu's discussion, as we have seen it, to see how he has come to these conclusions about modern legislation. The discussion of climate permitted Montesquieu to distinguish the aspects of human nature most subject to universal physical laws—namely, the passions. For this reason the passions can properly be called passive. They happen to us from physical causes. Insofar as people are subject to the passions alone—in hot climates, for example— only force can get people to act in a way that would satisfy the end—such as food, sex, survival—implied by their natural inclinations. People are entirely subject to their passions, and the order that is imposed is the result of fear—another passion—

being enforced by a despot. Everyone is a slave. Those who are so subject to their passions, are so inactive that they would not survive unless ruled despotically, are natural slaves.

In kinder climates, people are not simply subject to physical necessity, to their passions; they act for themselves, and they have spirit and characters. The terrain provides natural physical channels for that activity, so that varied characters are formed. As hunters, herdsmen, and farmers develop their activities into ways of life, they acquire the characters of savages or barbarians and finally become the men of the ancient cities. Singular regimes are founded by those who have these characters and who in turn develop their character further and more firmly. In this pre-modern, pre-Christian situation, the varieties of the human spirit are exemplified by different societies. Each society exemplified, supported, and defended a kind of human activity, a form of the human spirit. In so doing, it had no qualms about ordering itself so that those who exemplify that spirit were favored, and others supplied the goods necessary for its exhibition.

The premise of such a society is that the population can be divided into those who can come to express spirit, as that society understands it, and those who cannot. Those who cannot must be constrained, be ruled, in a manner appropriate to their limitations. They are not educated to be the citizens; rather, they are made to supply the materials that the citizens need. The distinctions that Montesquieu draws are those between slaves or servants, who did the jobs that provided the goods needed, and free men; between women, who raise families, and men, who serve or lead public lives; and between citizens and other free men, such as craftsmen, whose level of activity could not reach that of the citizenry itself. The citizens who act in the spirit of the country also have their passions engaged in that activity; they love their country and have political virtue. The economic and familial arrangements have been organized so that their attention and love are turned toward the republic and toward the particular activity that characterizes it.

The question arises as to whether identifiable portions of the population do fall into appropriate categories and, if so, will they do so in the proportions required to sustain the state. In book 15,

Montesquieu suggests that some people might always require despotic power to get them to work and that some jobs might always require despotic power to get someone to do them. In book 16, he suggests that families most easily consist of women, who are provided with the leisure required to care for and educate children, and of men, who in turn needed to be able to think that the children are theirs. In book 17, we are again reminded that even in a despotism, there is some political person who is distinguished from the rest of the population. Even in the worst situation, in which people are affected most profoundly and equally by a natural circumstance, these distinctions must surface.

Once the natural circumstance permits the development of peculiar ways of life and then of the governments built upon those ways of life, these distinctions are amplified and shaped to that end. There is great variety in such governments—that is, republics. The variety contrasts with the universality and the similarity of despotisms. The variety is based on the range of human spirits, purposes, and goods and on the fact that nature does not offer a preference for one but that it even offers contradictory demands, which must be resolved by some human choice as a political life that is not despotic comes into existence and maintains itself. There is a suggestion that the particularity of these spirits can point and has pointed toward universality in the preferability of a particular way of life—for example, in the Roman conquests and in the various philosophic sects of the ancients.

Montesquieu asserts that Christianity denies the truth behind any arrangement that amplifies these distinctions for the sake of a specific spirit. Christianity demands, by contrast, total control of the passions, so that a Christian can worship a spiritual God with his spirit. This demand for total control of the passions and worship of the spiritual God is asked equally of everyone. Everyone is presumed to have a spirit of which the highest demands can properly be made. The sociability implied in a society composed of such people is undifferentiated: everyone is equal, and all are equally open to one another and to God. Then there can be no natural slaves, because no one is thought to be without spirit, so that he or she can be properly ruled despotically. Women must be admitted to the sacraments of the church, and women cannot be kept entirely private. If all people's spirits are measured by that of God, they are all equal in their inadequacy, and in the end, they are all the same. Sociability is universal.

Montesquieu suggests a variety of grounds for this universality and equality: for example, the equal intelligence of book 1; the natural equality of people who have no society; something in the movement of the Romans from their singular devotion to warfare to universal empire; and the movement from the peculiar philosophic sects of the ancients to the universality of Christianity. The singularity of a particular political life is vulnerable to pressures toward universality, both from above and from below. Christianity adds greatly to the pressure, while it offers to form a whole life for everyone by controlling all of the passions for the sake of the universal divine spirit. Once Christianity—or perhaps its predecessor, Roman universality—became prevalent, Montesquieu seems to think that it is not possible or advisable to try to revive the particular political orders based on the development of particular spirits. If the strictest control of the passions and the highest devotion can be asked of everyone, it is difficult to understand how a population can be organized to support the particular spirit of a particular people, leaving most people behind and in support of the particular way of life. Although the ancient understanding of political life as particular and spirited was plausible, any incorporation of that understanding into the modern circumstance will require legislation and legislators who will act indirectly. Those who are preferred will always have at least some doubt as to their preferability.

In regard to both economic and religious questions, Montesquieu sees a situation in which political law—the direct ability of the ruler to give a particular, singular shape to his country—is either impotent or despotic. Montesquieu searches for and describes other modes of legislation that revive something of political control in this new environment, an environment that is created in large measure by the pressure toward universality inherent in Christianity. In his discussion of economic things, Montesquieu comes to terms with the cessation of economic life that is ordered directly to political ends. Families, parcels of land, occupations, and even slavery can no longer be put in places that would move the political purpose forward. Rather, they must be dealt with indirectly, by laws that set limits for economic activity and that try to help pick up the pieces as economic activity changes shape and direction. Similarly, religion is no longer a simple support or supplement to particular mores; rather, it offers a general worship, which is in direct competition with the political order for both the hearts and the spirits of the people. Christianity also judges and promotes families in regard only to whether they are constructed to control the passions so that people will devote their spirits to God, but not to whether they support a particular spirit in the citizens. In a Christian country, politics cannot be built on families constructed for its needs. Montesquieu accepts the Christian monopoly on the form of family life, while he expands the role of the civil law in ways designed to make those families more suitable to social and political life. Without the direct intervention of political law, families are pushed toward forms that are more compatible with political ends.

The problem remains of the shape and character of the government itself—once it can no longer directly give form and support to a particular spirit. Without some natural spirit, government may well be caught between the justice based on retribution of equal intelligences and that based on equal passions. Montesquieu finds this spirit in the freedom of the Germanic tribes and in a way of governing that encourages it in the indirect, divided, and balanced rule that they developed. Just as in the ancient republics the problem was to expand the spirits so that they could see the possibility of community with a wider range of others, the problem in this situation is to specify, limit, and make a particular political community possible. This analysis of the problems behind setting up and continuing a government informed, as we shall see, the view of American politics in *The Federalist,* among many of those who attended the Constitutional Convention, and of Alexis de Tocqueville as he came to examine this curious new republic.

7

MODERATE AND FREE GOVERNMENT: THE UNITED STATES CONSTITUTION

Those who proposed the Constitution of the United States saw the problem of legislation in much the same terms as Montesquieu had. First, the free government they pursued was moderate government, government under law, whose activities would be directed by the ends of that government, rather than limited government, government whose purposes would be limited to guaranteeing or promoting natural rights. The problem was not to limit sovereignty, but to shape its use. Second, they thought that they were facing a situation in which moderate government must be based on the many, must be republican, and could only be achieved through representation. They were Montesquieu's modern legislators, faced with a situation in which the virtues required for good government—both among the rulers and the ruled— could not safely, without despotism, be developed directly. Better, then, James Madison suggests in *Federalist* number 10, that we should do our best to ensure indirectly that the population be shapeless, that it have neither a regular majority nor a regular minority. To be moderate, such a government must somehow be given an orderly life of its own. To be free, that orderly life must somehow encourage or require the deliberation characteristic of free men governing themselves. Here we have reached the third point—namely, that the structure of the government must be relied upon to give the government its character and purpose; the separation of power and the balance of power must control, educate, and direct political action.

We shall now take up these three topics, using primarily *The Federalist* and Madison's notes on the Constitutional Convention as our sources. Madison, as well as many of the others, read and admired both Montesquieu and many people who were influenced by him, particularly the Scots of the Scottish Enlightenment. These facts, in themselves, demonstrate nothing about influence,

148

because these persons certainly read many other things. What I would like to do here is to measure the points of similarity and suggest that this match between Montesquieu and the considerations of the Constitutional Convention and in *The Federalist* not only makes the argument for Montesquieu's influence but also helps us to achieve a better understanding of the relation between the topics that the delegates considered.

The presentation of the argument for the constitution in *The Federalist* follows a pattern that Montesquieu could well have suggested. First, *The Federalist* takes up the need for union, a union as energetic and powerful as the proposed one. Circumstances both require and make possible such a government. The circumstances considered are the institutions and life of Americans in 1787 and the foreseeable future, not those of men in nature. Americans require a powerful free government, but not one that is explicitly limited by the natural rights of individuals. Second, that government is to proceed by representation in such a way that the character and actions of the representatives will not be directly dependent on those of the population. Third, the representation is to be divided, balanced, and checked so that the government will be moderate—and free—that is, stay within the bounds appropriate for this free government. The character of that freedom and thus of the forms appropriate to it are the topics here.

MODERATION

The propositions "that the means ought to be proportioned to the end; that every power ought to be commensurate with its object; that there ought to be no limitation of a power destined to effect a purpose, which is itself incapable of limitations"(*Fed.* no. 31) run throughout the first thirty-six papers of *The Federalist*. In these papers, the need to provide for the common defense brings along an array of powers to the federal government, particularly the power to raise and maintain an army and the power to tax directly. Given the limitless possibilities for actions that the government might need to take, its powers must be just as limitless. But this proposition is coupled with the argument that adherence to this principle will encourage adherence to the law, "that nations pay little regard to rules and maxims calculated in their very nature to run counter to the necessities of society. Wise politicians will be cautious about fettering the government with restrictions that cannot be observed, because they know that every breach of the fundamental laws, though dictated by necessity, impairs that sacred reverence which ought to be maintained in the breasts of rulers towards the constitution of a country, and forms a precedent for other breaches, where the same plea of necessity does not exist at all, or is less urgent and palpable" (*Fed.* no. 25). No disjunction is envisioned between a governmental power that has no formal limits and one that observes the law. That is, *The Federalist* sought a government that was moderate in Montesquieu's sense, a government that will follow the laws, that will stay within the bounds implied by its purposes as it deals with the circumstances that affect it.

This moderate government had to be republican, not monarchical or mixed. The assessment that the new government had to be republican was based on an analysis of the character, or the genius, of the people, about which there was little disagreement. Madison simply remarked that "it is evident that no other form would be reconcilable with the genius of the people of America; with the fundamental principles of the Revolution; or with that honorable determination which animates every votary of freedom to rest all our political experiments on the capacity of mankind for self-government" (*Fed.* no. 39). Americans begin with the assumption that mankind's capacity for self-government must be the basis of their government. The English had demanded that a body of the legislature be formed on this basis, but the Americans demand that the whole government be formed upon it. The American circumstance gives force to that demand and the assumption on which it is based. The population has no shape that can be used to give shape to a government; it has no king, nobility, or commons. In arguments over the suitability of using England as a model during the Constitutional Convention, it was often said that England was of limited use as an example because it was a mixed government, based on ranks and orders that had existed for a long time.[1] Even if monarchical, aristocratic, or democratic tendencies existed within the state or if they always existed in all governments, they had not come to offer a sufficient shape to the population to make such mixing possible.[2] In addition, one criticism was to point out that a proposal might lead to the development of a nobility and a people as distinct bodies. Thus, more than one office could not be held by one person; and although sumptuary laws designed to keep the appearance of equality were admired, they were put aside with little conversation.[3] A nobility, and thus a monarch, were prohibited. The consequence of ending British rule, forbidding the development of a nobility and a monarchy, and not encouraging the development of an egalitarian democratic citizenry was to leave the population formless, without any distinctive orders. America had to become explicitly the popular government that Montesquieu saw lying behind the English government, with its radically weakened orders.

In *Federalist* number 10, Madison defends the very formlessness of the American population as the condition of republican politics, arguing that the very size of the United States would encourage its continuation by making difficult the most likely formation, that of democratic majorities. But Madison's remarks in the Constitutional Convention make it clear that he saw the distinction between the northern and the southern states—that is, between societies based on slavery and those based on the work of free men—as central to the country at the time of the Constitution. In a late effort to establish representation in proportion to the population, he says: "It seemed now to be pretty well understood that the real difference of interests lay, not between the large & small but between the N. & Southn. States. The institution of slavery & its consequences formed the line of discrimination."[4] Slavery produces an inherited, stable distinction between people which is quite contrary to the assumption that no permanent distinctions existed in the underlying population upon which this moderate republic was to be built. One is led to wonder whether Madison thought that the union and its size could overcome the distinction caused by slavery.

Let us turn briefly to the Lockean prerogative to clarify the distinction between this moderate government based on mankind's capacity for self-government and a limited government based on a notion of equal natural right. "This power to act

according to discretion, for the publick good, without the prescription of the Law, and sometimes even against it, *is* that which
is called 'Prerogative'."[5] Locke goes on to say that in the infancy of
governments, almost all of government was prerogative. The law
of a country, then, is a kind of codification from experience of the
judgments about the proper applications of natural right in the
circumstances of a particular country. The best rulers present the
greatest dangers to the law and Locke offers no remedy other than
the appeal to heaven, or the sense of the majority that they are
weary of such rule.[6] There is no suggestion here, as there was in
The Federalist, that the law could somehow contain the responses to
extraordinary circumstances. If the law is to be able to contain and
even shape the responses to these unforeseen events, it must hold
within itself some principles of action, or purposes, that can direct
its response to every circumstance. To obey that law—to be
moderate—is to act according to those principles, or purposes, in
any circumstance.

In this moderate government, the character of the government
is primarily thought to be a result of the government itself. The
character of the people is such that the government must be based
on a general assumption that mankind is able to govern itself. The
population is and must remain structured, so that the generality of
that assumption is not contradicted by the development of orders
or of a constant majority. But there is no effort to turn that people
into a citizenry. Although the characteristics of the citizenry—of
the voting public—are touched upon, they remained peripheral to
the discussions of the shape of the American government. This
concern for the underlying shape of the population, the lack of
direct concern with a citizenry, and ultimately an interest in the
effect that the government will have on the population characterize
the approach to legislation that Montesquieu proposes for moderate governments in the modern situation.

The discussions of citizenship—of the suffrage—in a government based on the people take place only indirectly (*Fed.* no. 52).[7]
The census that is to establish the number of people to be divided
by the proportional representation in the House of Representatives; the criteria for voting for members of the House of Representatives, the only officers who were to be directly elected; and
the addition of new states—all raised the issue of who was to be

considered a citizen. The question of the census was considered in the context of a discussion of whether to apportion representation by some measure of wealth or by population. The agreement to count "other persons" as three-fifths of ordinary persons was interpreted by some as a compromise with the view that wealth was to be included in the criteria for establishing the basis for representation.[8] A brief discussion of the possibility of limiting the suffrage for members of the House of Representatives to freeholders raised sore issues, including that of counting a slave as three-fifths of a person, late in the convention, when these issues seemed to have been settled.[9] Finally, an objection to admitting new states on equal grounds with the old in unlimited numbers was met with the observation that their inhabitants would be "our children & our grand Children"; so that objection was not revived.[10]

The shape of political life—its kind of moderation and its purpose—was not thought to be a direct consequence of things external to the political organization itself, neither of the principle that governments are properly limited to certain activities nor of the character and principles of the citizenry. Rather, the Constitution seems to have been based on an assertion that limits engender distrust for the law and that care must be taken to see to it that the population acquire no set shape or characteristics that would lead to or require expression in the political life. In a country such as America, where the basis for government is assumed to be popular, only representation makes it possible for a moderate political life to take a particular direction.

REPRESENTATION

"The true distinction between these [ancients] and the American Governments lies *in the total exclusion of the people in their collective capacity* from any share in the *latter,* and not in the *total exclusion of the representatives of the people,* from the administration of the *former*" (*Fed.* no. 63). Here, representation must bear the entire burden of giving shape and therefore moderation to the government. The intermediate powers of the monarchy have altogether disappeared. The sovereignty of the monarch was exercised only through those intermediate powers. In England the representatives of the people were limited by the remaining nobles and "les grands," but in America the sovereignty of the people was to be exercised only through its representatives. The government was to be purely republican.

The way the distinction between reason and passion is drawn in *The Federalist* offers an understanding of the purpose for the distance that this representation creates between the represented and the representative institutions. In *Federalist* number 10, Madison argues that the large size of the new union and its representative structure will control the effects of factions. Factions are understood to be "a majority or minority of the whole, who are united and actuated by some common impulse of passion, or of interest, adverse to the rights of other citizens, or to the permanent and aggregate interests of the community" (*Fed.* no. 10). The passions of the public are thought to act more effectively in groups of a certain size. They cannot move easily across a vast country, and they cannot move as efficiently in a smaller group, although even the small House envisioned in 1787 was suspect: "The truth is that in all cases a certain number at least seems to be necessary to secure the benefits of free consultation and discussion and to guard against too easy a combination for improper purposes; as, on the other hand, the number ought at most to be kept within a certain limit, in order to avoid the confusion and intemperance of a multitude. In all very numerous assemblies, of whatever characters composed, passion never fails to wrest the scepter from reason. Had every Athenian citizen been a Socrates, every Athenian assembly would still have been a mob" (*Fed.* no. 55).[11] Passions affect groups of men in the same way. The danger is in having passions make groups with identical views, in having them sweep across a democratic assembly: "When men exercise their reason coolly and freely on a variety of distinct questions, they inevitably fall into different opinions on some of them. When they are governed by a common passion, their opinions, if they are so to be called, will be the same" (*Fed.* no. 50). The passions tend to cause unanimity, but reason divides men.

This view of the relation between passion and reason in politics runs quite counter to the most frequently encountered enlightenment view in which the private interests and the passions divide men who would be unified, and even unanimous, if their prejudices did not obscure the reasonable view, which was assumed to be singular. Reason in *The Federalist* does not seem to be an abstract truth to which everyone should aspire. Here, as in Montesquieu, the passions lead to unanimity, to despotism. This reason, like Montesquieu's spirit and the deliberation of monarchies, points toward particular purposes and action, not directly to the universal and the divine. Size, representation, and the division of powers—all serve to break up the unanimity that is the result of the passions and to encourage the variety of reason—that is, to discourage tyranny or despotism and to encourage liberty. The government was sufficiently buffered that it had the possibility of developing a life and a spirit of its own that would ensure its moderation and give it character and purpose.

A look at the way the Constitutional Convention resolved its most famous disagreement—that between the big and the small states over whether the states should be represented equally or in proportion to their population—will clarify the extent to which it was thought that a government formed by representatives was a consequence of the organization of the institutions—the separation and balance of powers—not a result of the relation between the representatives and the represented.

The dangers envisioned—foreign intervention, foreign alliances, smaller confederacies, wars among the states, the destruction of commerce—would be a consequence both of the failure of the convention to come up with an adequate plan for union and of a union that relied upon the enforcement of general laws upon recalcitrant state governments. Such enforcement would amount to war and thus would lead to all the evils that follow from the end of the union. Somehow, enforcement, both executive and judicial, had to be localized and individualized, either by creating federal enforcement institutions that would be capable of acting on individuals and federal courts that would have jurisdiction over offenses against that administration of the laws or by using state administrations and state courts or by using a combination of the two.

It was very difficult to imagine how to establish an upper house, a senate, in a union based either upon individuals or upon representation from each state in proportion to its population.[12] The view that such a body was necessary to check the passions of the electorate as those passions swept uniformly over the body politic and to restore the diversity of genuine political debate (*Fed.* no. 50) did not indicate a way to create such an institution in a society that had no nobility and had no intention of encouraging the development of one. The Virginia Plan—the first proposal before the convention—resolved this difficulty by suggesting that the second branch should be elected by the first from nominations made by the state legislatures. That proposal does not seem to have been seriously considered by the convention. One suspects that this was because such layering would have removed the second house too far from the people whom its members were to represent and because the arrangement would have violated the view that separation of powers could only be achieved when each power had an independent basis or source for that power. That is, the convention was not as willing as were the authors of the Virginia Plan to extend the distance between the people and their representatives. But if members of the second chamber were to be elected by the state legislatures, it became difficult to imagine how this would produce a smaller deliberative body than the House. The constant juggling of figures at the Constitutional Convention indicated how difficult it would be to produce a smaller body in which each state would have at least one member and in which the number of members from each state would be proportioned by its population.

All these problems paved the way for compromise, but no compromise would have been possible if the convention had been full of men who thought that the character of the government was a direct consequence of the way in which the representation was organized. William Paterson of New Jersey, who presented the New Jersey Plan, which settled representation equally among the states, used a notion of representation early in the Convention that suggests the understanding on which compromise could be reached. According to Madison's notes, Paterson said: "It has been said that if a Natl. Govt. is to be formed so as to operate on the people and not on the States, the representatives ought to be drawn from the people. But why so? May not a Legislature filled by the State Legislatures operate on the people who chuse the State Legislatures? or may not a practicable coercion be found."[13] Paterson's own notes for his speech put the matter thus: "Will the Operation of the natl. Govt. depend upon the Mode of Representation. — No — it depends upon the Quantum of Power lodged in the leg. ex. and judy. Departments — it will operate individually in the one Case as well as in the other."[14] Although Paterson's is the clearest expression of the opinion that the way in which the new national government can be expected to operate is an altogether different question from the way it is related to the people, some implicit opinion of this sort must underlie the compromise that made the new government possible.

In his introduction to the discussion of the institutions of the new government, Madison puts the issue as one between the institutions that are essential for the requisite stability and energy in a government and those that are due to liberty and to the republican form (*Fed.* no. 37). Adherence to republican form does not seem necessarily to either increase or decrease the possibility of a stable and energetic government. He ends by limiting the name republican to the government that "derives all its powers directly or indirectly from the great body of the people, and is administered by persons holding their offices during pleasure for a limited period, or during good behaviour" (*Fed.* no. 39). The particular method—through the states, individual votes, or appointment by representatives of the people—does not seem to matter. Thus, Madison can go on to call the proposed government partly national and partly federal and the result of a compromise, without compromising the energy and stability of the resulting national government.[15]

Here we have a view of the situation of the legislator like that envisioned in *The Spirit of the Laws.* Moderated, ordered rule is the aim. But the passions move the democratic base, and rule in the United States is to be republican, to have its ground in that base. One can hope that in America the base is so big that it cannot move as a whole. This fear of the simple, direct rule of the passions—of despotisms, whether democratic or princely—is shared with Montesquieu. So, here, representation is not designed to reflect the opinions of the people directly. Rather, the distance from the population, which is made possible by representation, is the source of popular moderate government.

LIBERTY

Although American government was established on the basis of the understanding that only self-government was honorable, it is only the government itself that made it possible to engage in that activity. The spirit of the people took shape within the divided and balanced governmental institutions. The division of powers was intended both to break up the unanimity of the democratic passions and to be the mechanism that would give the government a life of its own. By breaking up the passions, the division of powers serves, as do size and representation, to curb the virtually random wills or desires that pass through a democratic populace, making it as much a despot as a single man when he imposes his momentary whims on a people. In this sense it ensures moderation. But *The Federalist* did not stop with this moderation; the government was further designed to promote good government. The question remains of the content of that government and its relation to liberty. In England, Montesquieu says the division of powers has created a liberty that is a result of balanced passions and leads to action in no particular direction. That division was ordered in respect to the problems of government so that when it was forced by circumstances to move and to rule, it did so coherently. That is, the balances were constructed with reference to the problems of rule, as we have seen. Here it seems that the American government is being designed to go further in this latter direction than Montesquieu's English government—American liberty is meant not only to control the passions for the sake of moderation and liberty and to try to ensure some coherence in the rule itself but also to direct action and to teach something about the character of good government. In the American republic, as in Montesquieu's monarchy, one's honor comes to be identified with one's place, and finally, perhaps habit will lead to character.

The structure of the division of power that was proposed in the Constitutional Convention was not and could not be based on a division into ranks and orders of the people. A division of power that does not rely upon a division in the people is characteristic of republican rather than monarchical moderation. But the manner in which republican power is divided points toward the kind of republican government. In order to understand the purpose of those who wrote the constitution for this republican government, we should, following Montesquieu, inquire into the shape of the division of power: the sources of division, the grounds for attachment to the government or some part of it, and the effect of the division itself.

The first and most evident way of separating the branches of the government is for them to have different origins. The executive and the two branches of the legislature have different modes of origin in the people. Only the independence of the judiciary is to be ensured more by the conditions of its existence than by those of its appointment. It is hard to understand how these different modes of election by a formless population could produce representatives who would be peculiarly interested in or able to perform their tasks. In addition, there is no reason to believe that they will rest even somewhat content with the portion of governing they were elected to do. To the extent that they consider themselves the representatives of the people, they will tend toward expanding their realm to the whole of ruling. This predisposition of the representatives of the people to think of themselves as the whole of government is also one of the grounds for the expectation that the branches will compete with each other for influence over governmental activities. Republican government requires something more than different sources in the people to produce a government of divided and balanced power, rather than one of competing democracies.

A different notion of separate powers shaped the Virginia Plan, in which all of the other offices of the government derived directly or indirectly from a House of Representatives whose membership was to be proportional to the population and was to be elected directly by the people. George Washington's one public remark at the convention was, on the last day, to speak in favor of a motion to decrease the maximum size of a district for the House of Representatives.[16] This concern about the House of Representatives as the popular body was shared by Alexander Hamilton and Madison, who often remarked in *The Federalist* that the legislature was potentially the most influential branch, whose first office was in the House.[17] This could be an effort to increase the influence of the large states or to establish greater democracy. This could also be the result of a lingering view that the House would be *the* elected body, which survived the formation of a constitution in which the president, the Senate, and the House were separated by their varied sources of election from the people as well as by their tasks. This suggests that these men's view of the Constitution had its source in their understanding of the Virginia Plan. There the structure required for separate powers depended not upon separate sources in the people, but upon the internal shape of the powers of the government themselves.

A look at the proposal in the Virginia Plan that there be a council of revision—a council, made up of members of the executive branch and the judicial branch, that was to have a veto on legislation—will shed some light on the Federalists' view of how the powers could be kept separate. Madison brought up this suggestion a number of times during the convention, in spite of the fact that it never was given serious consideration. Madison's argument was that executive and judicial activities are similar in ways that make it important for the similarity to be recognized institutionally, so that these activities can be effectively separated from each other. Both the executive branch and the judicial branch are to enforce the laws, whether generally upon the people as a whole or upon specific offenders. Neither is likely to enforce laws that it disagrees with unless it knows that those laws have substantial support in the other branches of the government. These possibilities can all be weighed, or tried out, in a council of revision.[18] "Judicial self-restraint" can be seen as a rule that says that the judiciary should act as if there were a council of revision, as if it should not oppose the overwhelming opinion of the executive or the legislature. In this view, the branches of government are kept separate by acknowledging and giving an appropriate shape to the points at which their tasks overlap. These conjunctions are ordinarily called "balances."

Balanced and separated powers can be distinguished. They operate separately in a monarchy, in which separate powers, whatever their purposes, are easy to maintain because those who participate in them are separated by the principle of inheritance. Balancing, or adjusting, relations among those powers is difficult in a monarchy because the members of each branch are not at all interchangeable. They are bred to their place. Montesquieu's discussion of the separation of powers in England takes both these points of view: the House of Lords relies upon inheritance to separate it, and people are assumed to move between support for the executive and support for the legislature, depending upon the advantage they can expect at any time. These two branches share powers. This alternation is balanced by the stability of the House of Lords. In a republic, the separation of power can only be maintained through sharing in parts of ruling and through the tension that results from that sharing. Madison writes: "I shall undertake in the next place, to show that unless these departments be so far connected and blended as to give to each a constitutional controul over the others, the degree of separation which the maxim requires, as essential to a free government, can never in practice be duly maintained" (*Fed.* no. 48). In sum, in the American republic, the separation of powers has to be maintained through their controls over one another—that is, through the aspects of governing that they share.

We are accustomed to speak of the "checks and balances" of our Constitution, but it is useful to consider the possibility of distinguishing between the two. "Checking" at the Constitutional Convention seems to have referred to relations between the two chambers of the legislature—that is, to relations between the more immediate representatives of the people. This seems to have been the customary usage at the convention, but Hamilton remarked that "a democratic assembly is to be checked by a democratic senate and both these by a democratic chief magistrate."[19] These checks are related to the popular passions that are opposed to the reasonable views of political action. They are designed to check those passions, both as they move from the people to the legislature or the executive and as they act within the legislative bodies themselves.[20] Hamilton says that "gentlemen differ in their opinions concerning the necessary checks from the different estimates they form of the human passions."[21] These checks, then, serve to stop the passions of the public or of the legislatures when they are acting as democratic publics. These aspects of this government of checks and balances are what produce a stalemate, although perhaps a stalemate between the democratic passions is enough to give some room for the development of reasoned opinions, for deliberation.

In order to examine this last possibility, we need to return specifically to the understanding of the way the officers in the government will act within the structure of the government. Security for the balance of powers, or for the separation of powers, "consists in giving to those who administer each department the necessary constitutional means and personal motives to resist encroachments of the others. . . . Ambition must be made to counteract ambition. The interest of the man must be connected with the constitutional rights of the place" (*Fed.* no. 51). If ambition is to counteract ambition and defend the separation of power, the ambition of the man must be attached to—that is, identified with—the power and the status of the branch of government of the office he holds. Hamilton's argument that the officers of the new national government will not bother with the things that are in the province of state governments makes clear his view that the powers of the new government are required in order to attract the ambitious men to its working and its defense.

The regulation of the mere domestic police of a State appears to me to hold out slender allurements to ambition. Commerce, finance, negotiation, and war seem to comprehend all the objects which have charms for minds governed by that passion; and all the powers necessary to these objects ought in the first instance to be lodged in the national depository. The administration of private justice between the citizens of the same State, the supervision of agriculture and of other concerns of a similar nature, all those things, in short, which are proper to be provided for by local legislation, can never be desirable cares of a general jurisdiction. It is therefore improbable that there should exist a disposition in the federal councils to usurp the powers with which they are connected; because the attempt to exercise those powers would be as troublesome as it would be nugatory; and the possession of them, for that reason, would contribute nothing to the dignity, to the importance, or to the splendor of the national government. (*Fed.* no. 17)

There is no guarantee that in other times, when other opinions reign, ambition will not become attached to these objects as well. But the point is that the purposes and powers of government itself are what attract the ambitious.

Ambition, once attracted, is schooled by the institution that attracted it and by the one that it serves, as is the case with the honor of the nobility in a monarchy. Both ambition here and honor in Montesquieu imply an impulse to think very well of oneself, and to be thought very well of by others, an impulse that is virtually without content. Ambition in a monarchy is transformed into honor as men demand recognition for the preferences and distinctions to which they are born (3.7). Here, Hamilton seems to presume that ambition attaches itself most easily, most naturally, to political action and particularly to political action that involves the evident use of power. Montesquieu says that honor's shape—that is, the things considered honorable—was a consequence of the education that began as one entered the world (4.2). The ranks of the nobility taught the noblemen and their followers how they ought to value themselves, taught them an array of rules about proper behavior which could even lead them to disobey the prince in order to defend their honor. In England, according to Montesquieu, the legislative and the executive offered no direction to those who adhered to them, so that the government's end was liberty in the sense of the government's offering no shape for men's lives; the men were uneasy, uncertain about their place and character. In the American republic, the government itself, and particularly its branches, attract the ambitious men and give shape to their ambition. When the government is said to be based on "that honorable determination which animates every votary of freedom to rest all our political experiments on the capacity of mankind for self-government" (*Fed.* no. 39), the ambitious are challenged to follow this notion of honor and to try to perform this feat, to succeed in this experiment.

The American division of power is explicitly functional; it is based upon the different processes that are a part of any rule—

namely, making a rule, enforcing that rule, and judging those who offend against it. What Locke calls the federative power and what Montesquieu calls the execution of the law of nations here is absorbed altogether into the general notion of rule. The explicit separation of judging from executing and then the investment of that judging in a body of judges—a judiciary—distinguishes this division of power first from Locke and then from Montesquieu. Once the division of powers is seen as the separating out of parts of a single function, then each branch of government can be shaped from the point of view of performing its function well; each branch can be held responsible for its part in prudential government; and the whole can be seen, not as a result of competing parts, but as the whole of rule. In *The Federalist,* the ends of this government are said to be both justice and the common good, with justice being understood as the protection of the minority and with the common good being understood as something like what we have called good government, or the capacity to act on the genuine interests of the whole.[22] However, these ends are to be brought about for Americans by their own actions; Americans are to learn to act and to act within a government that constrains them to provide these ends for themselves. That lesson and that practice are embedded in the division of powers. Let us now take a brief look at the three branches of government from this point of view.

The House of Representatives, as the most numerous and directly elected branch, is the most subject to the democratic passions. It can either participate in the passions sweeping the nation, or those passions can be generated within the microcosm of democracy that is any assembly (*Fed.* no. 55). The House must, therefore, be checked by the Senate; the House itself must be kept to a reasonable size; and its internal structure must be such that representatives can become legislators. "No man can be a competent legislator who does not add to an upright intention and a sound judgment, a certain degree of knowledge of the subjects on which he is to legislate" (*Fed.* no. 53). So, the members must be elected for more than one year—two in this instance—and must be eligible for reelection. "A few of the members, as happens in all such assemblies, will possess superior talents; will, by frequent re-elections, become members of long standing; will be thoroughly masters of the public business, and perhaps not unwilling to avail themselves of those advantages" (*Fed.* no. 53). The knowledge of local interests and circumstances does not need to extend any further than the extent to which they are related to the national government (*Fed.* no. 56), and each representative will have to acquire much information about all the other states (ibid.). It seems likely that those who are distinguished as representatives will themselves be somewhat distinguished and that in each case a representative's "pride and vanity attach him to a form of government which favors his pretensions and gives him a share in its honors and distinctions" (*Fed.* no. 57). Republican government presupposes not only depravity but also the "other qualities in human nature, which justify a certain portion of esteem and confidence" (*Fed.* no. 55). In the House, it seems that provisions are made to check the most egregious democratic passions, to give a reason for proud and ambitious men to think themselves appreciated in this government, and then to provide the space required for good legislation. The notion seems to be that the men, once they have been started by their vanity or pride, will move into these positions and take up the aspect of rule available to them and will learn to use it if need be.

The Senate was conceived as a step further along this same path. It moved further in the direction of supporting those aspects of deliberation over legislation that require a greater extent of information and stability of character, wisdom, knowledge of the means by which that object can be obtained, permanence, the order and stability that makes a government truly respectable (*Fed.* no. 62), and a due sense of the national character, in defense of the people against their own temporary delusions (*Fed.* no. 63). These characteristics are to be encouraged by the criteria of age and length of citizenship, by the duration in office and by the rotation of election, and by the smaller size of the body itself, as well as by the relation with the executive in foreign affairs and appointments. The Senate's power to try cases of impeachment is grounded in this greater capacity for serious deliberation. "The necessity of a numerous court for the trial of impeachments is equally dictated by the nature of the proceeding. This can never be tied down by such strict rules, either in the delineation of the offense by the prosecutors, or in the construction of it by the judges, as in common cases serve to limit the discretion of courts in favor of personal security" (*Fed.* no. 65). Here the things that made the House work as a deliberative body are intensified, thus producing a space for genuine respectability to take hold, while the Senate is defended against its worst tendencies. There is, again, the notion that men exist who have the character to do that job, either as a result of their prior education or of the education that comes from holding offices defined in terms of rule—that is, from trying to act within a political space that gives them a chance to learn to deliberate by doing so, by trying out the avenues that are opened, and by coming against those that are closed.

In thinking about the presidency, it is helpful to remember that executing the law is closer to judging than it is to legislating. Both executive and judicial functions enforce the laws that are enacted by the legislature. Their proper interest in the law is in the consequences that its enforcement will have on the country or on the law itself. This perspective helps to explain the demand at the convention both for democratic election and for independence from direct electoral constraints. Thus, Hamilton could suggest, at the convention, an executive elected for life and, in *The Federalist,* could defend a process in which the "sense of the people" is filtered through the men who are most capable of analyzing the qualities adapted to the station (*Fed.* no. 68). He goes on to say:

> Talents for low intrigue, and the little arts of popularity, may alone suffice to elevate a man to the first honors in a single State; but it will require other talents, and a different kind of merit, to establish him in the esteem and confidence of the whole Union, or of so considerable a portion of it as would be necessary to make him a successful candidate for the distinguished office of President of the United States. It will not be too strong to say, that there will be a constant probability of seeing the station filled by characters preeminent for ability and virtue. (*Fed.* no. 68)

As for judges, independence assures that the president will be remote from the democratic passions, but "the best security for the fidelity of mankind is to make their interest coincide with their duty." This is true for the "love of fame, the ruling passion of the noblest minds" (*Fed.* no. 72). If men are not given the space to finish what they have begun, "the most to be expected from the generality of men, in such a situation, is the negative merit of not doing harm instead, of the positive merit of doing good" (ibid.). The combination of unity, duration, adequate provision for support, and competent powers is conducive to energy in the executive, "a leading character in the definition of good government" (*Fed.* no. 70). The executive will act, he will move energetically, if his task and powers are defined so that there is space for him to act. The preeminent men who are chosen are to be given the scope that their ambition requires; otherwise, their best cannot be expected and their worst may well be feared.

A judiciary of judges who hold the office for some time is necessitated by the existence of a constitution. Once a constitution exists which is distinguished from ordinary laws passed by the legislature, the possibility of a conflict between the two kinds of laws emerges. "If there should happen to be an irreconcilable variance between the two, that which has the superior obligation and validity ought, of course, to be preferred; or in other words, the Constitution ought to be preferred to the statute, the intention of the people to the intention of their agents" (*Fed.* no. 78). The interpretation of the laws is the province of the judges, not of juries, so the judges become an important part of the constitutional balance here, although they were not in Montesquieu's England. To get men with the courage and knowledge required to perform these functions, the independence of the judiciary must be assured by tenure for good behavior. The check on the judiciary's misuse of this virtually unlimited charge is that they depend upon the executive and the legislature for enforcement. They have no force or will; they simply have judgment (*Fed.* no. 78). In the cases of both the executive and the judiciary, there seems to be an idea that the space for political action will itself be attractive to the ambitious, even to those whose ambition is appropriate to the job, and that the checks will protect the country from the ambition of bad, or even of incompetent, men.

The division of powers in the United States Constitution can be said to be aimed toward liberty in a variety of senses. First, the constitutional structure provides a kind of liberty for those involved in it. The structure keeps them from going too far, from doing things against the fundamental law and thus making others do things against it; and it leaves them a space within which to act freely. In Montesquieu's account of English liberty, that space had no particular shape—that is, no specific kind of activity was preferred by the constitution. The politically active citizens who were not in the House of Lords switched their allegiance from the executive to the legislature as the changing circumstances seemed to them to warrant such action. In the United States Constitution, liberty as an end is understood somewhat differently. The division of powers is based on a separation of the functions of rule. The balance is between those who are engaged in each function and who see themselves and their honor, or vanity, in terms of the actions of the branch of government performing that function. Balance is achieved through that identification, as in a monarchy, rather than through changing sides, as in Montesquieu's version of the English constitution. Liberty, in the United States Constitution, can be seen, not as an absence of direction, but as self-government. Rule by those who are to be ruled—that is, self-government—is divided, balanced, checked, and put back together in a constitution whose end can be best described as deliberation, as that self-government itself.

The question remains of the relation between these representative political institutions and the population at large. Montesquieu called this the liberty of the citizen; Hamilton called it limited government. The separation must be maintained between a formless population and a representative government whose shape is defined by the needs of rule itself. The issue here is the safety of the citizens or, as Hamilton put it, the danger that the legislature will go beyond its bounds. The judiciary serves to protect the citizens from this overreaching, just as, in Montesquieu, the independence of the judiciary is the requirement for moderate government. The issues here are first those of habeas corpus, bills of attainder, the definition of treason, jury trials in criminal cases—all of which were in the original constitution before the Bill of Rights was added. In Montesquieu, the freedom to write, to speak, and to think is an extension of this first line of protection. For Montesquieu, the most dangerous crimes, those against the country itself, or against religion, raise the possibility of infinite prosecutions unless the prosecutions for political acts are defined carefully as for acts, not thoughts, and those against religion are left to the religions themselves. One cannot go in search of crimes that cannot be seen in public without endangering the security of the citizenry. In this sense the Bill of Rights is an amplification of the rights that already exist in the Constitution, as Hamilton claimed, and could in principle be read back into them as circumstances required. From another, a more Madisonian, point of view, keeping the government from a direct concern with questions of opinion and religion can make it less likely that those issues will divide the population into groups or factions that would make governing more difficult.

In sum, the shape of the representative institutions—the division of powers—offers an environment within which both political education and deliberation can take place, protected both from the passions of the population and from those of the representative bodies themselves. Various questions come to mind as a consequence of seeing the Constitution in this context. Tocqueville came to the United States in the years before the Civil War, and he raised the question of the character of a people whose regime neither supported nor tolerated any systematic distinctions.[23] For Tocqueville, the representative institutions were one among a variety of institutions and practices that exercised in Americans the capacity for self-government, giving them all a way to exercise their freedom. The ubiquity of the habit of governing oneself, particularly in small matters, makes it possible for representative government to work. The entire political education is not thought to take place within the division of powers. Once civil war had broken out, it would no longer do to hope that slavery could be dealt with indirectly; the national government had to insist on some national terms for citizenship, on equality. That is, the Civil War marked the failure and raised the possibility of a transformation in the structure of this moderate, representative government of divided powers. The question then becomes the manner and the extent to which that event and the resultant amendments to the Constitution transformed the government. The issue that endures is the extent to which it is possible, or even desirable, to maintain the distance between governing and sovereignty, between deliberation and rule.

8

TOCQUEVILLE'S DEMOCRACY

For Alexis de Tocqueville the democracy of his time was a new thing: it generated a new kind of man, and it created new political problems. Montesquieu helps us to understand the point of view with which Tocqueville began, but it is Tocqueville who seems, in effect, to extrapolate from Montesquieu's Frenchmen and Englishmen in book 19 to a new kind of democracy and a new democratic man.

He sought its character in America, where it had been free to develop its nature, without having to overcome a king and an aristocracy. Tocqueville, to the astonishment of Americans, begins *Democracy in America* with an examination of the inheritance laws, in which he makes clear that property is altogether individual and alienable. No groups are selected out for more property or for particular kinds of property; the underlying population is not structured by the needs of a certain government to encourage a particular kind of people. There are no political laws to maintain the wealth of the great families or to keep a body of citizens equal. Then, Tocqueville's version of democracy seems to be a way of expressing clearly and in public, after the Revolution, the view that it is impossible to found governments on a notion of the natural differences among men. In France, the Revolution had overturned all the orders of the monarchy, and by 1830, when Tocqueville set out for the United States, it had become clear that in contrast to the situation in England, the orders of the monarchy could not be depended upon to execute and reform the rule of the people.[1]

Here we shall turn primarily to the second volume of *Democracy in America,* where Tocqueville's concern is more with the characteristics of democracy itself than with those of American democracy. But first let us try to see the problem of the nature of this democracy as Tocqueville envisioned it. First, we shall look briefly at the way he positions democracy in time and in comparison to other regimes; this examination will clarify the extent to which he shared Montesquieu's point of view. Second, we shall try to get some perspective on the democratic character that Tocqueville presents, initially by comparing it briefly to the ancients and then by examining at greater length the terms that his predecessor, La Bruyère, used to compare the character of the ancients to those of his own time. Then, we shall finally be in a position to turn to *Democracy in America.*

Tocqueville divides the social and political world into that which is democratic and that which is aristocratic. These terms seem to describe both social conditions (*états sociales*) and political organizations.[2] In a discussion of the great parties and their relative absence in America he remarks: "These opinions were as old as the world, and one finds them under different forms and dressed with various names in all free societies. The one wants to restrain popular power and the other to extend it indefinitely" (1.2.2). That is, what the social condition and the political organization share is a way of thinking, feeling, and acting.[3] In his book on America, where the point of view is explicitly democratic, Tocqueville explains aristocracy in terms of an effort to control, or limit, democracy.

Elsewhere, when the point of view requires a more explicit analysis of aristocracy, Tocqueville says that aristocracies have ranks based upon the existence in societies of some goods—for example, birth, wealth, knowledge—which all citizens cannot share. What these aristocratic goods have in common is that they can be the lot of only a small number of people and that, therefore, they give all those who possess them separate tastes and exclusive ideas.[4] Then, equality of condition in a democracy means that no such good is recognized as the basis for ranking people, and therefore no such exclusive tastes and ideas follow. There is only one rank in a democracy. Here one can see clearly Tocqueville's link between social condition, in which some good either is or is not selected as the basis for the distribution of other goods, and political condition, in which those who have the selected good make up what are, in effect, the rulers and the citizenry. One could see Tocqueville's explanation of the French Revolution in the conflict between the increasingly bureaucratic rule of the monarchy, the democratization of society, and the remaining political and social privilege of the aristocracy.

Ancient democracies, like ancient oligarchies and aristocracies, are all, in Tocqueville's terms, aristocracies. Even the democracies distinguished people by birth, by whether or not they were born free. From this point of view the ancients were charting differences among aristocracies. This usage is similar to Montesquieu's use of the term *republic*. It seems that Tocqueville, like Montesquieu, is suggesting that among the ancients the difficulty lay in seeing any commonalty; but among the moderns the difficulty lies in cultivating those who have the characters required for various actions. That is, the tendency was toward aristocracy among the ancients but toward democracy among the modern governments.

In the Introduction to *Democracy in America,* Tocqueville begins with a monarchy characterized by the law that established primogeniture—that established the landed property of the noble families (1[intro.]; 1.1.2 and 3).[5] Tocqueville suggests repeatedly that Christianity was behind the constant pressure toward equality between families that destroyed the feudal social condition. He says that inequality began as the clergy opened its order to those who were not noble. He calls equality of conditions a "providential fact" which inspired in him a "religious terror" (1 [intro.]). In writing about American slavery, he says: "Christianity had destroyed servitude; the Christians of the sixteenth century have reestablished it; however, they have only admitted it as an exception in their social system, and they have taken care to restrict it to only one of the human races. They have thus made a wound on humanity less large, but infinitely more difficult to cure" (1.2.10). Modern slavery was different from the inequality that Christianity had destroyed. He asserts that Americans have understood the real character of Christianity—namely, support for democracy—and that the French identification of the clergy with the nobility is not necessary (1.2.9). Not only was the French Revolution the end of a long development toward equality; it also acted in "relation to this world precisely in the same manner as religious revolutions acted in view of the other; it has considered the citizen in an abstract fashion, outside of all particular societies, just as religions consider man in general independent of country and time."[6] If the Christian religion was the impetus behind the destruction of the feudal distinction, it should not be surprising that the political revolution that this process culminated in acted as if it were a religious revolution.[7]

In this analysis of the modern situation, Tocqueville is following along Montesquieu's assessment of modern equality and its causes, although considerably more directly and rapidly. The question that remains is the character of this new democracy and its susceptibility to despotism.

At their most positive, Plato and Aristotle describe democracies as being full of all the virtues without any ordering of those virtues. In *The Republic,* Plato has Socrates say of democracy: "It is probably the fairest of the regimes. Just like a many-colored cloak decorated in all hues, this regime decorated with all dispositions, would also look fairest, and many perhaps, like boys and women looking at many-colored things, would judge this to be the finest regime. . . . it contains all species of regimes.[8] While discussing the claims of oligarch and democrat to rule, Aristotle writes in *The Politics*: "The many, of whom none is individually an excellent man, nevertheless can when joined together be better—not as individuals but all together—than those [who are best], just as dinners contributed [by many] can be better than those equipped from a single expenditure. For because they are many, each can have a part of virtue and prudence, and on their joining together, the multitude, with its many feet and hands and having many senses, becomes like a single human being, and so also with respect to character and mind."[9] Even if all these bits do not come together into any order or a good order, as the democrats claim, the effect of democracy for Aristotle is pointless action, not inaction. When democracies turn bad, they turn toward using the political for private and lesser purposes, not toward withdrawal from action. In this regard, Thucydides says of Pericles: "He told them [the Athenians] to wait quietly, to pay attention to their marine, to attempt no new conquests, and to expose the city to no hazards during the war, and doing this promised them a favorable result. What they did was the very contrary, allowing private ambitions and private interests, in matters apparently quite foreign to the war, to lead them into projects unjust both to themselves and to their allies—projects whose success would only conduce to the honour and advantage of private persons, and whose failure entailed certain disaster on the country in the war."[10] At their best, the ancient democracies were blamed for having had too much variety, too many directions, and too little unity for the best things; at their worst, they were blamed for having had too much action in the wrong directions—in the private interests of the many—too little thought to the good of the whole, and too little virtue.

Tocqueville finds, however, in these characteristics of democracy, not its criticism, but its hope. He writes: "For me, far from reproaching equality with the indocility it inspires, it is primarily for that, that I praise it. I admire it when seeing it deposit at the bottom of the spirit and the heart of each man this obscure notion and this instinctive tendency toward political independence, thus preparing the remedy for the evil that it has given birth to. I attach myself to it on this side" (24.1). Tocqueville seems to want to revive the activity of the ancient democracies. The new evil is even worse.

This assessment—namely, that something so fundamental had happened to human character that a new analysis was necessary—is not unique to Tocqueville. Let us turn briefly to La Bruyère, one of the French *moralistes* who thought about this new character. La Bruyère, in the middle of the seventeenth century, looked at his fellow Frenchmen, particularly the fashionable and the noble, compared their vices to those of the Athenians as described by Theophrastus, and found a new human situation whose internal map he tries to suggest in a book of brief thoughts and descriptions.[11] He writes, for example:

Everything is foreign in the dispositions, mores, and manners of most men: one who has spent his life distressed, irascible, avaricious, fawning, submissive, hard-working, self-seeking, was born lively, peaceful, lazy, ostentatious, with a proud courage, and far from all baseness: the needs of life, the situation in which one finds oneself, the law of necessity forced nature and caused these great changes. Thus such a man cannot be defined in the end and in himself; too many things external to himself altered him, changed him, overcame him; he is neither precisely that which he is or that which he seems to be.[12]

Here men are not what they are or what they are thought to be. Circumstances have made men extremely complicated creatures. La Bruyère traces out a variety of these complications in a variety of circumstances, but our interest here is in the situation, the circumstance, that he thought he and his subjects were facing.

The first thing to notice is that by nature men are not necessarily virtuous, nor are all the characteristics of men whose nature has been forced wholly bad. That is, natural men can be lazy and ostentatious; the others are hardworking. Theophrastus's Athenians, with whom La Bruyère begins his book, are taught to be more virtuous by a description of their vices that makes them appear ridiculous. They, it seems to be presumed by Theophrastus, will laugh or be shamed by this description and will try to stop doing similar things.[13] But nothing is so straightforward once the nature of men has been forced. They are no longer what they seem to be or what they think they are, so such simple ridicule is not likely to affect them. Rather, one must apply oneself to the vices of the spirit, to the corners of the heart, and to the whole interior of man in order to discover the principle of his malice and of his weaknesses.[14] Even if men have not changed in respect to the heart and the passions, the paths of their passions have become so much more complicated, that to affect them, one must trace the passions to their origin, their principle, rather than remark satirically upon their effects in action.[15]

The chapter titles of La Bruyère's *Characters* cut across France in a variety of ways: the central chapters are the public divisions— the city, the court, the greats, the sovereign; the preceding chapters take up a number of considerations that have been thought to be private—such as personal merit, women, the heart, society or conversation, wealth; the succeeding chapters are titled "Man," "Judgments," "Fashions," "Some Usages," and "Sermons"; they take up categories that are applicable to all of the previous considerations. The first chapter and the last chapter take up the spirit, in works of literature and in respect to God. These categories overlap and cut across each other; they offer no possibility of a society or of political life that is ordered along a single purpose.[16]

In one instance, La Bruyère compares France to Rome, saying: "Among us the soldier is brave, and the lawyer [homme de robe] is learned; we do not go further. Among the Romans the lawyer was brave and the soldier was learned: a Roman was both soldier and lawyer."[17] The French division gives a man a function, not a character. "A man who has been given a place no longer uses either his reason or his spirit to regulate his conduct and his attitude to others; he takes his rule from his post and his estate: from this follows forgetfulness, pride, arrogance, harshness, and ingratitude."[18] The implication here is that there is great pressure on these people to act in ways that are not natural to them. As in the earlier quotation, they are forced by their condition and become less reliable and more complex people. Then there is something unnatural about the ranks and orders of the French monarchy and perhaps about any ranking that assumes a similar division in character. These orders produce a certain pressure and artificiality, which makes them over the long run unreliable supports for a government. In a remark making fun of the "greats" who use the names of ancient heros, he says: "It is already too much to have the same religion and the same God as the people; how can they be called Peter, John, or James like the merchant or the worker? . . . Let them appropriate the twelve apostles, the first martyrs (what people, what patrons)."[19] Underneath the divisions is the unity before the Christian God, which always casts doubt upon the reliability of those very divisions. Here we have Tocqueville's and Montesquieu's view of the French monarchy, expressed in terms of a discussion of exactly the way in which those strains worked within the monarchy at a time when it was thought to be stable and reliable. It is no wonder that Tocqueville admired La Bruyère's perspicacity.

La Bruyère says about those who have spirit: "An author seeks futilely to make himself admired with his work. The fools [sots] sometimes admire, but they are fools. Those persons with spirit have within themselves the seeds of all the truths and all the sentiments, nothing is new to them; they admire little, they approve."[20] This distinction between those who have spirit and the fools occurs frequently in La Bruyère's works. Those who have spirit are in tune with themselves and the world; they may or may not be virtuous. The fools are those who connect themselves to the arbitrary standards of the social world. They are constant and yet unreliable. "The fool is an *automaton,* he is a machine, he is a spring, the weight shifts him, moves him, turns him, always in the same direction to the same extent; he is uniform and never alters . . . . what appears the least in him is his soul, it does not move, it never stirs, it is in repose."[21] But the reliability is altogether dependent upon the machine, or the place, that give him a direction and a motion. He possesses none of his own. In these considerations, La Bruyère comes closest to those that shaped Montesquieu's view of the way monarchies and the English government worked and to Tocqueville's problem with democracy. Is there only a democracy of fools, attached to their places and their equality as they were attached to their places and their inequality; or is there a democracy of "manly equality," of men of spirit and freedom, whose movement comes from their souls, rather than from their places?

The authors of *The Federalist,* as we have seen, fear the passions that sweep across the citizenry of a democracy or even through the halls of the legislature. They seek to dissolve, to halt, and to break up those passions by the large size of the republic, its federal organization, and its division of powers. Their purpose is to slow down the thinking of the people and the representatives of the people so that there will be room for deliberation. The authors do so in some considerable measure by removing political discussion to representative institutions, where it can be shaped and directed, and, one suspects, by hoping that the others will be content with electing those officials as political acts. The authors share the distress of the ancients with the constant action, the meaningless innovation, and the lack of any real deliberation in democracy. But they seem to most fear the similarity of those passions as they move through the population. Something causes these democrats to be alike, not different, thus making it possible to fear a tyrannical democracy. The problem is to refine the basis on which the people govern themselves, not to encourage them to try to do so. There is no sign at all of any worry about inactivity, solitude, or withdrawal.

To understand Tocqueville's reasons for fearing a peaceful, moderated, soft democratic despotism, we need to turn, not to the first volume of *Democracy in America,* in which Tocqueville analyzes the reasons for the success of the American democracy, but to the second volume, in which he extrapolates from the American practice to try to characterize this modern democracy itself.[22] The thoughts, sentiments, mores, and politics of democracy are taken up in turn in the four parts of Tocqueville's second volume, and we shall follow Tocqueville here.

Tocqueville begins the first part of the second volume of *Democracy in America,* on the thought of Americans, with a discussion of the similarities between the way that Americans think and the Cartesian method. Americans are unconscious Cartesians. "Each is, therefore, enclosed strictly within himself and tries to judge the world from there" (2.1.1). They look for clarity; they distrust both forms and authorities. As they are accustomed to relying on evidence that is available to them, they like to see very clearly the object with which they are concerned; they then uncover it, as far as they can, from its wrappings; they take away all that separates it from them; and they remove all that hides it from their view, so as to see it from close up and in broad daylight. This disposition of their spirit (their turn of mind) soon leads them to distrust forms that they consider "useless and inconvenient veils put between themselves and the truth" (2.1.1). After a democratic revolution, like the one in France in 1789, the structures of their common life were torn apart, "leaving men to themselves and opening before the spirit of each of them an empty and almost limitless space" (2.1.1). The Cartesian spirit destroys accepted ways of understanding and acting by its insistence on the clarity of vision of the individual and then by its insistence that reason is always universal.

According to Tocqueville, the next step for these democrats is to move toward some generalization. If there is to be a society and, even more emphatically, if that society is to prosper, "all the spirits of the citizens must always be assembled and held together by some principle ideas" (2.1.2). Even if people are considered singly, the shortness of their life and the limits of their spirit make it necessary for them to adopt some opinions that they have not demonstrated for themselves to be true. Not their wills but the inflexible law of their condition constrains men to do this (2.1.2). If people cannot examine all of their own opinions and if they see no one superior to themselves from whom they can adopt opinions, they will adopt the opinions of those around them. The tendency of democrats to consider the similarities, but not the differences, among people and to think in generalizations reenforces their tendency to adopt one another's opinions. Every characteristic or action is generalized or is discarded as not being serious or as not being moral if it cannot be generalized. If everyone thinks this way, there will come to be a general opinion whose virtual unanimity will guarantee its acceptability. Ways of thinking that cannot be generalized are discarded. To summarize, "There are only very particular and very clear ideas, or very general and very vague notions; the intermediate space is empty" (2.1.18).

Montesquieu, too, portrays the modern situation in Cartesian terms. A particular intelligence is confronted with universal laws, but that justice is inappropriate for humans. People require some limits to justice and some internal impulse toward one another's well-being in order to act justly. Tocqueville, instead, portrays a people who are trying to be Cartesians, who have come up against the difficulty that Montesquieu portrays: they have no internal direction, and they have no source of community with others. They then tend to withdraw into themselves and into the tiny society of family and friends with whom they surround themselves. Democracy constantly gathers each person back into himself "and threatens finally to enclose him entirely in the solitude of his own heart" (2.2.2) Montesquieu finds direction and community in the activity of the human spirit, whether it be particular and natural or general and Christian. Tocqueville finds a source of activity in political freedom, but the anchor of that freedom is less clear.

Tocqueville's attitude toward the notion of political rights will help us see his relation to those political thinkers who grounded their thought in natural equality. For the latter, natural right and political right follow from natural equality. For Tocqueville, this concentration on the similarity and the equality of men at the expense of their evident differences is a peculiarly modern thought. "Those among the Greeks and Romans with the most profound and extensive genius were never able to come to the idea, both so general and so simple, that men are similar and that they have an equal right to liberty which each of them has upon birth; and those same Greeks and Romans did their utmost to prove that slavery was natural and that it had always existed"

(2.1.3). Tocqueville's perspective on the notion of right permits him to see it as a way of connecting an individual with the principle behind the political order, as a way of improving his character. In the first volume of *Democracy in America*, Tocqueville says: "After the general idea of virtue, I know of nothing more beautiful than that of rights, or rather these two ideas are mingled. The idea of rights is nothing but the idea of virtue introduced into the world of politics" (1.2.6). In worse times, the notion of rights may have to be anchored in interest. "If, in the middle of this universal collapse, you do not succeed in linking the idea of rights to personal interest, which offers itself as the sole moveable point in the human heart, what will then remain to govern the world, if not fear?" (1.2.6). The notion of rights can be used to link individual interest to political virtue. An individual gets some view of himself as a member of a particular society through the idea of rights, even if that view is grounded in the beginning on self-interest.

Our contemporary corruption of the terminology of natural right is quite within Tocqueville's understanding of the way in which Americans use the notion. Almost every group that wants something from the government claims that it has a right to that thing. We have heard of the rights of neighborhoods, of women, of small farmers, of businessmen, as each group seeks to improve its position. The tactic is to claim a right and then to give a reason why the place currently occupied by the group does not coincide with its contribution or its virtue.

In his section on the movement of the intellect in democratic America, Tocqueville continues to describe the tendency toward thinking about generalizations, rather than particular things, using abstractions such as equality and countries, rather than men, as the actors in the story. Here he reflects on his position and his own writing: "I have often made use of the word equality in an absolute sense; I have in addition personified equality in several places, and thus I have come to say that equality did certain things or refrained from doing certain things" (2.1.16). Democratic historians "even take away from peoples themselves the ability to modify their own lot, and they submit them to an inflexible providence or a kind of blind fatality" (2.1.20). Those same historians also give "voluntarily force and independence to men united in a social body. It is necessary to keep from obscuring this idea, because the issue is to raise souls not to manage to beat them down" (2.1.20). For Montesquieu, the modern situation requires that people be thought of as parts of general movements, whether economic or historical; but that same situation requires that somehow people come to think of those same generalities in ways that give them a sense of their efficacy and their capacity to direct those same movements. But Tocqueville, in contrast to Montesquieu, seems to regard this as a matter of style's suiting circumstance, rather than of taking circumstance into account. Tocqueville's solution has a quality of the arbitrary, of daring the fates, which reminds the reader of Tocqueville's admiration for Pascal, as well as for Montesquieu and Rousseau.[23]

If the thoughts of democratic people move between themselves and generalities about similar people, then their sentiments, or feelings, must be directed toward themselves or toward themselves and others as a part of some general grouping. Unlike aristocrats, they are not likely to devote themselves to another person or another person's cause. Tocqueville starts the second part of the second volume of *Democracy in America,* "The Influence of Democracy on the Sentiments of Americans," with this notion. He is deeply concerned about the effects of having democrats turn their affections inward, and he appraises the various possibilities for getting them to turn those sentiments toward their associations with other people. Only by turning to groupings with others can democrats arouse those tendencies within themselves that point to something higher, or better, than self-satisfied self-preservation.

Montesquieu and Tocqueville share this vision that democratic individuals are separated from one another, are isolated within themselves, and act from their passions and their need for something to which to attach themselves. Montesquieu's Englishmen, who could move without difficulty from support of the king to support of the legislature, who did not quite know who they were out of office, who had no sense of beauty or style, but who turned instead to eccentricity; and his Frenchmen, who attended only to the infinite variations in fashion and position—both are less well-developed versions of Tocqueville's American.

The activity of Montesquieu's English and French takes place within a framework that constrains and directs them, but they are without resources outside of that framework.

Tocqueville begins his discussion of the sentiments of democrats by asserting that their equality leads to a love of equality itself, "the principal passion which agitates men in these times" (2.2.1). By contrast, love of liberty is neither peculiar to nor inevitable in democracies. Equality itself does not lead people in democracies toward concern for others. Neither, as we have seen, does the pattern of thought of democrats as they generalize from their own experience, from their solitude, without conversation with others. Tocqueville calls these people individualists, thus marking a new human ill: "Individualism is a calm and considered sentiment which disposes each citizen to isolate himself from the mass of his fellows and to withdraw into the circle of family and friends, so that after having thus created for himself a small society to his taste, he voluntarily abandons the great society to itself" (2.2.2). Democracy not only "makes each man forget his ancestors, but it hides his descendents from him and separates him from his contemporaries; it throws him ceaselessly back upon himself and threatens to finally enclose him entirely in the solitude of his own heart" (2.2.2). This sentiment is distinguishable from vanity and from egotism, both of which include an implicit comparison with some external standard that one claims or hopes to meet. As is the case with Montesquieu, the capacity to move outside of one's own feelings, or heart, is identified with strength of spirit: "Sentiments and ideas are not renewed, the heart does not expand and the human spirit does not develop except by the reciprocal action of men upon one another" (2.2.5). The thought and feelings, as well as the spirit, of men are weak if they do not interact on these levels with others. Alone, people are, and feel themselves to be, weak. This weakness immobilizes them, and immobility comes to make action seem both inconceivable and impossible.

Tocqueville thinks this impasse can be broken when people join together. In so doing, they break up the formless space outside of the individuals. Such people begin to be able to identify principles of action beyond themselves: "By dint of working for the good of his fellow citizens, one acquires in the end the habit and the taste for serving them" (2.2.4). Later in this part, Tocqueville explains further: "That which makes us superior to the beasts in this is that we employ our soul to find the material goods toward which instinct alone guides them. In man, the angel teaches the brute the art of satisfying himself. It is because man is able to raise himself above the goods of the body and even to scorn life, a matter of which the beasts have not the least idea, that he can multiply these same goods to a degree they cannot conceive" (2.2.16). Even a move toward shared thought about how to improve one's material well-being is a step toward recognizing and using one's humanity; thus, Tocqueville regards such democratic notions as self-interest properly understood as extremely useful to the development of the humanity of democrats.

One can conceive of what Tocqueville expects from voluntary associations in a democracy by imagining that his Cartesian individuals are appearing at a meeting with those they believe agree with them about something. Each individualist has come to certain views by generalizing from his own thoughts. Because he cannot imagine others' being different from himself, he thinks that they would come to the same generalizations. Descartes himself generates God, the universe, and men from his own thought; there is no consideration of the possibility of the need to check that thought with whatever might be "clear and distinct" to another person. One can only imagine a series of speeches reiterating opinions that have already been formed from such people when they meet in a group. They would not be persuasive because persuasion requires an accurate perception of one's audience, its character, and its opinions. In order to persuade, one must know that one's audience is not the same as oneself. Such a group would be without motion. However, in small and informal organizations, in contrast to larger and more formal ones, talk seems virtually inevitable. As people talk to one another, they begin to respond to one another; they even try to imagine the train of thoughts and the feelings of others. Each steps out of his individuality, stretches his sentiments, and strengthens his spirit. This new sympathy requires that one forget oneself, however briefly. To extend one's sympathy, one must acknowledge some commonly understandable purpose; one must develop one's spirit or mind, as well as one's heart. Understanding is no longer a result of the clarification and the generalization of one's own thoughts; it becomes communication in words with others.

The question remains of the standing of that communication. Tocqueville does not seem to care greatly what purposes the groups pursue; it is simply the pursuit of a common purpose that improves democratic character. But Tocqueville does not move, as does Rousseau, to the notion that freedom and a common purpose are properly set into the formality of a general will. Thus, the making of a common purpose itself cannot be the whole of political life, as it is for Rousseau. Tocqueville suggests both that the taste for the infinite and the love for what is immortal have an immovable foundation in human nature and that no matter how equal men are in respect to their material well-being, "there will still remain the inequality of intelligences, which, coming directly from God, will always escape from the laws" (2.2.12 and 13). Here are the grounds for preferences, for inequality. One can hear Rousseau complaining about the alienation of the people's sovereignty in these purposes whose content is something other than their commonalty.

These associations of the like-minded serve another purpose: "A political, industrial, commercial, or even scientific and literary association is an enlightened and powerful citizen who cannot be bent at will or oppressed in the shadows and which, while defending its particular rights against the exigencies of power, saves the common liberties" (2.4.7). Whatever difficulties are overcome and whatever lessons are learned in joining a voluntary organization, the organizations themselves serve a further purpose in a democracy. Upon reflection, one realizes that these organizations differ from those that establish a polity. They need not embody all the human variation within a country; rather, they join those already inclined to agree but leave out the others. From this point of view, it seems that Tocqueville is struggling through associations to reproduce the democracy of the Greeks—Plato's many-splendored city, filled with a variety of people. Tocqueville appreciates and encourages those institutions that could encourage such a democracy. People have reached for a whole variety of principles and ways of life in the variety of voluntary associations. In so doing, they have come out of their isolation and grandiosity into opinions that can be shared with and protected by others of a like mind. Each of these organizations is, in effect, a person of different character and different opinions, acting within the country.[24]

In the third part of the second volume of *Democracy in America,* titled "Influence of Democracy on Mores Properly So Called," Tocqueville turns to the question of the transformation of those relations that were central to the old regime: relations between those in different ranks or countries; relations within a family between men and women, between adults and children; relations between masters and servants; relations between warriors and the civilian population. Some remarks of Tocqueville's from the first volume may help us understand the point of view with which he begins this analysis. According to Tocqueville, the whole of the education of men in America is directed toward politics; in Europe its principal end is to prepare one for private life. The multiple teachings of Montesquieu's monarchy have collapsed into the monopoly of the new egalitarian politics in America and into the distinctions and domesticity of the familial in Europe. The members of America's nuclear families are pushed out toward the practice of politics and into a form of sociability appropriate to politics in their family life. Americans almost always carry the habits of public life into private life (1.2.9). Europeans, who have no such impulse toward and practice of political sociability, import private sociability into political life. "In Europe, we often have the ideas and habits of existence of private life enter into public life, and as it happens to us to pass suddenly from the interior of the family to the government of the state, we are often seen to discuss the great interests of society in the same manner that we converse with our friends" (1.2.9). Tocqueville here contrasts the feudal importation of private life into public life with the democratic importation of public life into the private one.

Implicitly the question at issue here in *Democracy in America* is the nature of those impulses that lead men to live in families. If the old regime built upon a notion of a family in which some protected, some worked, some cared for children, and some prayed, the question is the extent to which that shaping of the impulses of men was a result of the regime. What is left of those relations in a democracy which seems to recognize none of these differences, even those that seem most natural? From this point of view, Tocqueville's analysis in this section is concerned with a theoretical question, not simply with the character of Americans. Montesquieu, as we have seen, asks this same question in the context of the circumstance of the most extreme climate—the hardest, rather than the most generous, circumstance.

Tocqueville begins, as does Montesquieu, with the observation that those who are considered human are, in a democratic society, not simply those with whom one shares a rank or even those with whom one shares a government; rather, it is all of humanity. Pity extends only as far as those who are thought to be human. "Mme. de Sévigné did not conceive clearly what it was to suffer when one was not a gentleman" (2.3.1). La Bruyère remarks—with what irony is a question: "One sees certain wild animals, male and female, scattered over the country, black, livid, and burned by the sun, who are attached to the land they dig and turn over with an unconquerable stubbornness; they have a sort of articulate voice and when they stand up they show a human face and they are in effect men."[25] La Bruyère here reflects the ambiguity of the monarchical division: the others may well be human, but identifiable humanity is linked to one's own sort. Tocqueville then claims, in contrast, that in a democracy, when there are no established distinctions among people, the people are less attached to each other; they lack the elaborate politeness of aristocratic societies; they are hard to dispose of in conversation; and they are both extremely scrupulous and very demanding, especially abroad, where they face the question of how to fit into an inegalitarian society.

Democracy leaves people with only their common humanity and natural pity upon which to base a common life. Other sentiments, or habits of the heart, that connect them with particular other people have been eclipsed. Americans act as if they feel a natural pity for one another, when their interests do not come into conflict with the actions required by such a pity (2.3.4). This is a consequence of people in a democracy all feeling themselves "subject to the same weakness and the same dangers, and their interest, as well as their sympathy, make it a law for them to lend each other mutual assistance, when needed" (2.3.4). Like Rousseau, Tocqueville does not seem to think that natural pity is sufficient support for political life, but again Tocqueville turns toward investigating the characteristics of other relations that can be revived or reorganized in this new situation.

Tocqueville takes up a consideration of the effects that democracy has on the relations between a servant and his master within the family. The final result of relations between servant and master in an aristocracy is a strange confusion of the two existences, which is both touching and ridiculous (2.3.5). But "among democratic peoples, the servant and the master are very close; their bodies touch ceaselessly, their souls do not mix; they have occupations in common, they almost never have common interests" (2.3.5). They live parallel lives that do not touch. They share neither sentiments nor interests. This unstable, tenuous relation is duplicated between landowners and tenants, between employers and employees. These familial relations, now a part of what has become a public economic life, offer democrats no direct feeling for each other either through their sentiments or through their interests. These people share nothing within themselves.

Families in a democracy emphasize the contractual relations between equals and deemphasize the natural relations of dependence—whether it be of children and parents, men and women, or old and middle-aged. By so doing, they limit the family to the generation that is raising children, to the nuclear family, as we would now put it. In summarizing the first eight chapters of this third section, Tocqueville writes: "Democracy stretches social links, but it tightens natural links. It makes families closer while at the same time it separates citizens" (2.3.8). One is reminded of Montesquieu's ironic remark that Justinian had thought he was basing his laws on nature when he abrogated all the laws that kept the Roman families together over generations.

Tocqueville then raises the question of women because women, he says, determine mores (2.3.9). The American judges his wife by saying that "her spirit is as able as a man's of discovering the naked truth, and her heart firm enough to follow it; and they have never sought to place her virtue any more than his under the protection of prejudice, ignorance, or fear" (2.3.12). But this view has not led Americans to thinking that women are like men. Rather, Americans, according to Tocqueville, "do not believe that a man and a woman have the duty or the right to do the same things, but they show the same regard for the role of each of them and consider them as beings whose worth is equal although the destiny differs" (2.3.12). Thus, Tocqueville says that Americans have effected a compromise between their belief in equality and a view of natural differences.

Tocqueville completes part 3 with a discussion of questions of manners, gravity, national vanity, agitation, honor, ambition, public employment, revolutions, war and peace, and finally, the army. These considerations are linked through the question of the extent to which perceptions of differences impel action. In each of these considerations the reader is shown an example of the last remnants of activity resulting from thinking well of oneself. Tocqueville writes: "Far from thinking that we had to recommend humility to our contemporaries I would want to try to give them a more vast idea of themselves and their species; humility is not healthy for them; what they lack the most, in my view, is arrogance. I would voluntarily surrender several of our small virtues for this vice" (2.3.19). Arrogance is a vice that should be cultivated in democratic countries. It leads to a larger view of the human soul through the willingness to view with pride the contents of one's own.

This enlarging of the soul is Tocqueville's prescription for democrats. They must encounter each other, take into account each other's sentiments, and perceive each other's purposes—and perhaps, come to share feelings and purposes. In the old regime, natural, familial differences were the basis for the ranks and orders. These differences gave people both a ground for sympathy and people who were to be identified as human. But in a democracy, these relations are reduced to the minimum. They do not suffice to bring out men's humanity. In part 4, Tocqueville says that on the basis of democracy alone, the only power to emerge would be a government whose despotism "would be more extended and softer and would degrade men without tormenting them" as in earlier times (2.4.6). Eventually such a democracy "would strip each one of several of the principal attributes of humanity" (2.4.7). Political liberty is his prescription for this new despotism. That liberty would rely on the old democracy, on the "indocile equality," on the "obscure notion and instinctive penchant for political independence deep in the spirit and heart of each man" (2.4.1).

Here Tocqueville seems to see a progression from the democratic man who, like Tocqueville's American and Montesquieu's Englishman, is free because he occupies a space defined by a government of decentralized or divided powers within which he is free to act, to the democrat who, like the despot, is enclosed within his own house and has no space for action. The democrat's spirit, like that of the despots and the slaves of old, has no avenue for action, but his passions, unlike those of the despots, are also limited, not by exhaustion, but by the timidity that results from his position as one among many.

Tocqueville concludes: "I think that, in the democratic centuries which are opening, individual independence and local liberties will always be a product of art. Centralization will be the natural government" (2.4.3). Art, or human making, is required to halt the natural course of events. But on what material is it to work? Tocqueville refers regularly to the attributes of humanity, to differences in intelligence, to higher things, to the taste for the infinite and the immortal. These are not notions that distinguish one group of people from others. They are attributes of individuals. But they do point to those higher things that differentiate people, rather than those lower, material, and passionate things that they can all be said to have.

Tocqueville claimed to have stood impartially between the claims of equality and of inequality, of democracy and aristocracy. One way of understanding this claim is to reflect, as he does at the end, upon the differences between God and men. Of God, Tocqueville wrote in the beginning of the second volume:

> God does not consider the human species in general. He sees separately with only one glimpse all the beings of which humanity is composed, and He perceives each one of them in the resemblances which bring him close to all and the differences which isolate him from them.
>
> God, then, does not need general ideas; that is, He never feels the necessity of enclosing a great number of analogous objects under the same form in order to think of them more easily. (2.1.3)

Generalities are at best a second-rate way of thinking. They are a way of dealing with human weakness. This mental weakness, not the human spirit, moves people toward groups and toward thinking in generalities. Tocqueville remarks at the end that he takes pleasure in regarding a group of people that is defined by its grandeur or smallness, wealth or poverty, wisdom or ignorance, but that his pleasure is due to his weakness, because he must differentiate a group in order to contemplate it. "It is not the same for the eternal and all-powerful Being whose eye necessarily includes the total of things and who sees distinctly, yet at one time, all of the human species and each man"(2.4.8). All generalities, even the boundaries of a particular country and government, are artificial; therefore, democrats are no more correct than aristocrats; yet one can see that the impulse that Tocqueville calls providential in the beginning undermines the smaller aristocratic groupings for the larger democratic ones. Here, although Tocqueville appears, in contrast to Montesquieu, to be unable to see any real ground for particular groupings of people, he inhabits Montesquieu's modern world.

9

CONCLUSION

Political life is life in-between, in-between the universality of nature and passions and the universality of God, or the best. Its goods are limited, particular. Moderate government lives within those limits, while free government offers us a space within those limits for our own individual deliberation and action. The problem in establishing and preserving these moderate governments is how to keep them from dissolving into some universal, and thus despotic, principle. In our time, Christianity holds everyone to the highest standards, thus making the particular good of politics seem arbitrary and second-rate. But politics must somehow embody its particularity in this society. Montesquieu's book teaches us to understand this situation. Tocqueville and those who wrote and defended the United States Constitution, particularly Madison, were just the sort of readers that Montesquieu wanted. They deliberated about the best possibilities in their circumstances. First of all, Montesquieu gave them a notion of the circumstances, the context, within which they should deliberate. Governments have places within which one can understand their possibilities—both moderate and despotic. This context, these limits—or the shape offered for political thought and action—makes such reflection possible. In a similar way the constitution of a free government makes possible moderate and free political action. That is, Montesquieu has devised a context for a modern prudence.

Now we can see clearly how far Montesquieu has moved from the alternative offered in his early work, *Dialogue de Sylla et d'Eucrate,* which I mentioned briefly in chapter 1. There, Montesquieu presented a confrontation between the attractive ambition of Sulla and the doubtfulness of his interrogator, Eucrate. Sulla remarks, for instance: "The gods, who have given most men a cowardly ambition, have attached almost as many evils to liberty

191

as to servitude. But whatever the price of this noble liberty, it must be paid to the gods."[1] Montesquieu has Eucrate answer, after Sulla makes a number of such statements: "My lord, it is fortunate that the heavens have saved mankind from a number of men like you; born for mediocrity, we are overwhelmed by sublime spirits. It costs all the others too much for one man to be above humanity."[2] Politics, as we have seen, is not to be measured by that which is either above or below it: in either case, the consequence is despotism. It must be measured against its own possibilities. But one might well ask about the "sublime spirits," those who can say with Montesquieu that "still I do not believe that I have totally lacked genius. When I have seen what so many great men in France, England, and Germany have written before me, I have been filled with wonder, but I have not lost courage. 'And I too am a painter,' have I said with Correggio" (Preface). Montesquieu does not deny the existence or the importance of such souls; but he does assert their dangerousness, the damage that they can do to decent, everyday political life.

In *The Spirit of the Laws,* Montesquieu pushes this conclusion further, applying it to the philosophical legislators, to Aristotle, Plato, Machiavelli, More, Harrington, and a crowd of writers who "found disorder wherever they did not see a crown" (29.19). "The laws always meet the passions and the prejudices of the legislator. Sometimes they pass through and are colored; sometimes they remain there and are incorporated" (29.19). There is no reason to think that legislators, even legislators of this rank, are without the passions that can color or even overwhelm their thought.

Music, Montesquieu claims, enters the spirit through the body. "It is a mean between the physical exercises the render men harsh and the speculative sciences that render them savage" (4.8). As we have seen, that music made their soul "feel softness, pity, tenderness, and sweet pleasure" (4.8). This claim is most clearly directed to softening the harshness of the Greek warriors in the ancient republic. The remark about the savagery of the speculative sciences seemed to be an aside. But now we can suggest that music may well also be necessary to make philosophers sociable, to make them, like the warriors, feel their commonalty with other people. They remain men, not intelligences.

Finally, we must reconsider Montesquieu's discussion of the great virtue of aristocrats and the magnanimity of the nobility in a monarchy. The problem in aristocracies is to get the aristocrats to constrain themselves. They can do so "either by a great virtue that makes the nobles in some way equal to their people, which may form a great republic; or by a lesser virtue, a certain moderation that renders the nobles at least equal among themselves, which brings about their preservation" (3.4). The great virtue of the nobles seems to be that they ask no more than that which they give to the people. Moderation is a kind of imitation of such virtue; in moderation the nobles ask no more than they are willing to give to each other. Great virtue and moderation mean that the goods of the society are not at the disposal of the ruler and are not organized in terms of his needs. The magnanimity of the prince in a monarchy sheds light and glory on his subjects. "Each one has, so to speak, a larger space; he can exercise those virtues that give the soul not independence but greatness" (5.12). This magnanimity, like great virtue, is claimed, not for oneself, but for the light that it sheds on others. Perhaps these are the virtues required of the great legislators—as well as of the aristocrats.

NOTES

CHAPTER 1. INTRODUCTION

1. In the years just before he wrote this work, Montesquieu had extensively interviewed a Chinese man living in France. See Robert Shackleton, *Montesquieu: A Critical Biography* (Oxford: Oxford University Press, 1961), pp. 11–12; see also *Oeuvres complètes de Montesquieu,* ed. M. André Masson, 3 vols. (Paris: Les Édition Nagel, 1950), 2:927–943, hereafter cited as Nagel. The translations from Montesquieu's *Dialogue de Sylla et d'Eucrate* (Nagel, 1.3:355–363) are mine.

2. Montesquieu, *The Persian Letters,* trans. George R. Healy (Indianapolis, Ind.: Bobbs Merrill, 1964). I have used this translation in the text.

3. Frederick M. Keener, in *The Chain of Becoming* (New York: Columbia University Press, 1983), pp. 183–193, takes a similar point of view, although he does not go so far as to say that this enlightened thought may characteristically distance the thinker from his subject and subjects.

4. Nagel, 1.3:559.

5. Thomas L. Pangle, *Montesquieu's Philosophy of Liberalism* (Chicago: University of Chicago Press, 1974). Beginning with a different interpretation of book 1 by identifying Montesquieu with a more traditional view of natural law, Mark Waddicor, in *Montesquieu and the Philosophy of Natural Law* (The Hague: Martinus Nijhoff, 1970), proceeds in much the same way, trying to make of the book an exposition of the consequences of a position taken in the natural-law tradition.

6. Bernard Manin, in "Montesquieu et la Politique Moderne," *Cahiers de philosophie politique,* no. 2–3 (1985), pp. 157–229, also takes this point of view.

7. Basia Miller, "Montesquieu's *Esprit des Lois*: Elements of Non-Linear Composition" (Ph.D. diss. prepared for Department of Romance Languages, University of Chicago, 1988); see also Roger Lauffer, *Style rococo, style des lumières* (Paris: Librairie José Corti, 1963), and Jacques Proust, *L'Objet et le text: Pour une poètique de la prose française de XVIIIe siècle* (Genève: Libraire Droz, 1980), pp. 295–311.

8. See Destutt de Tracey, *A Commentary and Review of Montesquieu's "Spirit of the Laws,"* trans. Thomas Jefferson (New York: Burt Franklin, 1969; reprinted from 1811 ed.), for a remarkably uninhibited effort to recast Montesquieu into a more traditional Lockean liberal.

CHAPTER 2. NARRATIVE

1. For a full discussion of all this see Shackleton, *Montesquieu*, pp. 240–243; Nagel, Introduction to vol. 1; and Montesquieu, *De l'esprit des lois,* 4 vols. (Paris: Les Belles Lettres, 1950), texte établie par Jean Brèthe de la Gressaye, 1:xliv–lxii, lxxxv–xci.

2. This reference is to a book and chapter in *The Spirit of the Laws.* The translations are from a draft of a new translation by Anne M. Cohler, Basia C. Miller, and Harold Stone, to be published by Cambridge University Press in the series History of Political Thought, edited by Quentin Skinner, Richard Tuck, and Raymond Geuss.

3. The word for both in French is *plusieurs,* whose primary meaning in *The Spirit of the Laws* and in the eighteenth century was "many."

CHAPTER 3. SPIRIT

1. See Bernard Groethuysen, *Philosophie de la Révolution française précédé de Montesquieu* (Paris: Librairie Gallimard, 1956), pp. 75–76, especially.

2. 2 Cor. 3:7–8. The translations from the Bible are from the Revised Standard Version.

3. Rom. 7:6.

4. Martin Luther, *Christian Liberty* (Philadelphia: Muhlenberg Press, 1943), p. 25.

5. René Descartes, *Meditations,* no. 3.

6. David Lowenthal, "Book One of the *Spirit of the Laws,*" *American Political Science Review* 53 (June 1959): 485–498.

7. In his translation of Plato's *Republic* (New York: Basic Books, 1968), Allan Bloom translates the Greek word *thumos* as "spirit," arguing that the peculiarly political passion for justice is a consequence of anger, the ordinary meaning of that word. Although Montesquieu uses a notion of spirit for the human characteristics required for politics, this spirit does not begin with anger.

8. The Greek emperors were the Christian emperors of the Eastern Empire.

9. Judith N. Shklar, in *Ordinary Vices* (Cambridge: Harvard University Press, 1984), p. 43, argues that for Montesquieu cruelty was first among the evils; rather, it seems to me, he says that only under despotic rule is punishment the first mechanism of justice.

10. See 24.17, where Montesquieu compares the Germans to the Malayans and ends by remarking that in Malaya, where there is no reconciliation, the guilty party wounds and kills whomever he encounters.

11. By contrast, Sheila M. Mason, in *Montesquieu's Idea of Justice* (The Hague: Martinus Nijhoff, 1975), pursues Montesquieu's presentation of justice in book 1 and in some early writings as if this justice were the standard for politics.

12. See Anne M. Cohler, "Montesquieu's Perception of His Audience for the *Spirit of the Laws*," *Interpretation* 11, 3 (Sept. 1983): 317-332, for an account of how this view shaped Montesquieu's rhetoric.

13. That Montesquieu understood some of its limitations is clear from some remarks he made about similar scientific results in papers presented to the Academy of Bordeaux. He said that "these systems [are] no sooner set up than they are overthrown" (Nagel, 3:52) and that "one must not seek a reputation from these kinds of papers; they neither get it nor do they merit it" (Nagel, 3:117).

14. Robert Shackleton, "Le Manuscrit de la Bibliothèque Nationale," Nagel, 3:567-577.

15. For a contemporary discussion of this situation, which does not contradict Montesquieu's view, see *The Lombard Laws*, trans. Katherine Fischer Drew (Philadelphia: University of Pennsylvania Press, 1973), pp. 6-14.

CHAPTER 4. MODERATION

1. Aristotle, *The Politics*, trans. Carnes Lord (Chicago: University of Chicago Press, 1984), p. 36 (1252b1).

2. Paul Vernière, in *Montesquieu et "L'Ésprit des lois" ou la raison impure* (Paris: Société d'Édition d'enseignement supérieur, 1977), and Catherine Larrère, in "Les Typologies des gouvernments chez Montesquieu," in *Études sur le XVIIIe siècle*, ed. J. Ehrard (Clermont, France: Université de Clermont II, Faculté des Lettres et Sciences Humaines, Association des Publications de la Faculté des Lettres, 1979), take up the problem of the two classificatory systems. Nannerl O. Keohane, in "Virtuous Republics and Glorious Monarchies: Two Models in Montesquieu's Political Thought," *Political Studies* 20, 4 (Dec. 1972): 383-396, does not see this context for the kinds of governments.

3. See Melvin Richter, "Despotism," in *Dictionary of the History of Ideas* (New York: Charles Scribner's Sons, 1973-74), vol. 2, pp. 1-18, for a description of the meanings *despotism* has had. It has been identified with the rule of slaves, with that rule in which ruler and ruled have the least in common.

4. Here one is reminded of contemporary theories of totalitarianism in which examples of regularity or freedom are said not to be real but to be part of the totalitarian process.

5. This notion of democratic despotism remains closer to the notion of democracy of the ancients than to the notion of despotism that Tocqueville developed as an extension of the character of people in a modern democracy (see chapter 8).

6. Montesquieu seems to suggest that the end of privacy in Plato's *Republic* is an extension of the notion of government inherent in the ancient republic.

7. For Rousseau, as for Montesquieu, the citizens of a republic invest their passions, their "amour propre," into the community of citizens. In the *Social Contract*, Rousseau in effect offers a pattern, a form, for the proper shape of

those wills. See Anne M. Cohler, *Rousseau and Nationalism* (New York: Basic Books, 1970), pp. 135–151.

8. In 6.5, Montesquieu refers to Machiavelli's assertion that the people as a body should judge crimes against itself.

9. Yet Marat took Montesquieu to be an ally; he took Montesquieu's willingness to offer thoughts about legislation as an education in republican citizenship: see *Éloge de Montesquieu, présenté à l'Académie de Bordeaux le 28 mars 1785, par J. P. Marat*, introduction by Arthur de Brézetz (Libourne, France: B. Maleville, Librairie—editeur, 1883).

10. Anne M. Cohler, "Introduction," in Montesquieu, *The Spirit of the Laws,* trans. Anne M. Cohler, Basia C. Miller, and Harold Stone, to be published by Cambridge University Press; and Judith N. Shklar, *Montesquieu,* Past Masters Series (Oxford: Oxford University Press, 1987).

11. A. Lloyd Moote, *The Revolt of the Judges: The Parlement of Paris and the Fronde, 1643–1652* (Princeton, N.J.: Princeton University Press, 1971).

12. Franklin Ford, *Robe and Sword* (New York: Harper & Row, 1965), pp. 222–245.

13. The difficulties inherent in this effort to describe the institutions of a monarchy are illustrated in the history of this phrase. In the only existing manuscript—a draft, not the manuscript submitted to the printer—the powers are simply "intermediate": see *De l'ésprit des lois,* ed. Jean Brèthe de la Gressaye, vol. 1:45 and notes. Within this chapter (2.4) the expression becomes "intermediate, subordinate," and finally "intermediate" as it is repeated.

14. Claude de Seyssel, *La (Grande) Monarchie en France,* Nannerl O. Keohane, in *Philosophy and the State in France* (Princeton, N.J.: Princeton University Press, 1980), p. 394, sees a closer connection between the two views of monarchy.

15. See Pensée 2266.

16. The extent to which Montesquieu valued this mode of thought is emphasized by some remarks in the *"Défense."* Of his critic he said, "I say only that metaphysical ideas are extremely confused in his head, that he has no capacity to make distinctions, that he does not know how to make good judgments, because he sees only one thing when he should see many" (Nagel, 1.2:453–454). Of the author himself he says, "He believed his inquiries useful because good sense consists largely in knowing the nuances of things" (ibid., p. 456).

17. The members of the parlements either bought or inherited their jobs, but they did, in principle, have some relevant education.

18. See Georges Benrekassa, *Montesquieu* (Paris: Presses Universitaires de France, 1968), and Suzanne Gearhart, *The Open Boundary of History and Fiction* (Princeton, N.J.: Princeton University Press, 1984), for two works that treat the types of government somewhat similarly, as convergences of a cluster of relationships.

19. See Keith Michael Baker, "Politics and Public Opinion under the Old Régime: Some Reflections," in *Press and Politics in Pre-revolutionary France,* ed. Jack Censer and Jeremy Popkin (Berkeley: University of California Press,

1987), pp. 205-246, for an account of the notion of universal communication in the years before the French Revolution.

20. See Daniel Roche, *Le Siècle des lumières en province* (Paris and the Hague: École des hautes études en sciences sociales, Mouton Éditeur, 1978), for an analysis of the way in which the provincial academies were organized, which makes it clear that this notion was well known in the circles in which Montesquieu traveled.

21. That Montesquieu saw the forms of government this way makes it understandable that people have read him both as an aristocratic liberal of the old regime and as an advocate of modern liberalism. See, for example, E. Carcasonne, *Montesquieu et le problème de la Constitution française au XVIIIe siècle* (Paris: Les Presses Universitaires de France, 1927), and Mark Hulliung, *Montesquieu and the Old Regime* (Berkeley: University of California Press, 1976).

CHAPTER 5. LIBERTY

1. Thomas Hobbes, *Leviathan,* ed. Michael Oakeshott (Oxford: Basil Blackwood, 1960), p. 84 (pt. 1, chap. 14).

2. See also 26.20: "Liberty consists principally in not being forced to do a thing the law does not order, and one is in this state only because one is governed by civil laws; therefore, we are free because we live under civil laws."

3. David Spitz, "Montesquieu's Theory of Freedom," in *Essays in the Liberal Ideal of Freedom* (Tucson: University of Arizona Press, 1964), pp. 28-35.

4. See John Plamenatz, *Man and Society* (Harlow, Essex, Eng.: Longman, 1963), pp. 284-291, and C. P. Courtney, *Montesquieu and Burke* (Oxford: Basil Blackwell, 1963), pp. 59-64, for their defense of Montesquieu's account of British politics as it was practiced when he visited and observed. William Blackstone, in his *Commentaries on the Laws of England,* relies heavily on Montesquieu's account of the division of powers in England.

5. John Locke, *Second Treatise of Government,* rev. ed., with an introduction and notes by Peter Laslett (Cambridge: Cambridge University Press; reprinted by Mentor), p. 410, para. 146.

6. One can only wonder whether this implies a criticism of the French *parlements,* which were permanent bodies that judged.

7. See 8.15-20 in *The Spirit of the Laws* for Montesquieu's discussion of the proper sizes of the various governments; and for the treatment of size in *The Federalist* see p. 154.

8. Both Edmund Burke, in his "Speech to the Electors of Bristol" (3 Nov. 1774), and David Hume, in his "Idea of a Perfect Commonwealth," in his *Essays, Moral Political and Literary,* presumed and advocated a considerable distance between the population and the representatives. This notion of constructing a space in which the representatives could think and act in a way that was not possible for the population at large was remote from the thought in France at that time: see Keith Michael Baker, "The Idea of Representation at the End of the Old Regime," in *The Political Culture of the Old Regime,* ed. Keith

Michael Baker (Oxford: Pergamon Press, 1987), pp. 469–492; this is Vol. 1 of *The French Revolution and the Creation of Modern Political Culture,* 3 vols. (1987–).

9. This is possible in a system in which the notion of proof requires a judgment between two competing views, not a positive judgment as to the event: see 29.11 and p. 139.

10. See Martin Diamond, "The Federalist," in *History of Political Philosophy,* ed. Leo Strauss and Joseph Cropsey (Chicago: Rand McNally & Co., 1963), pp. 573–593, for an account of *The Federalist* that is remarkably close to this account of English government.

CHAPTER 6. LEGISLATION

1. Emile Durkheim, *Montesquieu and Rousseau: Forerunners of Sociology* (Ann Arbor: University of Michigan Press, 1965); Raymond Aron, "Montesquieu," in his *Main Currents in Sociological Thought* (New York: Basic Books, 1965), pp. 11–56; Louis Althusser, *Politics and History* (London: NLB, 1972), pp. 13–109; Henry J. Merry, *Montesquieu's System of Natural Government* (West Lafayette, Ind.: Purdue University Press, 1970)—all view Montesquieu as having intended, if not quite accomplished, to take these things on their own, that is sociologically or historically.

2. From this point of view it is no great surprise that these and the books on nature and slavery (14–17) were what commanded the attention of Adam Ferguson, in *History of Civil Society* (Philadelphia: A. Finley, 1918); Adam Smith, in *Lectures on Jurisprudence* (Indianapolis, Ind.: Liberty Classics, 1982); and James Madison's teacher, John Witherspoon, in *Lectures on Moral Philosophy* (Princeton, N.J.: Princeton University Press, 1912).

3. When Tocqueville later claimed, in *The Old Regime and the French Revolution,* that evidence showed that the French peasantry did own much of the land, he was referring to a claim of the Revolution that Montesquieu could have endorsed.

4. Montesquieu, *Considerations on the Causes of the Greatness of the Romans and Their Decline,* trans. David Lowenthal (New York: Free Press, 1965), p. 123 (chap. 13).

5. *Pensées,* 1711 (Pléiade 380).

6. Nagel, 1.2:458.

7. Shackleton, *Montesquieu,* pp. 356–377.

8. See 28.40–41, where Montesquieu considers the courts that acted in accord with canonical law and then stopped as "a kind of light appeared and they no longer existed."

9. See Catherine Volpilhac-Auger, *Tacite et Montesquieu,* in Studies on Voltaire and the Eighteenth Century, no. 232 (Oxford: Voltaire Foundation, 1985), for an account of how Montesquieu used Tacitus in his consideration of the character of the Germanic tribes.

10. Here one can see the attraction of this discussion to someone like the Abbé Mably, *Collection complète des oeuvres de l'Abbé Mably* (Paris: Ch. Des Grière,

1795), vol. 1, pp. 374–382, 389–399, who moves another step further to say that no real constitution—that is, a republican one—had yet been established in France.

11. Here one can see good reason for Burke's admiration of Montesquieu. See Edmund Burke, "Appeal from the New to the Old Whigs," in *Works* (Boston: Little, Brown, 1889), vol. 4, pp. 211–212.

CHAPTER 7. MODERATE AND FREE GOVERNMENT: THE UNITED STATES CONSTITUTION

1. *The Records of the Federal Convention of 1787,* ed. Max Farrand, 4 vols. (New Haven, Conn.: Yale University Press, 1937), Pinckney, 1:397–404; Madison, 1:421–423; Hamilton, 1:424–425.

2. Ibid., Franklin, pp. 82–83.

3. Ibid., 2:284–287, 344, 606–607.

4. Ibid., 2:9–10; see also 1:476 and 486 and 2:370–374 for an illustration of the ease with which a discussion of this issue could begin.

5. Locke, *Second Treatise of Government,* p. 422, para. 160.

6. Ibid., pp. 424–425, paras. 165–166; see also the discussion in *Federalist* no. 49 of Jefferson's suggestion of an appeal to the people.

7. Here the criteria are for the representatives, not for those who were to select them.

8. Farrand, *Records,* 1:201, 579–582.

9. Ibid., 2:201–224.

10. Ibid., p. 3.

11. See also 62, 63, 78.

12. See also Gordon Wood, *The Creation of the American Republic, 1776–1787* (Chapel Hill: University of North Carolina Press, 1969).

13. Farrand, *Records,* 1:179.

14. Ibid., p. 187.

15. In *Federalist* no. 44, the states are actually referred to as "intermediate powers"; see also Farrand, *Records,* Dickenson, 1:87, 156–157; and Forrest McDonald, *Novus Ordo Seclorum: The Intellectual Origins of the Constitution* (Lawrence: University Press of Kansas, 1985), pp. 228–232.

16. Farrand, *Records,* 2:644.

17. Ibid., pp. 553–554.

18. See *Federalist* no. 73 for the more customary opinion that the conjuction provides an avenue for the executive to corrupt the judiciary.

19. Farrand, *Records,* 1:310.

20. Ibid., p. 421 (Madison on private passions).

21. Ibid., p. 289.

22. See David Epstein, *The Political Theory of "The Federalist"* (Chicago: University of Chicago Press, 1984), for a good discussion of these notions.

23. Tocqueville did not take any particular interest in *Federalist* number 10. See James T. Schleifer, *The Making of Tocqueville's "Democracy in America"* (Chapel

Hill: University of North Carolina Press, 1980), p. 116; and John C. Koritansky, "Two Forms of the Love of Equality in Tocqueville's Practical Teaching for Democracy," *Polity* 6, 4 (Summer 1974).

CHAPTER 8. TOCQUEVILLE'S DEMOCRACY

1. François Furet, "The Conceptual System of Democracy in America," in *In the Workshop of History,* trans. Jonathan Mandelbaum (Chicago: University of Chicago Press, 1984), pp. 167–196; Alexis de Tocqueville, *Oeuvres complètes,* in progress (Paris: Gallimard, 1951–), vol. 13, pt. 1, pp. 225–238. References to Tocqueville will be to this edition. References to *De la démocratie en Amérique (Democracy in America)* will hereafter be cited parenthetically in the text by volume, part, and chapter (e.g., 1.2.2). The translations are mine.

2. For a discussion of Tocqueville's own efforts at defining these terms formally see Schleifer, *Making of Tocqueville's "Democracy in America,"* pp. 10–12; 263–274.

3. See François Furet, *Interpreting the French Revolution* (Cambridge: Cambridge University Press, 1981), p. 155.

4. Tocqueville, *Oeuvres Complètes,* 2.1.45.

5. Ibid., 2.1.37. It is in this context that one should understand Tocqueville's great interest in American inheritance law, which made any such noble families impossible.

6. Ibid., 1.1.89.

7. See Marvin Zetterbaum, *Tocqueville and the Problem of Democracy* (Stanford, Calif.: Stanford University Press, 1967), for an exposition based on the view that Tocqueville's depiction of this tendency toward equality as providential was a rhetorical device to ensure a discussion based on equality as the ground of government.

8. Plato, *Republic,* p. 235 (557d).

9. Aristotle, *Politics,* p. 101 (1281b).

10. Thucydides, *The Peloponnesian War* (New York: Modern Library, 1934), p. 120 (65).

11. See Schleifer, *Making of Tocqueville's "Democracy in America,"* pp. 31–32, for an example of Tocqueville's attention to La Bruyère.

12. La Bruyère, *Les caractères,* "De l'homme," in *Oeuvres complètes* (Paris: Gallimard, 1951), p. 300 (18). The translations are mine.

13. La Bruyère, "Discours sur Théophraste," p. 14.

14. Ibid., p. 16.

15. Ibid., p. 13.

16. Roland Barthes, *Essais critiques* (Paris: Editions du Seuil, 1964), suggests a similar understanding of the organization of the book.

17. La Bruyère, "Du mérite personnel," p. 99 (29).

18. La Bruyère, "De la cour," pp. 230–231 (51).

19. La Bruyère, "Des grands," p. 255 (23).

20. La Bruyère, "Des ouvrages de l'esprit," p. 76 (36).

21. La Bruyère, "De l'homme," pp. 337–338 (142).

22. The second volume was printed in 1840, five years after the first volume, Tocqueville read widely in political philosophy during those years: see Schleifer, *Making of Tocqueville's "Democracy in America,"* p. 26.

23. Tocqueville, *Oeuvres complètes,* 13.1.418: "I live every day with three men, Pascal, Montesquieu, and Rousseau."

24. Michael Hereth, *Alexis de Tocqueville: Threats to Freedom in Democracy* (Durham, N.C.: Duke University Press, 1986), concentrates on Tocqueville's use and advocacy of the political rhetoric required for such persuasion.

25. La Bruyère, "De l'homme," p. 333 (128).

CHAPTER 9. CONCLUSION

1. Nagel, 1.3:558.
2. Ibid., p. 560.

INDEX

Alexander the Great, 130
Ambition in *The Federalist,* 162–163,
  166–167
Aristotle, 18, 67, 122, 173, 192
Associations, in Tocqueville,
  182–185
Athens, 121, 154
Augustus (Roman emperor), 130
Aurangzeb (Mogul emperor), 129

Balance
  in England, 1, 9, 17, 104–114
  in *The Federalist,* 160–168
  and moderation, 10, 17, 170
  in Rome, 18, 81–82
  See also Division of powers
Barbarians, new laws of, 59
Bayle, Pierre, 26, 131
Bill of Rights, 108, 168–169
Boulainvilliers, Henri de, 85
Brunhilda (Merovingian queen), 62
Burgundians, 60

Calvinists, 141
Capetians, 30, 31, 32, 61, 87, 88,
  136, 141
Caractères (La Bruyère), 174–177,
  186
Carolingians, 26, 32, 61, 87, 88
Carthage, 23
Catholics, 117, 131
Charlemagne, 32, 62
Charles VII (of France), 63
Charles Martel, 32, 141

Checks in the United States,
  161–162, 167. *See also* Balance;
  Division of power
China, 21, 22, 54, 71, 80
  as moderated despotism, 73–75
Christianity, 14, 191
  in China, 74–75
  and chivalry, 103, 137
  and equality, 19, 50, 74, 80, 85,
    96, 101, 102
  and equality in La Bruyère, 176
  and equality in Tocqueville,
    172–173, 189–190
  and love, 43, 100
  and otherworldliness, 14, 26, 43,
    58, 59, 83–84, 131
  in republics, 80, 95
  and restraint, 26, 42–44, 57
  and Rome, 83, 126–127, 130,
    134
  and spirit, 9, 34–35, 42–43, 55,
    179
  theologians and, 24, 57, 130–131
  and universality, 11, 43, 54–55,
    56, 65, 85, 100–101, 132,
    145–147
  See also Divine law
Cicero, Marcus Tullius, 140
Citizens
  as associations in Tocqueville,
    184
  in *The Federalist,* 152–153
  See also Republics
Civil law, 11, 17, 27, 29–31, 32, 35,
  47, 51, 55–64, 72, 89, 104,
  106, 121, 131–135, 147